"I squealed with joy when I learned that Darra was writing this book, and the results are even more magnificent than I could have imagined. *Beyond the North Wind* is at once vividly passionate and methodically researched—a love letter to Russian cooking and hospitality."

—**BONNIE FRUMKIN MORALES**, chef/owner of Kachka and author of *Kachka: A Return to Russian Cooking*

"This is Darra Goldstein's masterpiece. Not only is this book full of invaluable research, it is also brimming with warm words and love for real Russia—its people and their wonderful food and unique culture."

—**OLIA HERCULES**, author of *Mamushka*

"In this beautifully written, gorgeously photographed volume, Darra Goldstein captures both the archaic soul of old Russia and the hip new global zeitgeist. Her love letter to the mysterious Russian North brims with revelations, from recipes I can't wait to make—dandelion blossom syrup! pumpkin pancakes!—to intimate portraits of cooks, erudite historical essays, and insightful travel notes. Part recipe collection, part cultural anthropology, part poetic evocation of place, this is the best kind of cookbook: one that conjures an entire culture at the table."

—**ANYA VON BREMZEN**, author of *Mastering the Art of Soviet Cooking*

For Leila, global traveler, kitchen sorceress, beloved daughter

"Don't put off till supper
what you can eat at lunch."

—ALEXANDER PUSHKIN (1834)

Darra Goldstein

Photographs by Stefan Wettainen

BEYOND THE NORTH WIND

Russia in Recipes and Lore

TEN SPEED PRESS
California | New York

CONTENTS

THE FLAVORS OF RUSSIA

I've been thinking and writing about Russian culture and cuisine for almost a lifetime, nearly fifty years now. And all that pondering has led me to a moment of understanding Russian food in a new way—a kind of gathering revelation, and one that happens to jibe beautifully with our current dietary trends. It's a discovery of the extraordinary in the ordinary, which came to me while cooking with ordinary Russians in ordinary towns, provincial cities, and remote villages. My aim in writing this book, in devising and testing recipes, has been to unearth the most deeply Russian flavors, not only by uncovering ancient practices but also by riffing on traditional recipes and ingredients to emphasize elemental tastes and make them modern. I sought to discover the benefits of austerity rather than its limitations—how a harsh climate, poor soil, and limited availability of foods can foster an astonishingly complex cuisine characterized by exhilarating flavors and innovative techniques. Ignoring the obvious dishes—the French-inspired haute cuisine of the tsarist past and the kitschy dishes of the Soviet era—I want instead to showcase the Russian foods that are organic and honest, many of them old foods that feel new again in their elegant minimalism.

I also want to dispel the false impression that Russian food is heavy and bland, basically borscht and potatoes. The truth is, borscht is Ukrainian, and potatoes weren't widely planted in Russia until the mid-nineteenth century, so neither one is intrinsically Russian. What is Russian is the thousand-year-old practice of fermentation, the pickling and culturing and curing of vegetables, grains, fish, and dairy products that enabled the Russians to survive their long winters. It's the sour tang of kvass and sourdough rye bread and the comforting earthiness of whole-grain porridges. It's the foraged mushrooms and berries that each year are transformed into a dazzling array of pickles and preserves. It's the wanton glory of Russian pies with their myriad shapes, crusts, and fillings. It's a surprisingly sophisticated cuisine, despite the country's harsh climate and seventy years of Soviet misrule. Writing this book has renewed my love for Russia, and I hope it inspires you, too.

A NOTE ON INGREDIENTS

Most of the ingredients called for in this book are easy to find in grocery or health-food stores. Others, like sea buckthorn and caviar, can be ordered online. You'll find a list of sources at the back of the book.

Unless otherwise noted, I use unsalted butter, large eggs, Diamond kosher salt, and unbleached all-purpose flour throughout the book. When rye flour is specified for baking, I use light rye for a fine texture, though dark rye can be substituted.

Cultured butter is always an option when making Russian food, since it adds a desirable, slightly sour tang that can offset the richness of other ingredients, as in my whitefish roe spread (see page 76). Commercial butters from Vermont Creamery and Ploughgate Creamery are excellent, or you might try making your own from the recipe on page 78.

Many recipes call for sunflower oil. You can use any good-quality sunflower oil for frying, or substitute another neutral vegetable oil. In other dishes, especially whenever sunflower oil is used as a garnish, you should make sure it is cold-pressed in order to achieve a distinctively Russian taste. Good brands include Hudson Valley Cold Pressed Sunflower Oil from New York state and Full Sun Cold Pressed Sunflower Oil from Vermont.

Dried mushrooms star in many Russian recipes. The king of them all is the bolete, aka cèpe or porcino, but it's fine to use other dried mushrooms you might have on hand, such as black trumpets, morels, oyster mushrooms, or even a mix.

Classic Russian dill pickles are made by immersing cucumbers in brine to undergo lacto-fermentation. Brined pickles, or what I call "sour pickles" in this book, taste radically different from American dills that have been made with vinegar. Whenever a recipe calls for sour dill pickles, seek out brined pickles from a delicatessen or the refrigerated section of grocery stores, where you'll find good commercial brands such as Bubbies.

A handful of recipes call for foraged ingredients, such as dandelions, cherry leaves, and black currant leaves. Except for the dandelion blossoms needed to make the syrup on page 59, these ingredients aren't crucial to the recipes' success, though they'll enhance both flavor and texture.

МАСЛО подсолнечно
нерафинированное

CHASING THE PAST

IT'S

midnight at the edge of the frozen Barents Sea, yet the world is in motion. Ice pellets skitter along the strand; the northern lights undulate across the sky. I'm two hundred miles north of the Arctic Circle, in February, and I don't think I've ever felt a wind more fierce. Russia's legendary winter enfolds me— the cold and the snow that defeated Napoleon, the famed "General Winter" that conquered the Wehrmacht. But really, it's not so bad—in fact, it's enthralling. The cosmic display is riveting in its shape-shifting forms, its wondrous streaks and saturations. Eventually I tear myself away and trudge back to the guesthouse in the dark, tripping over snowdrifts, hoping not to lose my footing or my way. Indoors at last, I take ten minutes to shed my clumsy felt boots and multiple layers of clothing. My fingers are frozen stiff—I finally feel what that cliché means. The unheated anteroom doesn't help me thaw, and after the invigorating outdoor air, the smoke hanging in the room feels suffocating. Men are banished here to smoke, in this middle kingdom between comfort and cold.

Once inside the house, I begin to feel cozy. The kitchen windows are steamy with condensation. I pop into the bathroom, which doubles as the laundry room. It's filled with plastic tubs of all sizes in fluorescent shades of pink, blue, and green. Tattered dish towels hang from makeshift clotheslines, their wide-eyed, patterned puppy dogs oblivious to the trays of kitty litter below. Someone has pulled the floral shower curtain back from the freestanding shower stall, and there, right on the base of the stall, I find a huge pot of Kamchatka crab legs. Truly enormous, straight out of a 1950s sci-fi movie. If I were to lie down side by side with one of these monsters, its leg span would be longer than I am. I decide not to try it.

It occurs to me that the steam must be from the boiling seawater into which these legs will soon descend. And sure enough, within fifteen minutes, the crabs are on the table, along with shot glasses of vodka, bowls of melted butter, and a basket of bread. Who needs anything more? By the time we finish cracking the giant crab legs and dipping them in butter, it's past 2 a.m. I decide to take a shower to get completely toasty for bed. The guesthouse is silent. The shower curtain is once more in place. I pull it aside only to find the crab pot, now empty, back in the stall. But there's room for us both, and so I step in. As the hot water rains down, I'm enveloped in a mist of salt and crab—far more aromatic and restorative than any spa treatment I've ever enjoyed. Afterward, I tumble into bed and think, "Yes, I really am in the Russian North!"

THE ALLURE OF THE ARCTIC

But what, really, was I doing on the Kola Peninsula? Jutting into the Arctic Ocean, it's one of the literal ends of the earth—next stop, North Pole. I thought of the early polar expeditions on foot and on skis, which usually ended in disaster. I thought of Mary Shelley's Frankenstein chasing his monster over the ice. I reconsidered the phrase "going to extremes."

It was no accident that I'd traveled to the remote village of Teriberka, braving the narrow tundra road from Murmansk whose formidable snowdrifts almost forced us to abandon the journey. Until the Soviet Union collapsed, Teriberka had thriving cod and haddock fisheries. Now the village was nearly deserted and—thanks to the Golden Globe–winning film *Leviathan*—synonymous with corruption and despair. But the extremes of this place invigorated my senses: the light and colors in the crystalline sky, the glimpses of ethereal beauty amid squalor and decay. The soothing aroma of braised elk softened the Arctic air. Yet a deeper reason had propelled me to the Kola Peninsula. It was here, in this isolated part of Russia, that I hoped to get beyond the outside influences that had shaped both imperial Russian dining and proletarian Soviet fare. I wanted to find the elemental flavors underlying traditional Russian cuisine. I was deliberately chasing the past.

It all started for me with blini, those irresistible pancakes that Chekhov described as "plump as the shoulders of a merchant's daughter." True blini aren't the dry, bite-size morsels passed at cocktail receptions, mere vehicles for smoked salmon. The original Russian pancakes are lacy, with the robust flavor of buckwheat and pocked with pores to soak up melted butter. Saucer-size blini are one of Russia's most ancient dishes, dating back to pre-Christian times, when they were baked on hot stones at the spring equinox. Shaped into rounds in the image of the sun, they beckoned the return of solar warmth after the long, dark winter.

Not surprisingly, the pagan people living in this northern region practiced a cult of the sun until Christianity was introduced in the tenth century. Their early beliefs still echo today through the round golden blini traditionally prepared for *Maslenitsa*, the Butter Festival marking a farewell to winter that evolved into a weeklong pancake indulgence before Lent—an all-out celebration that included troika and toboggan rides, ritualized fistfights, and kissing fests. Images of light and sun abound in Russian folktales, where the trees in distant magical kingdoms hang heavy with golden apples, and a single feather from the elusive firebird is incandescent enough to illuminate an entire room. One hero, Ivan Tsarevich, undertakes impossible quests to the mythical Kingdom under the Sun, an earthly paradise where the sun always shines. In other tales, a crystal mountain shimmers, and crystal bridges radiate light. Within these stories, passed on for more than a thousand years through poetry and song, lies a meaning deeper than fantasy,

expressing the Russians' collective ancestral memory of a northern land close to the sun representing paradise on earth. Some geographers have suggested that this utopia wasn't just wishful thinking, arguing that before the last ice age, the climate of the North was far more temperate than it is today, that deep in the past, the seasons may not have cycled into such relentlessly harsh winters. There may indeed have been warmth, radiant light, and lush vegetation even at this northernmost fringe of Europe.

Hints of this splendid land can be found in the name of the Kola Peninsula, which evokes *kolo*, an ancient Slavonic term for the sun. There are reminders, too, in the winter solstice holiday known as Kolyada, when Russians celebrate the shortest day of the year and the rebirth of the sun by baking gingerbread in the form of goats, birds, cows, and bears to bring good fortune. The Russian version of the Gingerbread Man, Kolobok, is round as the sun, a shape that allows him to tumble freely through field and meadow until he's outwitted by a clever fox.

In the nineteenth century, dozens of spiraling stone labyrinths, believed by some anthropologists to trace the orbit of the sun, were discovered on the Solovetsky Islands off the southwestern coast of the Kola Peninsula. The abundance of solar associations in folklore and in life, coupled with the mythical geographies recorded by Herodotus and Pliny the Elder, led some Soviet researchers to conjecture that northwestern Russia was the site of the legendary realm that the ancient Greeks considered the cradle of civilization: Hyperborea, the land "Beyond the North Wind," where the sun always shone and people lived to a thousand years without discord or sorrow, in a land so divine that the sun god Apollo himself traveled there. Hyperborea was a place of spiritual centeredness where people lived in harmony with nature, absorbing positive energy from the sun as well as from the magnetic North Pole. Hyperborea was considered the birthplace of human ingenuity, of technology. Is it a coincidence that the earliest Russian sagas describe ingenious towers inside which shimmered the sun, moon, and stars?

Such luminous mythology may seem a long way from Teriberka's visible decay, but even as the abandoned fisheries and desolation bespeak the death of Soviet life, Russia's past—the distant past—seems very much alive. My travels to Russia's Far North, including the Kola Peninsula and the Arkhangelsk region to the east, revealed a deep connection to bygone eras. Beyond the cities lie villages lost in time, virtually unchanged for hundreds of years, where the inhabitants still use traditional masonry stoves for cooking and heating, and still fetch water from the river. Most do enjoy electricity, thanks to diesel generators, so they may also have TV. And it's not that they are unaware of the present; they've simply chosen to live by different rhythms. These villages are most accessible in winter when the roads are covered with a smooth surface of ice and snow. Summer travel is slowed by potholes, ruts, and streams; also by small rivers that must be forded or crossed on a rickety ferry with a cable attached to each end. As for the spring mud season, it's best to stay home.

Those who have chosen to remain in the North are a resilient and hospitable people, and because of their isolation, many of the dishes they prepare descend uninterrupted from Russia's medieval culinary practices. Surprisingly little has been written about the inhabitants of this region. Why, you might wonder, would anyone voluntarily settle in such a far-flung place? For one thing, the Mongols didn't venture this far to the north and west, so the region never fell under the subjugation of the Golden Horde, which other Russians endured for more than two hundred years. Neither was the cruel system of serfdom in place as it was in Russia proper. So, despite the harsh climate and difficult farming conditions, life in this remote region offered freedoms that were impossible elsewhere.

Beginning in the ninth century, Russians began arriving from the south, from the principality of Novgorod. The resulting intermarriage with the indigenous inhabitants—including the Sami—gave rise to a distinct population still known today as the Pomors, literally "those who live by the sea." They farmed the water, harvesting not only fish and shellfish but also river pearls that were sent to Moscow to decorate the headdresses of wealthy women. "The sea is our field," the Pomor saying goes. By the twelfth century, the local population had perfected the art of obtaining salt from the marshes along the coast, long before cast-iron evaporators came into use. Unlike in warm climates where salt is evaporated by the heat of the sun, the Pomors froze the salt out of water. They devised a process that involved cooling the saltwater very slowly to ensure that the ice that formed was nearly pure water, with the salt concentrated in the brine. The process was tricky as well as laborious. If the water cooled too quickly, the salt would get trapped within the ice, but when the operation was properly carried out, it resulted in solid crystals of salt.

Another large wave of Russians arrived in the Far North in the sixteenth century, this time from Muscovy, escaping the depredations of Ivan the Terrible. Even more fled north after the great seventeenth-century schism in the Russian Orthodox Church. Like the American West, this region offered an area of relative independence. Here in the distant North, far from the religious and political center of the country, devout Russians were able to practice their Old Believer faith. The majestic Solovetsky Monastery, built in the fifteenth century on the largest of the Solovetsky Islands, became an Old Believer stronghold. The monks on Solovki (the colloquial name for the islands) coaxed extraordinary vegetables from the soil, including cabbages that grew so flavorful in the midnight sun that they were known as "Solovetsky apples."

The Solovki monks also developed salt works so large and so lucrative that their monastery became Russia's second-wealthiest religious community. Although we'll never know the provenance of the salt tasted by German

ambassador Adam Olearius on his seventeenth-century visit to Moscow, his journal records that it smelled of violets. (Today, artisans are reviving the art of salt production, and Slow Food, the international grassroots organization that promotes local foodways, has added mineral-rich White Sea salt harvested by traditional methods to its Ark of Taste.) In addition to selling their salt, the monks used it to preserve the fat herring they fished from the White Sea's cold waters in late summer and fall. Layered in brine often flavored with coriander, their herring was so prized that barrelsful were sent straight to the table of the tsar. Sadly, the herring catch is now in decline due to global warming, but my husband and I were lucky enough to taste it at Solovki's Kayut-Kompaniya Café, where Svetlana Mashkova serves fresh herring both pan fried and exquisitely poached. I felt positively royal as I savored its moist, oily flesh. Svetlana also makes an exceptional version of the beloved Russian fish soup *ukha*, with local salmon, cod, and halibut, spiked with a little fresh cod liver. That's a lot of omega-3s—one secret to staying healthy in the North.

Besides eating fish, the Pomors foraged all sorts of wild berries to turn into fruit juices and the lightly fermented beverage known as kvass, to bake into pies and to puree into sauces, puddings, and porridges. Cloudberries especially were prized as a scurvy preventative. Gathered in August, they were piled into a tub set in the swampy ground and then covered with branches and leaves. After the first frost, when the ground had firmed up enough to move the heavy tub, it was retrieved from the swamp and the cloudberries were brought home for long keeping. The great English naturalist John Tradescant was astonished by the abundance and variety of berries he encountered near the city of Arkhangelsk, the center of trade on the White Sea. He described excellent cloudberries, lingonberries, cranberries, blueberries, bilberries, bird cherries, and red, white, and black currants, and he went on to pronounce Russian honey the best in the world.

The Solovetsky Islands enjoy extraordinary bounty and an extraordinary history. These days, to get there, you can simply hop on a flight from Arkhangelsk. Alternatively, you can reach Solovki as my husband and I did—eleven hours by train from Murmansk down the Kola Peninsula to Kem and then two hours by ferry across the White Sea. Because the sea is frozen for a long eight months of the year, the ferry runs only seasonally, a limitation that has helped keep Solovki pristine and its isolation profound. As you arrive, you see huge granite boulders rising starkly out of the sea, trees stooped from the wind, and stone labyrinths dotting the shores, remnants of the ancient cult of the sun. And then, as the ferry rounds a bend, you catch sight of the magnificent monastery.

The islands' beauty and remoteness, coupled with the monastery's holiness, have made Solovki a mythical place. Yet it is also a place of deep sorrow. Ivan the Terrible exiled "misbehaving" priests to these islands, and Peter the Great imprisoned criminals in the monastery's dank dungeons. After the Russian

Revolution, the Bolsheviks used the once-sacred site to perfect the system of labor camps that grew into the Gulag. Some of the prisoners—the lucky ones—were put to work salting fish, though it was hardly the stuff of the tsar's table. The great scholar Dmitri Likhachev, imprisoned on Solovki in the 1920s, described the islands as an otherworldly place lying between heaven and earth, where the endless summer horizons yielded to winter's oppressive fog, relieved only by the majesty of the northern lights. Today there's a different sort of apparition to behold, one that recalls the pre-revolutionary past: women dressed in buttoned-up blouses, long skirts, and headscarves who have come as pilgrims to this site. They stroll the paths in contemplation, seemingly oblivious to the brawny, shirtless workers around them, many with voluminous beards. Such beards were once a sign of religiosity and faith—one reason why Peter the Great ordered men to be clean-shaven, and why the dissident writer Alexander Solzhenitsyn wore a beard defiantly in Soviet times.

On the monastery grounds, we encountered a lithe man in a Tolstoyan shirt playing the gusli, an ancient zitherlike instrument. As we paused to listen to its sweet notes, the man stopped playing, eager to explain at length how music opens the soul, especially when it coincides with the ringing of the church bells. He then took a hard look at me, set his instrument down, placed his hands on my shoulders, and gave me the same instructions that, oddly enough, I'd once received as part of media training in New York City: "Don't incline your head to the side," he admonished. "You will breathe better and see the world more clearly if you hold it upright." Maybe it was the rarefied northern air or the fact that for a couple of weeks afterward I didn't tilt my head to the side as I'm—dare I say—inclined to do, but I really did begin to feel as though I was seeing the world anew. Could that magical Russian air be bottled? I was surprised to find that in a wildly roundabout way it already has been. A summer spent in the Russian North inspired the Moscow-born parfumier Ernest Beaux to create the legendary Chanel No. 5. As he recalls in his memoirs, he went "beyond the Arctic Circle at the time of the midnight sun, when the lakes and rivers release a perfume of extreme freshness. I retained that note, and replicated it."

THE OLD IS NEW AGAIN

The past is on full display throughout the rural Russian North, where the ruins of enormous collective farms stand side by side with small private farms. These small farms are run by a younger generation of Russians who, previously cut off from traditional practices, are now actively working to uncover and revive the old ways. In an ironic turn of history, their artisanal activity was spurred by the political sanctions imposed by the European Union, the United States, Australia, and Canada in 2014 after Russia's forced annexation of Crimea. These sanctions led to economic turmoil and shortages, and ultimately inspired young agrarian entrepreneurs to produce food to fill the void—a case of unintended beneficial consequences. At least in the realm of food, the sense of excitement and hope for renewal is palpable, with old recipes and forgotten cooking techniques being rediscovered and developed in sophisticated new ways. As for ingredients, the outside world needs to know more about Russia's culinary treasures, particularly those from the North: the lamb that has grazed in salt marshes, as distinctive in flavor as Normandy's lauded *agneau de pré-salé*; the springtime vendace (a whitefish) and smelt whose flesh carries a hint of cucumber; the Barents Sea urchins pulled from icy waters in September. Sea buckthorn, once gathered only in the wild, is planted commercially for use in all manner of drinks, savory sauces, ice cream, and other desserts. Fireweed leaves are fermented into flavorful green and black teas whose nutritive properties are stunning. *Stroganina*—shaved frozen whitefish or salmon—contains ice crystals that melt on the tongue in a shiver of delight. And why shell out money for almond milk when you can make your own lactose-free beverage from oats? Humble oats were a continuing revelation in my Russian journeys. Slightly malted, then dried and ground into a fine flour called *tolokno*, they make a crisp topping for blini. The same flour can be transformed into a hearty dessert when mixed with sweetened berries or baked with farmer's cheese, sour cream, and a little honey. We ate oats fermented into porridge and oat bran whipped up into pancakes. These dishes are some of Russia's oldest, yet they also fit right into our contemporary tastes with their emphasis on fermentation, wellness, and natural products.

Here was the food of Russia I'd been searching for. Nowhere is this reinvention more visible than at two popular restaurants in Murmansk, at the top of Russia, above the Arctic Circle, where New Russian cuisine has taken hold. Like its Scandinavian cousin, New Nordic, this approach to food reaches back, celebrating local ingredients and time-honored methods of preparation. At Tsarskaya Okhota (The Royal Hunt), chef Svetlana Kozeiko serves soul-satisfying roast elk with spelt porridge and an ethereal mousse of aspen mushrooms, along with celery root and a sprinkling of fruit ash—powders made from dried blackberries and lingonberries that add a colorful touch to the plate's autumnal palette. Across town, at Restaurant Tundra, chef Sergei Balakshin presents Barents Sea scallops in their shells with seaweed, the bright coral roe still intact. And if the words "cod liver" conjure up memories of childhood torture, you should try Sergei's radical makeover. Mixed with scallion and egg, then shaped into a croquette that is breaded and fried, Sergei's cod liver is nothing short of divine. In a traditional yet contemporary turn, food doubles as medicine in black salt made by charring coriander-scented bread, caraway, and thyme;

in syrupy jam made from tiny pinecones, its slightly menthol flavor soothing the throat; and in vitamin-rich "hunter's tea" steeped with lingonberry, raspberry, cloudberry, sea buckthorn, thyme, and mint leaves. And we can't overlook the flavored vodkas that Russians have been infusing with herbs, spices, and fruits for hundreds of years, each infusion, from horseradish to cranberry, guaranteed to cure various ills. Both Tsarskaya Okhota and Tundra offer signature flavors that can be ordered in flights. For dessert lovers, there's Svetlana's *smetannik*—four thin rounds of honey cake layered with a tart sour cream filling and topped with black currant sauce; and Sergei's extravagant torte made with flour ground from dried Siberian bird-cherries and garnished with chanterelle ice cream. These chefs' riffs on classic dishes display the culinary revitalization that occurs whenever new foodstuffs, ideas, and techniques are introduced. They also show that traditional Russian food is alive, not moldering in the pages of old cookery books.

KIMZHA

The picturesque village of Kimzha is a bumpy five-hour drive from Arkhangelsk over kidney-bruising roads. Named one of the hundred most beautiful villages in Russia, Kimzha is home to the world's northernmost functioning windmill, once used for milling barley. A second windmill has been turned into a museum. Wooden and deeply weathered, the mills rise up starkly from the fields, their inverted shapes almost otherworldly, not at all like the cheerful windmills we associate with the domesticated Dutch landscape. Log houses with ornately carved wooden details extend along the village's single central lane, traversed by cows as well as people. The church, an early-eighteenth-century marvel of Northern wooden architecture, stands dilapidated above the river, which remains the only source of water for Kimzha. A number of garden hoses attached to pumps draw drinking water from the river, but more often people use buckets.

The village's isolation has enabled it to retain both its beauty and its archaic foodways. We were met by three generations of women, all energetic and eager to share their knowledge. First up, even though it was early afternoon, were welcoming shots of the homemade *brazhka* they distill from local barley. The women explained that it's their drink of choice, and they compete with neighboring villagers to determine whose distillation is best. The color of dark caramel, *brazhka* tastes like tawny port. After a few shots, we were all giggling with joy at this impromptu celebration. Lena, the youngest member of the troika, had already fired up the masonry stove in preparation for our visit. As soon as we arrived, she put newly dug potatoes into a cast-iron pot with some water and set it in the back of the stove. She briefly boiled some cod steaks, then stripped them

of skin and bones before flaking the fish into a large earthenware casserole. Using long tongs, she retrieved the potatoes from the oven, cut them into cubes, and added them to the cod along with butter, sour cream, and a generous sprinkle of salt. After ten minutes in the oven, the fish was done. We ate it straight from the casserole, gleefully scooping up the fish with pieces of bread to capture the buttery juices—no forks allowed.

Next it was time for *shan'gi*—small, open-faced pies similar to what Russians elsewhere call *vatrushki*. Yevdokia, of the middle generation, had soaked some cracked barley in sour milk overnight to soften and swell. She mixed in melted butter, then made a soft dough with finely ground rye flour, sour cream, and a little baking soda (admittedly a modern touch). Yevdokia deftly rolled the dough out into rounds, which she topped with the barley filling and brushed with a thin smear of sour cream, using a large duck feather. Into the hot oven they went. While the pies baked, Lena explained the distinctly local way of preparing coffee— in a samovar. In the eighteenth century, coffee arrived in the town of Mezen, to Kimzha's north, via Siberia's network of rivers. Because no one knew how to prepare this novel beverage, the townspeople made it in the vessel they knew best, the samovar. They salted the water lightly; if they did use sugar, it was in the form of a sugar cube held between the teeth. (The sensation of a sugar cube melting as hot liquid flows through it is immensely pleasurable, but years of drinking tea or coffee this way spells bad news for teeth.) Lena made us coffee in the samovar, adding a little cinnamon and salt. As soon as the water boiled, she let the coffee stand for a few minutes. Meanwhile, the pies had come out of the oven. Yevdokia brushed them with butter till they glistened, then carried the pan to the table, where an "omelet" made with the morning's fresh milk and eggs awaited us. This omelet was more like a shimmery custard, which on cooling had settled into two layers—the finest example of curds and whey I've ever tasted, with a dreamy texture like that of junket.

Kimzha sits above the river amid lush meadows, beyond which rise dense forests that harbor wildfowl and game, mushrooms and berries, and hives of wild bees. Seemingly endless expanses of pines, aspen, and birch line the narrow road that cuts through often-swampy terrain and provides the sole link to the outside world. The forests are public and wild, featuring wondrous rock formations and magnificent caves coated inside with sparkling ice even in the heat of summer. Locals who know the forests led us to secret springs and waterfalls whose water they consider healing (I made sure to douse myself) and showed us their secret places to gather the health-giving chaga that grows on birch trees, as well as wild plants for herbal teas—lemon balm and lingonberry, woodland strawberry and yarrow, meadowsweet and thyme. Foraging is a way of life for these northerly Russians. It's a necessary knowledge and a deep connection to the land and to their identity.

THE POETRY OF PLACE

The first time I traveled to Russia was in my imagination, when I was five. I'd discovered, deep in my parents' closet, a small, barrel-shaped wooden cup with low reliefs of onion domes painted in shades of cream and pale yellow. I loved that little cup for its promise of romance. No matter that my grandmother, a Russian Jew, had escaped a terrible life in that country. A few years later, when my little brother ruined the cup in a chemistry experiment gone awry, I felt devastated. I remember clutching the cup, now streaked with burn marks and covered with sticky residue. Only then did I notice the "Made in USSR" stamp on the bottom. The experiment had destroyed more than the cup.

Still, an allure held sway, and in college I jumped at the chance to study Russian. The language left me breathless at its beauty and sometimes tongue-tied from its consonant clusters. I yearned to experience the country itself. And so, in 1972, I found myself retracing Lenin's route from Helsinki to the Finland Station in Saint Petersburg, where the great man had so fatefully arrived to foment revolution. These were the Brezhnev years, the "Era of Stagnation," when the Soviet Union (USSR) was trapped in an apparently endless pattern of buoyant economic projections that fizzled. The promised prosperity never materialized. The store shelves remained empty, information with the outside world was strictly controlled, and contact with foreigners was sternly discouraged if not entirely forbidden. Nevertheless I soon managed to fall in with a group of disaffected Soviet youth who knew their way around the city and delighted in introducing me to the local street food served up from kiosks and mobile carts: *chebureki*, deep-fried meat pies oozing glistening fat; *ponchiki*, Russia's answer to Krispy Kreme doughnuts; and *trubochki*, cardboard-wrapped ice cream logs coated with chocolate that the Russians enjoy outdoors even when the temperature dips to twenty below. My new friends showed me that there really was more to Russia than meets the eye, that abundance and joy could lie hidden behind the façades of empty storefronts and sullen faces.

That initial taste of Russia left me hungry for more, but it wasn't easy to visit the Soviet Union without submitting to a tour group led by a watchful guide. I had to find another way in. So I signed on as a guide myself, working for the U.S. Information Agency (USIA), whose exhibits had been touring the Soviet Union since 1959, when Richard Nixon and Nikita Khrushchev famously bickered at the politically charged exhibition "The American Home." Our theme for 1978—"Agriculture USA"—was equally controversial since the USSR, to its embarrassment and shame, had to import American grain to keep bread on the table. I was in charge of the pickles and preserves stand, where we displayed actual blue-ribbon specimens from the Iowa State Fair. Over that long Moscow winter, the number of mason jars dwindled as I surreptitiously broke into them,

desperate for fruits and vegetables. Life got easier only when the exhibition moved south to Rostov-on-Don, where I reveled in freshly salted and dried fish from the Don River, washed down with mugs of toasty homemade kvass.

Within a few years, I was back in the USSR for dissertation research, this time with my husband. These were still the Brezhnev years, which seemed more stagnant than ever. Moscow was gray, as devoid of color in the sky as the stores were devoid of food. Sometimes we'd pass a shop with something in the display window, only to find it was a pyramid of nothing more than identical cans of mackerel, like a bad Andy Warhol joke. (To this day, I can barely manage to feed canned mackerel even to our cat, who loves it.) On the streets, people were bundled up, both literally and metaphorically. Their expressions were flat; their eyes guarded. Children in prams were swaddled, wrapped up tight in their cocoons. But by this time, I could distinguish between the public faces and the private ones. On the streets and in the workplace, people were shuttered. But at home, their eyes lit up, they sparkled, they laughed. Out came the vodka and the happily mismatched plates and glasses. From tiny private kitchens—and even shabby communal ones—emerged delicious food you couldn't find in the stores. Although the shops were empty, we were always regaled, because Russians instinctively pull out the stops for guests. The language of Soviet Russia distinguished sharply between the words for "to buy" and "to obtain," the latter conveying an unspoken history of heroic bartering and long hours spent traveling to the far reaches of Moscow by metro or bus and standing in seemingly endless lines. When so-called deficit items such as decent sausage or oranges or bananas appeared at kiosks or in the state-owned shops, people would queue for hours at a time, their position inked onto their hands lest anyone try to cut ahead. I often worried about the extraordinary effort and cost that went into putting together these meals.

American tourists who visited the stagnant Soviet Union came home with horror stories about the food they encountered—the limp cabbage, the wizened potatoes, the gristly chunks of meat. Their stories were true enough, since tourists were shepherded to state-run restaurants that were part of the vast, indifferent Soviet bureaucracy that didn't care whether the food tasted good or bad. But domestic life was different, and that's where the magic took place, for no one can spin culinary straw into gold quite like a Russian. Deprivation has taught Russians to coax flavor from whatever is on hand. And so we delighted in appetizers of dense, sour black bread; pickled herring; cold-smoked sturgeon and hot-smoked salmon; fingernail-size salted mushrooms with whole cloves and dill; chopped beets mixed with walnuts and prunes; flaky hand pies filled with scallions and eggs; half-sour cucumbers and pickled green tomatoes; tiny "hedgehogs" of pâté studded with Siberian pine nuts; and eggplant caviar. Even real caviar could be "obtained" in those days with a perk from the workplace, a pair of used blue jeans, or a favor from a friend.

And there were other characteristically Russian pleasures, such as clandestine midwinter picnics. During the Soviet years, the countryside around Moscow was off limits to foreigners, and special permits were needed even for literary pilgrimages to Leo Tolstoy's estate or Anton Chekhov's country house. As a student of Russian culture, I was dying to visit Abramtsevo, a late-nineteenth-century artists' colony that was central to the revival of Russian folk art. I wanted to see its handcrafted buildings and mosaic-rich interiors, to absorb the spirit of Modest Mussorgsky and Nikolai Rimsky-Korsakov, whose music was celebrated there. So our dear friends Nadia and Volodia concocted a plan. My husband and I were to dress as close as possible to Soviet style and remain silent and wooden-faced throughout the ride north from Moscow on the suburban train. We hopped off at the Abramtsevo station, trying hard not to display our excitement. It was the most glorious kind of January day, when the sky is a brilliant blue and the snow radiates light. The temperature was twenty below, but we were warmly dressed. We headed onto a forest path for the half-hour walk to the colony. As we entered a clearing surrounded by tall pine trees, Nadia declared it was lunchtime, and before our eyes, a feast materialized, as if from nowhere, like the tablecloth from Russian fairy tales that magically spreads itself—except that we couldn't sit down in the snow. We remained standing, shifting from foot to foot to keep our toes from stiffening. Out of Nadia's basket came roasted chicken, a jar of salted mushrooms, and another of salted cucumbers. Next emerged a loaf of sour black bread and little pies stuffed with cabbage and hard-boiled eggs. Lest we felt the cold on that wintry day, Volodia had thoughtfully packed a bottle of vodka, which we passed around and around, the fiery spirits immediately warming us. I wanted to shout with glee at the beauty of this picnic and of this day. But that would have been unwise. Even though we were alone in the woods, we were afraid to attract attention, so we expressed our joy in whispers and mime.

Brezhnev died while my husband and I were in Moscow. The streets were filled with thousands of soldiers, medal-laden bigwigs, and specially delegated workers who queued up to view Brezhnev's corpse, which lay in state at the House of Unions. People thronged into Moscow from afar, drawn to the center as much from anxiety as from a desire to connect. And then a new elderly leader was selected, followed by an even older one. We left the Soviet Union much as we had found it, slowly collapsing. More trips to the Soviet Union followed until I had a baby and no longer felt as footloose as before. By the time I next visited Moscow, in 1993, the USSR had vanished, at least in name, and I was seeing Russia for the first time. Cafés and restaurants were popping up everywhere, with full menus, the food skillfully prepared and swiftly and graciously presented. And yet the buildings were still crumbling and the sky was still gunmetal gray. As I had done so many times before, I spent long hours in the archives, leaving only when the reading room closed for the day. One evening I found myself racing to the metro in a downpour. The pavement was slippery underfoot, but I was so caught up in the day's discoveries that I paid little attention to my surroundings. Before I knew it, I'd turned from scholar to slapstick comedian performing a classic routine: a banana peel, a puddle, and I was flat on my ass, laughing at the absurdity. Bananas in Russia? Lying there in the puddle, I looked around and saw more banana peels. My first thought was, "Isn't it wonderful that there are now bananas in Russia, plentiful enough that their peels can be so carelessly discarded?" But almost immediately, a second thought came to mind—how could there be so much litter in Moscow? Where was the army of bent-over women sweeping the streets with their twig brooms?

That banana peel encapsulates for me a truth about Russia, a country I thought I knew so well; it's slippery. In Russia, things are seldom what they seem. The Russians have a good word for that: *pokazukha*, what we call Potemkin villages. As the story goes, Catherine the Great's lover Count Grigory Potemkin wanted to spare her the sight of her wretched empire, so when the empress sailed down the Dnieper River, he ordered picturesque façades to be built along the route. This story is likely apocryphal, if only because astute Russians have long made an art of reading between the lines, of discerning the reality beneath the veneer. But it contains a general truth: Catherine, like many of her subjects, was happy enough to be deceived. She played along. Over the decades I, too, became adept at the sort of parsing that helped me navigate the paradoxes of Soviet life. Even so, I was flummoxed sometimes. One evening in particular stands out. Friends had introduced me to Zhenya, a renowned heart surgeon, and when he invited me to dinner, I jumped at the chance. Given Zhenya's status, I assumed his quarters would be posh. I was shocked to discover that he lived in a communal apartment, sharing a kitchen and bath with nine other families. He was, he said, lucky to live alone—at least his twelve-foot-square room gave him personal space. A table, narrow bed, wardrobe, and shelves provided the only furnishings. By American standards, Zhenya had nothing to show for his achievements.

By the time I arrived at Zhenya's, I was starving. Years of experience in the Soviet Union had taught me never to eat before visiting because even when food was in short supply, it miraculously materialized in more than ample amounts for guests. So my heart fell when I glanced at Zhenya's bare table. A bachelor, a busy doctor—I should have known better. But within moments, he had retrieved a bottle of vodka and two shot glasses. He then pulled a jar from under his bed. "White mushrooms!" he cried triumphantly. "I salted them myself!" Not only had Zhenya preserved these mushrooms (which we prize as porcini), but he had also gathered them himself. The mushrooms had been brushed clean; layered with salt, peppercorns, bay leaves, and dill; and then left in a dark place to age for a month. They tasted of the earth. No vinegar puckered the mouth or distracted from their dusky flavor. Zhenya spooned the mushrooms onto small chipped plates. We toasted the bounty of the earth and our acquaintance.

Salted mushrooms and vodka are classic *zakuski*, appetizers that leave you thirsting for more. Zhenya soon excused himself to prepare the next course. Despite my offer to help, he wouldn't allow me to go near the kitchen— embarrassed, no doubt, by the grubbiness of the communal space. I settled down with a book of poetry, imagining the grease-spattered burners, the dented aluminum pots, the crowds of cockroaches, the overflowing garbage that too often made up the landscape of a shared kitchen. After twenty minutes, Zhenya reappeared, wielding a heavy cast-iron skillet that sputtered and steamed. It was in his simple gesture of setting down the hot skillet that I noticed his hands—a cardiovascular surgeon's hands that had foraged for mushrooms in the Russian countryside, Russia's metaphorical heart.

I shifted my focus to the skillet. Inside were cubes of potato fried in lavish amounts of butter along with whole cloves of garlic. The meal might have been a cardiologist's nightmare, but we dug right in, spearing the potatoes straight from the skillet, the fat dripping onto our chins. The potatoes were perfect: crackly on the outside, creamy within. New potatoes, hand dug in the countryside, again by the surgeon himself. And that was our meal. Nothing fancy or complicated, just mushrooms and vodka and potatoes, honest and plain. This was the poetry that lay behind the battered door to his cramped room.

TODAY'S RUSSIAN TABLE

For those who have never experienced it, what I call the poetry of Russian life might be impossible to imagine. When I published my first cookbook, *À la Russe: A Cookbook of Russian Hospitality*, in 1983, the political landscape was similarly fraught. It was still very much the Cold War. The *New York Times* had planned to feature my book, but on publication day, September 1, a Korean jetliner was shot down when it trespassed into Soviet airspace. Talk about Russian hospitality! The feature was pulled. Now, once again, Russia is eyed with great suspicion, and once again I find myself trying to convey what's so captivating about Russian culture and cuisine. So much has changed since Soviet times, and yet there's something undeniably immutable about Russian life.

Some of Moscow's high-end restaurants speak to this timelessness. Back when I was a USIA guide, I lived for two months in the Metropol hotel, just steps from Red Square and the Bolshoi Theater. Once a splendid art nouveau building, the Metropol was shabby by the 1970s, though you could still glimpse its great bones. Each morning I felt like a duchess as I swept down the hotel's grand staircase to the dining room where, with a little imagination, I entered into the faded elegance of the past. The domed ceiling of leaded glass made the room feel like a conservatory, but the once-lush palms were now spindly, the massive chandelier covered in dust. In true Soviet style, only a few standard dishes from the multipaged leather-bound menu were available to order. Certainly not the elegant Salade Olivier with hazel grouse and crayfish tails created by chef Lucien Olivier for Moscow's Hermitage restaurant in the 1860s. Over the ensuing century, this famous salad had morphed into the ubiquitous Capital Salad, a pyramid of boiled potatoes drenched with mayonnaise and studded with canned peas. At least the Metropol's version contained generous chunks of chicken.

The Metropol has now been restored to near-tsarist splendor. The restaurant boasts a "brand chef" who is happy to transport you to the past with Strawberries Romanoff, Ruinart champagne, and crystal bowls full of caviar served with mother-of-pearl spoons. Burbling water from the marble fountain and the gentle notes of a harp will soothe any jangled nerves that the champagne doesn't ease. Yet, gilded and opulent as its ambience is, the Metropol is no aberration in Russia. Moscow and Saint Petersburg, and increasingly other cities, are filled with fine-dining restaurants that display culinary sophistication as well as an understanding of hospitality and polished service that would stun anyone who spent time in Soviet Russia. Dozens of magazines, cookbooks, cooking shows, and culinary schools now showcase all kinds of food—international recipes, Russian peasant fare, and the sort of worldly meals once enjoyed only by the aristocracy.

When I wrote my first cookbook, I was enamored of the grand dishes of French-inspired haute cuisine named after Russian noblemen—rich preparations such as chicken Demidoff and Nesselrode pudding. Their names evoked a romantic vision of Russia that Americans still find beguiling: *Swan Lake*, Nijinsky, Nicholas and Alexandra, *Doctor Zhivago*. But much as I love my early enthusiasms, Russian food has evolved, and so has my taste. In the pages of this book, you'll find neither nineteenth-century haute cuisine nor such Soviet stalwarts as herring under a fur coat (pickled herring layered with boiled potatoes, carrots, and beets and wearing a generous coat of mayonnaise). Nor will you find the foods of the Soviet Republics that were absorbed as colonial cuisines into the Russian repertoire, such as Georgian chicken *tabaka* (crisp flattened chicken) and Uzbek *plov* (pilaf). These varieties of culinary practice remain rightful components of a broadly conceived Russian cuisine, but in this book I'm seeking the flavors and techniques that have characterized Russian cooking from the start. I'm digging deep into the old ways to showcase food rooted in the countryside, particularly in the remote regions where the extremes of climate have inspired an inventive, resilient, and earthy cuisine.

Along the way I also hope to dispel some myths and especially to correct the impression that Russian food exists in two extremes: elaborate dishes such as Beef Stroganoff and Veal Orloff versus plain old cabbage and potatoes. The Russia I describe here is a place not seen by Americans on TV or on tourist trips devoted to the country's major cities. Even those of us who have traveled to Russia many times can miss the current conjunction of the old and the new, guided as we are by our preconceptions. And because our political view of Russia tends to be equally binary, I try hard to provide through the prism of food a more nuanced view of the country and its culture—to offer a glimpse into private life in Russia, where the kitchen and the table, the dacha and nature, take center stage.

Having endured more than their share of horrific regimes, Russians are highly adept at devising ways to lead emotionally rich lives despite oppressive politics and sometimes-murderous governmental control. They define their lives not by their current autocrats but by the rhythms of the seasons and of the domestic sphere, of growing gardens and foraging, of time spent with dear friends and family. Birthdays, name days, anniversaries, and other celebrations are marked with food, commemorations as ingrained as the annual cycles of planting and harvesting. Isn't that really how we all live? Except for Russians the conditions are more extreme, and not only in climate. Russians know well that occasions of joy and pleasure can prove unexpectedly fleeting, so they've learned how to revel in them. What's striking about this moment in Russian life is that foodways are being renewed with such vigor and excitement, opening a window on the cultural and the culinary, the present and the past. Nostalgia and identity, deliciousness and diet, are the inspirations for today's vibrant food scene.

Fortuitously, Russia's culinary continuity—a through line that largely bypasses both Western and Soviet influences—happens to coincide with the diet most often touted as wholesome today: whole grains rich in fiber; cultured dairy products and fermented foods bursting with probiotics; vitamin-rich plants foraged in the wild. Some people think of Russian food as intrinsically bland, but it's not at all. An abundance of pungent horseradish and mustard gives Russian foods a powerful zing, and the love of all things sour adds a further layer of intensity, which is achieved by fermenting and culturing just about everything at hand. And then there are the pies, marvels in their own right. They appear in a multitude of sizes and shapes, with a dizzying array of fillings, from simple summer pies brimming with berries to the glorious fish pie known as *kulebyaka*. Rustic food means fresh farmer's cheese studded with radishes and scallions; hot cabbage soup enriched with caramelized onions; cold beet soup brimming with garden vegetables and dill; salted wild mushrooms scented with garlic and cloves; tart black currants stirred simply with honey for a midwinter boost of vitamin C; black bread toasted and fermented into refreshing kvass; vodka infused with the first birch buds of spring. These are the nurturing, transformative foods of the Russian heartlands.

1

DRINKS, PRESERVES, AND SAUCES

Sea Buckthorn Tonic

Облепиховый кисель

Russians love *kisel'*, fruit juice thickened with potato starch and barely cooked to ensure that its nutritive properties remain intact. *Kisel'* can be made as thick as a pudding or thin enough to drink, which is how I suggest making it here, with sea buckthorn, a kind of super fruit, filled not just with vitamins, amino acids, and antioxidants but also all of the omega fatty acids.

During the Soviet years, when medicine was hard to come by, Muscovites would seek out sea buckthorn berries from Siberia, which they believed would cure everything from the common cold to cancer. Like the Russians, I'm a bit obsessed with sea buckthorn. I adore the berry not only for its restorative powers but also for its tart, dusky flavor.

Kisel' is generally chilled before serving. But in the depths of winter, you might also want to try this drink hot, as I tasted it in the provincial city of Velsk, in a charming restaurant called Yuri's Courtyard. We'd arrived more than a bit ragged after a long overnight train ride. A steaming mug of this golden beverage perked me right up.

Sea buckthorn berries are available frozen. You can also use bottled juice (see Sources).

Serves 4 to 6

2 cups fresh or thawed frozen sea buckthorn berries (or ¾ cup unsweetened sea buckthorn juice)

2½ cups plus 2 tablespoons cold water

¾ cup sugar

2 tablespoons potato starch

Put the berries through a food mill, pressing down hard on the seeds to extract all the juice. You will end up with about ¾ cup of juice.

In a medium saucepan, bring the 2½ cups water to a boil with the sugar, lower the heat, and simmer for 1 minute. Spoon the potato starch into a small bowl and gradually stir in the remaining 2 tablespoons water to make a loose paste. Whisk the paste into the sugar syrup and bring to a full boil again. The mixture will thicken slightly. Whisk in the sea buckthorn juice, lower the heat, and simmer for 1 minute.

Serve immediately, or pour into glasses or bowls to chill in the refrigerator. It will keep for several days, covered, in the refrigerator.

Lingonberry-Cranberry Juice

Брусничный морс с клюквой

The Russians love berry juice so much that it has its own name, *mors*, which distinguishes it from other fruit juices. Before the advent of commercial sodas, Russians served berry juice at almost every meal, and it remains a popular refresher. Use red or black currants in place of some or all of the lingonberries or cranberries. You'll just need to adjust the amount of sugar, depending on your taste and the sweetness of the berries.

Serves 6

3 cups fresh or frozen lingonberries

2 cups fresh or frozen cranberries

6 cups water

½ cup sugar

2 tablespoons freshly squeezed lemon juice

If the berries are frozen, thaw them at room temperature. Put the berries through a food mill. You will end up with about 1 cup of juice. Set aside.

Scrape the berry pulp from the food mill into a large saucepan. Stir in the water and bring to a boil. Simmer, uncovered, for 5 minutes, then put the mixture through the food mill again. This time you'll get about 6 cups of juice.

While the juice is still hot, add the sugar, stirring until it dissolves. Then stir in the lemon juice and reserved berry juice. If you want the juice to be clear, pour the mixture through a fine-mesh strainer to capture the last of the tiny seeds. Transfer the juice to a 2-quart jar or lidded pitcher. Let cool to room temperature before placing in the refrigerator.

The juice keeps for a couple of weeks in the refrigerator. Stir or shake gently before serving.

Variation: Lingonberry-Beet Juice

Брусничный морс со свёклой

Serves 6

1½ cups fresh or frozen lingonberries

1 large beet (8 ounces), peeled and coarsely grated

6 cups water

3 tablespoons sugar, or to taste

2 tablespoons freshly squeezed lemon juice, or to taste

This garnet-colored juice is a light tonic for beet lovers. The lingonberries offer a nice boost and tart alternative to the apples and ginger typically mixed with beets at American juice bars. The amount of sugar and lemon to add depends on the age and sweetness of the beets, as well as your own preferences. If, after you've chilled the juice, the balance doesn't seem quite right, you can always adjust it then.

Follow the instructions for the lingonberry-cranberry juice, adding the grated beet to the lingonberry pulp and water in the saucepan.

AT THE DACHA

Technically speaking, a *dacha* is a Russian country cottage, used most often in the summer. But once you add the preposition *at*—"at the dacha"—that summer cottage becomes a state of mind, a kind of Eden. It's no longer just a building or the land it sits on. "At the dacha" evokes an immediate connection to the rhythms of nature and to being Russian, a source of security in a country where social upheaval and hunger remain within active memory. Russians are devoted to their dachas not only because they offer a respite from urban life, but because they enable self-sufficiency—the urge to sow and reap and forage and preserve in anticipation of the long winter to come.

Dachas aren't vacation homes where you just kick back and drink kvass. They're more often minifarms and gateways to the wild. In springtime, Russians gather the first mushrooms and wild greens of the season and turn over the newly exposed soil, reveling in its earthy smell. Then they plant. Midsummer is for picking berries and harvesting early potatoes and beets and crisp, refreshing cucumbers. With late summer come more mushrooms and wild berries and the sudden urgency of the garden harvest, when the real labor begins: the salting, pickling, drying, and brining; the preserving of fruits and infusing of vodkas. All this activity is crucial to Russian identity, based for a thousand years on being close to the soil, whether one's ancestors were landowners or serfs. The dacha offers an essential means of spiritual survival quite apart from the crucial food that is grown there. Even today, when Russians have access to grocery stores with ample produce, many continue to tend dacha gardens, if only to raise a crop of potatoes, a kind of insurance against bad times ahead.

Despite all the work involved, being at the dacha also affords relaxation. It means the midnight sun, long summer days that for months in the Far North never end. It means swimming in rivers and lakes, and simmering freshly caught fish over an open fire into the fisherman's soup, *ukha*. It means harvesting cucumbers and radishes and scallions and dill and dicing them into the cold soup called *okroshka* that's doused with a bottle of kvass. It means both freedom and tradition. This unstructured (or self-structured) life is a large part of the dacha's appeal.

Most dachas are less picturesque than the word "cottage" suggests in English. (The recent, modish term *kottedzh* describes the stylish country houses of newly affluent post-Soviet Russians.) The typical dacha is a modest wooden dwelling, something like an old-fashioned summer camp and usually in need of constant repair. So the feeling of leisure coexists with the do-it-yourself impulse to tinker and improve, to build new garden beds and fix leaky roofs or listing foundations. Because many dachas lack indoor plumbing, a *banya*—the Russian steam bath—adds to the charms of country life. The special smell of the dacha—drying herbs, especially dill, and fresh birch besoms for massaging the skin in the *banya*—mixes with the pleasant mustiness of old wood.

There are entire dacha communities tucked off the main roads where people collectively engage in summer pursuits. One such community lies near Severodvinsk, on the shore of the White Sea. To get there, we commandeered a taxi from Arkhangelsk, our driver cursing us for every mile we had to traverse on a road paved with crumbling concrete blocks. The road led past camouflaged Soviet-era military installations and endless forest. And then suddenly, there was a charming village of wooden houses and well-worn footpaths cutting through overgrown meadows ablaze with wildflowers. Each small house had a small plot of land intensively cultivated with gardens and fruit trees and berry bushes. The lushness obscured all the labor involved. For several seasons our host, Yuri, had carted in humus to enrich the sandy soil, laboriously working it in by hand. The rewards were great—cucumbers, tomatoes, beets, scallions, onions, carrots, garlic, potatoes, green peppers, and cabbage, inspiring a quick summer soup concocted by Yuri's wife, Alexandra, who flavored the vegetables with parsley, chervil, tarragon, and dill. She saved the garden's marigolds, dill crowns, and black currant, horseradish, and cherry leaves for her famous pickles. We worked together that day, adhering to traditional gender roles. Yuri and my husband constructed concrete forms for a new *banya*, while Alexandra and I made the soup, baked fish pies and berry pies, and put up pickles. We convened for tea around a smoky old samovar propped up in the garden. It was a beautiful, rhythmic, hardworking day.

Cultivated gardens are only part of the dacha story. "At the dacha" is also about foraging in forests and meadows for the wild mushrooms and berries with which Russia abounds. For Russians, foraging isn't a trendy pastime, it's a deeply embedded ritual defined by the seasons, the heat, and the rainfall. Each summer weekend, the commuter trains heading out to the countryside are jammed with foragers toting empty baskets and sacks, only to return later with their buckets and pails spilling over with mushrooms and berries. The mood is jubilant; the excitement palpable. Vladimir Nabokov captured the essence of the hunt in his memoir, *Speak Memory*. Though he describes his mother's foraging on their country estate (a far cry from the simple dacha life), the emotion she experiences from the hunt is universal.

One of her greatest pleasures in summer was the very Russian sport of *hodit' po gribi* (looking for mushrooms). Fried in butter and thickened with sour cream, her delicious finds appeared regularly on the dinner table. Not that the gustatory moment mattered much. Her main delight was in the quest. . . .

Rainy weather would bring out these beautiful plants in profusion under the firs, birches, and aspens in our park, especially in its older part, east of the carriage road that divided the park in two. Its shady recesses would then harbor that special boletic reek which makes a Russian's nostrils dilate—a dark, dank, satisfying blend of damp moss, rich earth, rotting leaves. . . .

This immersion in nature is what being at the dacha is all about. The forest floor and the stands of birch trees aren't a mere backdrop to the hunt. They are vital to the Russians' well-being. It's no surprise that the Russian words for *family*, *motherland*, *native*, and *dear* all share the same root as the word for *nature*. They are all one.

Infused Vodkas
Настойки

PEPPER VODKA
Перцовка

Makes 1 (750 ml) bottle

1 (750-ml) bottle high-quality vodka, such as Russian Standard, Stolichnaya, or even Tito's

1 hot red pepper, 4 inches long, such as cayenne or jalapeño

8 black peppercorns

2 allspice berries

1-inch piece cinnamon stick

2 tablespoons mild honey

Pepper vodka is one of Russia's most popular infusions. It packs a different kind of punch from horseradish vodka, with a nice hint of spice. This vodka infuses longer than the others I've included, so you'll want to taste it daily until it reaches the peak of heat that you like. I find it just right after three or four days, but you can infuse it for up to a week.

Transfer all but 2 tablespoons of the vodka to a wide-mouth 1-quart jar, reserving the original bottle. Remove the stem from the pepper and score the skin in three places to enable faster infusion. Drop the pepper into the jar.

Slightly crush the peppercorns, allspice, and cinnamon in a mortar with a pestle and add the spices to the jar. In a small bowl, stir the honey with the remaining 2 tablespoons vodka until the honey dissolves, then add it to the jar. Close the lid and allow the vodka to infuse at room temperature for at least 3 days. Strain the pepper and spices and transfer the vodka by means of a funnel into the reserved bottle. Chill well before serving. The vodka will keep indefinitely in the freezer.

continued

CHERRY VODKA

Вишнёвка

Makes 1 (750 ml) bottle

1 (750-ml) bottle
high-quality vodka

36 fresh, sweet cherries,
such as Bing

This delicate infusion capturing the flavor of summer is ideal for either a hot summer's day or a cold winter's night. The vodka takes on a subtle shade of pink from the infused cherry pits. Use the unused flesh to make a sweet cherry dessert, like clafoutis or cobbler.

Transfer the vodka to a wide-mouth 1-quart jar, reserving the original bottle. Pit the cherries, crush the pits with a mallet or meat pounder, and drop the pits into the vodka. Close the lid and allow the vodka to infuse at room temperature for 48 hours. Strain out the pits and transfer the vodka by means of a funnel into the reserved bottle. Chill well before serving. The vodka will keep indefinitely in the freezer.

HORSERADISH VODKA

Хреновка

Makes 1 (750 ml) bottle

1 (750-ml) bottle
high-quality vodka

1½ ounces fresh
horseradish root, peeled
(about a 2½-inch chunk)

This is my favorite vodka infusion, with just the right amount of bite. Mike Wiley, the brilliant chef at Eventide in Portland, Maine, describes his experience with it: "I had a nip of it with some smoked swordfish belly last night and looked up to find that I was standing in a column of golden light." It may not be holy water, but it's bracing!

Taste the vodka after 24 hours. If your horseradish isn't especially potent, you may want to let the vodka infuse for up to 48 hours.

Transfer the vodka to a wide-mouth 1-quart jar, reserving the original bottle. Cut the horseradish into 6 pieces and drop them into the vodka. Close the lid and allow the vodka to infuse at room temperature for 24 hours. Strain the horseradish and transfer the vodka by means of a funnel into the reserved bottle. Chill well before serving. The vodka will keep indefinitely in the freezer.

TARRAGON VODKA

Настойка на тархуне

Makes 1 (750 ml) bottle

1 (750-ml) bottle
high-quality vodka

1 small bunch tarragon (to
yield 3 cups loose leaves)

15 large fresh mint leaves

1½ tablespoons freshly
squeezed lemon juice

1½ teaspoons mild honey

The herbal notes of this vodka will beguile your guests. Although dill is
the quintessential Russian culinary herb, tarragon is enjoyed, too. Native
to Central Asia—probably Siberia—the plant is hearty, with an assertive
taste that's tempered here by the addition of mint, lemon, and honey. This
infusion turns a lovely pale green.

Transfer the vodka to a wide-mouth 1-quart jar, reserving the original bottle.
Strip the tarragon leaves from the coarse stems and chop them along with
the mint leaves. Place the leaves in a small bowl and stir in the lemon juice
and honey. Let sit for 20 minutes until the leaves turn moist, then add to the
vodka. Close the lid and allow the vodka to infuse at room temperature for
24 hours. Strain the leaves and transfer the vodka by means of a funnel into
the reserved bottle. Chill well before serving. The vodka will keep indefinitely
in the freezer.

BIRCH-BUD VODKA

Настойка из берёзовых почек

Makes 1 (750 ml) bottle

1 (750-ml) bottle
high-quality vodka

Scant ¾ cup birch buds

1 tablespoon mild honey

Birch trees and vodka! What could be more Russian? Here the two come
together in a single tasty shot. This infusion has a lovely herbal flavor that's
unexpected and just shy of bitter. It's the perfect springtime tonic, since
you have to pick the buds before they unfurl into leaves. Gathering them
is admittedly laborious, but it's a nice excuse to spend an early spring day
outdoors. And Russians swear by the healthful properties of birch buds,
which they believe cleanse the blood and counteract inflammation.

Transfer the vodka to a wide-mouth 1-quart jar, reserving the original bottle.
Muddle the birch buds with the honey in a mortar with a pestle and let sit for
30 minutes, then add to the vodka and stir well. Close the lid and allow the
vodka to infuse in a cool, dark place for 1 week, turning the jar occasionally to
keep the ingredients well mixed. Strain the birch buds and transfer the vodka
by means of a funnel into the reserved bottle. Chill well before serving. The
vodka will keep indefinitely in the freezer.

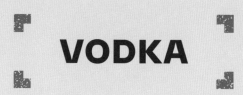

VODKA

Asked what comes to mind when they hear the words "Russian food," people usually say borscht, vodka, and caviar. Borscht is actually Ukrainian, but vodka and caviar are indeed iconically Russian—and ideal complements to each other. The spirit's crisp, clean profile delivers a refreshing counterpoint to the rich, buttery fish eggs. No indulgence is more Russian than a generous scoop of caviar followed by a toast—to peace, to friendship, to beautiful women—and a swallow. "Moderation in all things" is a Greek motto, not a Russian one.

Vodkas vary wildly depending on their base ingredient and how each variety is crafted. The spirit can be distilled from any fermentable ingredient (even from milk, in Vermont). Although Poland has perfected the art of distilling soft-tasting vodka from potatoes, I think the finest comes from grains such as rye, barley, or wheat. Vodka's transformative powers meant that it was originally used for medicinal purposes. Pulkheria Ivanovna, in Nikolai Gogol's story "Old-World Landowners," concocts variously infused spirits to cure every ill, including a vodka infused with the herb centaury to heal ringing in your ears or shingles on your face, and another with peach pits in case you've bumped your head against the corner of a cupboard or a table when getting out of bed and a lump's sprung up on your forehead.

Russia's love of alcohol is not only literary but central to Russian history. The twelfth-century *Tale of Bygone Years,* Russia's earliest chronicle, relates that when Grand Prince Vladimir debated which religion would best unite his new nation, he dismissed Islam in favor of Christianity, proclaiming "Drinking is the joy of Rus'." From the earliest times, the Russians enjoyed mead and kvass, lightly alcoholic beverages achieved through fermentation rather than distillation. They also produced fermented birch juice and beer. Distilled spirits, in the form of vodka, were introduced to Russia by the fifteenth century, either from the south, through Crimea, or from Western Europe along the Hanseatic trade routes—no one knows for sure. What we do know is that after domestic production began in the late sixteenth century, the drink—called *goriachee vino* (burning wine) or *khlebnoe vino* (grain wine)—gradually displaced the older beverages in popularity. The word *vodka* (a diminutive, affectionate form of "water") didn't come into common usage until the late nineteenth century.

It's hard to say who's to blame for the Russian proclivity for spirits—the vodka itself, or the government. Ever since Ivan the Terrible established the first taverns in 1553, Russian rulers have vacillated between lax and strict approaches to alcohol, at times encouraging its consumption to build up the state treasury and ease public unrest, at other times curtailing access. Vodka was already causing significant social problems by the seventeenth century, but the government, which enjoyed a virtual monopoly on its commerce, was loath to curtail production and lose revenue. In the early eighteenth century, Peter the Great used vodka to political advantage, plying his court and foreign diplomats with drink as a form of intelligence gathering. He introduced drinking games, convened a Drunken Synod in mockery of the Russian Orthodox Church, and famously forced his subjects to drink vodka from the Great Eagle goblet that held one and a half liters and that had to be drained on the spot.

Numerous attempts at prohibition proved unsuccessful. Temperance societies were considered such a financial threat to government income that they were banned and their proselytizers exiled to Siberia. But pervasive drunkenness was an equivalent threat, and in 1914, as Russia entered World War I, Tsar Nicholas I succeeded in making Russia the first country to institute prohibition. More recently, Soviet leaders Yuri Andropov and Mikhail Gorbachev attempted to regulate access to alcohol, generating widespread discontent, especially Gorbachev's 1988 restrictions, which led to a run on sugar, used to produce moonshine. The government compounded its problem by imposing a sugar ration, which was even more widely unpopular, since sugar was necessary for making the baked goods and preserves the Russians pride themselves on.

Being old-school, I prefer my vodka not too smooth or soft, but with a bit of an afterbite. I also avoid commercially flavored vodkas, preferring to infuse my own. Good vodka should have a pleasant aroma, with no hint of ethanol or oily finish. And it should be served ice-cold. I always keep bottles in the freezer, ready for immediate consumption. Unlike a cocktail, Russian vodka isn't meant for sipping—it's drunk straight, downed from a shot glass in a single swig. The sensation of the icy liquid coursing through your body is quite wonderful—warming in winter, refreshing in summer.

Unless it's abused, vodka is still considered healing. Russian friends taught me their fail-proof regimen for a cold. Just before bedtime, pour yourself a generous shot of *pertsovka* (pepper vodka), then slather a piece of black bread with honey and top it with thinly sliced raw garlic. After eating the bread and downing the vodka, wrap a warm scarf around your neck and crawl into bed. By morning you should be cured, though no one will want to come near you since you'll reek of garlic.

Summer Berry Compote

Компот из летних ягод

For Russians, compote is not a dessert but a drink to enjoy year-round. In winter they make it with dried fruits, and in summer with fresh ones. I favor this very berry-forward version: summer in a glass. I simmer the berries just long enough to flavor the water and don't usually strain them since they look so pretty and can be scooped from the bottom of a glass with a spoon. Any combination of berries works well for compote, so feel free to substitute red currants, blackberries, or sea buckthorn. Or you can use fruits, like peaches and plums, apples and pears, for a different flavor spectrum. In any case, you'll want to taste and adjust the amount of honey you add, depending on the fruit and your own sweet tooth.

Serves 8

8 ounces small strawberries, hulled

8 ounces gooseberries

8 ounces black currants

6 ounces raspberries

6 cups water

3 to 6 tablespoons mild honey

Place all the berries in a large saucepan with the water and bring to a boil. Lower the heat and simmer, uncovered, for 10 minutes. Remove the pan from the heat, stir in the honey, and allow the compote to cool to room temperature. Refrigerate for at least 2 hours before serving, well chilled.

Hot Spiced Honey
Сбитень

This ancient drink was once imbibed several times daily as a tonic, especially in winter. Medicinal herbs, like St. John's wort and fir tips, were frequently added, either to soothe or invigorate the system. Most often this spiced honey drink is nonalcoholic, though it becomes Russia's answer to glogg when the honey is simmered with brandy, beer, or wine. Hawkers with samovar-like urns slung over their shoulders used to ply Russia's streets, offering passersby a bracing drink for only a few kopecks, but like other old-fashioned figures, these *sbiten'* sellers disappeared after the revolution. Now, happily, this drink is experiencing a revival, and *sbiten'* tastes lovely even when sipped from a mug at home.

Serves 6

6 cups water

¾ cup mild honey

1½-inch knob fresh ginger, peeled and grated

3 cinnamon sticks

8 black peppercorns

3 whole cloves

6 allspice berries

6 cardamom pods

1 teaspoon dried mint or lemon balm, crushed

Lemon slices for serving (optional)

In a medium saucepan, bring all the ingredients except for the mint and lemon slices to a boil. Lower the heat and skim off any foam that rises to the surface. Add the mint and simmer the mixture for 15 minutes. Strain and serve, with lemon slices to cut the sweetness, if desired.

Tea with Sea Buckthorn and Honey

Чай с облепихой и мёдом

As you may have gathered, I have a thing for sea buckthorn. I just love its dusky flavor and tart jolt. If you're new to these berries and not ready to jump right in, you may want to begin gently by mixing them with honey and black tea. This recipe allows for near-endless variations, depending on the tea and the honey you choose. I sometimes use black currant–flavored tea to pair two of the berries I like best.

If you don't drink all of the tea right away, you'll find that it separates in the pot—but as soon as you pour it, the mixture comes together again. This tea is an excellent way to combine your daily doses of vitamin C and caffeine.

Serves 4

1½ cups fresh or thawed frozen sea buckthorn berries (see Sources)

2 tablespoons high-quality loose-leaf black tea

3 cups cold water

¼ cup mild honey

Put 1 cup of the berries through a food mill, pressing down hard on the seeds. You will end up with about ¼ cup juice.

Place the tea leaves in a medium teapot. Bring the water just to a boil and pour it over the leaves. Allow the tea to steep for 5 minutes, then strain it into a 6-cup French-press coffeepot (see Note). Stir in the honey and the remaining ½ cup berries. Allow the mixture to steep for 10 minutes, then press down on the plunger to push all the solids to the bottom of the pot. Serve immediately.

Note

Russian restaurants use French presses that are dedicated to tea so that the oils from coffee won't sully the taste. Part of the beauty of this drink also lies in seeing the berries shimmer through the glass. But if you have only a standard teapot, you can steep the tea in a heatproof measuring cup, then pour the strained tea into the teapot. Stir in the honey and berries and let the mixture steep again, then pour through a strainer into cups to serve.

BIRCH

The Russians love their birch trees, both visually and gastronomically. They even enjoy drinking what they call birch juice—the light, sweet sap of the trees—which tastes like bottled spring. American companies are now beginning to sell birch sap commercially, branding it as something new, with names like TÅPPE and Säpp that play on the allure of New Nordic cuisine. But birch trees have long been important to both the Russian pantry and medicine cabinet. Besides drinking birch juice straight, Russians turn it into lightly fermented kvass. They also make a lovely tisane, which is a little like wintergreen in flavor, by pouring boiling birch juice over fresh twigs and letting them steep. Birch buds are believed to have healing powers, especially when paired with vodka (see page 41).

Even more potent is chaga (*Inonotus obliquus*), a shiny, charcoal-colored fungus that grows on birch trees. Reputed to be a miracle food with antioxidant and anti-inflammatory properties, chaga has long been used in Russian folk medicine, either imbibed as an infusion or used as a tincture, and is even reputed to have cured the twelfth-century Grand Prince Vladimir of lip cancer. Though chaga's efficacy remains unproven, a compound called betulinic acid, derived from the bark of white birch trees, is frequently used in cancer treatment today.

During times of famine, Russians resorted to eating *zabolon'*, the inner bark of the tree. They boiled it until soft, then dried it and ground it into flour. Hoping to create an interesting recipe at home, I decided to experiment with *zabolon'*. With a sharp hunting knife, my husband cut off large shards of the inner bark. I boiled the bark for an hour, then strained it and used the liquid to simmer whole spelt berries. The resulting concoction had a slightly tannic and bitter taste, so I added some dried mushrooms that I'd reconstituted and sautéed in a little butter. Thanks to the mushrooms, the dish ended up tasty, but the recipe didn't make the cut for this book.

Russians have been finding uses for birch trees for hundreds of years. Each spring they pulled the pliable outer bark from the tree and wove strips of it into *lapti*, the traditional footwear of the peasantry. They also fashioned it into storage vessels—the bark's antiseptic properties discouraged insects and helped prevent spoilage. Burls were removed from the trees and carved into bowls, while the fresh, aromatic branches were (and still are) tied together into *veniki*, besoms used for slapping the skin to stimulate circulation in the Russian bath.

The birch also has deep cultural meanings. The word *birch* is grammatically feminine in gender, and the tree was often personified as a woman, its white bark poetically likened to a fair maiden's skin. In a holdover from pagan times, villagers would dress birch trees in women's clothing, then cut the trees down and leave them in newly planted fields to ensure a fertile crop. Young girls used to seal pacts of friendship by kissing under arches they'd made by bending young birch trees, or through wreaths they had coiled and hung on the tree's branches. These rituals were followed by a symbolic dance called the *beriozka* ("little birch tree"), in which they waved ribbons and branches. Springtime festivities culminated in feasts during which eggs were served to symbolize rebirth. Such practices likely inspired Igor Stravinsky's great 1913 ballet, *The Rite of Spring*.

In 1964 the Soviet government appropriated the beloved birch by naming the chain of state-run foreign-currency stores Beriozka, an irony not lost on the unprivileged populace. These stores offered foods and luxury goods that weren't generally available, and ordinary Russians without access to foreign currency were unable to shop in them, even forcibly barred from entering. When possession of foreign currency was legalized in the 1990s, the stores disappeared, liberating the image of the birch from cynical Soviet branding and restoring it more fully to its fond place in the hearts of ordinary Russians.

Flavored Salts
Ароматизированные соли

SPRUCE SALT
Еловая соль

**Makes about
2 tablespoons**

Several fresh spruce twigs
(enough to yield ¼ cup of
needles, about ¼ ounce)

2 teaspoons coarse
sea salt

This salt has a subtle woodsy flavor that enhances shaved salmon or any kind of meat. Although I've made spruce salt with fresh needles, I prefer the intensity of blackened ones, a technique I adapted from Gunnar Karl Gíslason's *The Hygge Life*. Gunnar blackens pine needles, but I find spruce more resinous and aromatic.

Preheat the oven to 500°F. Line a baking sheet with parchment paper.

While the oven is heating, strip the needles from the spruce twigs. Scatter the needles in a single layer on the prepared sheet and bake until just barely blackened, about 5 minutes. Be careful not to let them incinerate.

Transfer the needles to a spice grinder or mini food processor. Grind until medium fine. You should have about 1 tablespoon of powder. Add the salt and continue to grind until fine. Store in an airtight container for up to 2 weeks.

MONASTERY SALT

Монастырская соль

Makes about ¾ cup

¾ cup rolled oats

¼ cup coarse sea salt

½ teaspoon dill seed

½ teaspoon coriander seed

½ cup water

Vegetable oil, for the pan

Of the flavored Russian salts, I like this one best, even though it takes longest to bake. It takes its name from the monks who flavored their black salt with herbs from the monastery gardens. The salt is aromatic with dill and coriander, and a sprinkling of it on even the most mundane foods will greatly enliven them.

Preheat the oven to 500°F. In a small bowl, mix together the oats, salt, dill seed, and coriander seed. Pour the water over the mixture and stir. Let sit for 15 minutes while the oven is heating.

Grease a small cast-iron pan with a very light film of oil. (I use a 5-inch long-handled blini pan for ease of removing from the oven.) Transfer the oat and salt mixture to the prepared pan. Bake for 2 hours, until the mixture has turned into a hard charred disk.

Carefully remove the pan from the oven. Be prepared for a whoosh of smoke when you open the oven door. (I take the smoking pan right outside to let it cool, so I don't set off our smoke detectors.)

When the disk has cooled, lift it from the pan and break it into chunks with a mallet or meat tenderizer. (I find this easiest to accomplish in an old pan with sides so that bits of charred salt don't fly all over the kitchen.)

Transfer the chunks of salt to a mini food processor and grind to your preference, from medium-fine to fine. The salt can also be pounded the traditional way in a mortar with a pestle, but that's much more laborious. In either case, it's a good idea to sift the finished salt through a sieve to eliminate any lumps. Store in an airtight container for up to a year.

continued

BLACK SALT

Четверговая соль

Makes about ¼ cup

⅓ cup preservative-free rye bread, torn into small pieces (or substitute ⅓ cup of soaked bread left over from making kvass)

¼ cup coarse sea salt

Vegetable oil, for the pan

This stunning salt is also called "Thursday salt" because it was traditionally made once a year, on Maundy Thursday, the Thursday before Easter. As part of the great feast marking Easter Sunday and the end of Lent, hard-boiled eggs were served with black salt. The Russians continued to use the salt throughout the year for its healthful properties (see facing page). Black salt tastes great on bread and butter, and on baked potatoes. Use it in place of other finishing salts, like fleur de sel, to add a new depth of flavor to your food.

In a small bowl, soak the bread in hot water to cover for 30 minutes. Strain any excess water but don't press down on the solids. Return the moistened bread to the bowl and stir in the salt, mixing well.

Preheat the oven to 500°F. Grease a small cast-iron pan with a very light film of oil. (I use a 5-inch long-handled blini pan for ease of removing from the oven.) Transfer the bread and salt mixture to the prepared pan. Bake for 30 minutes, until the mixture has turned into a hard charred disk.

Carefully remove the pan from the oven. Be prepared for a whoosh of smoke when you open the oven door. (I take the smoking pan right outside to let it cool, so I don't set off our smoke detectors.)

When the disk has cooled, lift it from the pan and break it into chunks with a mallet or meat tenderizer. (I find this easiest to accomplish in an old pan with sides so that bits of charred salt don't fly all over the kitchen.)

Transfer the chunks of salt to a mini food processor and grind to your preference, from medium-fine to fine. The salt can also be pounded the traditional way in a mortar with a pestle, but that's much more laborious. In either case it's a good idea to sift the finished salt through a sieve to eliminate any lumps. Store in an airtight container for up to a year.

THURSDAY SALT

The Thursday before Easter (Maundy Thursday) is known in Russia as "Pure Thursday," a time for cleaning the house and cleansing the soul. A charred black salt called "Thursday salt" is ritually prepared beginning at midnight or first thing that morning, to help purify body and soul for the coming year. Devout parishioners bring the salt to church when it's still in brick form, to be blessed along with the traditional Easter sweets of *paskha* and *kulich*. Only after the blessing is the salt broken up with a pestle. In earlier times, Thursday salt was revered enough to be stored in an ornately carved saltcellar kept not in the kitchen area but in the "beautiful corner." This nearly sacred space in every cottage consisted of a table where guests were seated, with one or more icons positioned on a wooden shelf above so that they would be the first thing visitors saw when entering the cottage.

Thursday salt was not so consecrated that it wasn't consumed, however. Traditionally, Russians put great store in this black salt, believing that it cured all sorts of ills, from fatigue to poor circulation to inflamed gums, thanks to the blessing and the chemical transformations of the charring process. (Their centuries-old practice is interesting to contemplate in light of the current fashion for activated charcoal as a detoxifier.) The salt was also tied up with superstition, even among religious peasants, who safeguarded their homes by hiding, in a corner of the cottage, a bag with a pinch of salt that had been blessed by a priest.

Superstition was part of the salt-making process as well. The rye-salt mixture was shaped into a brick and placed in a birchbark shoe or wrapped in a thick linen cloth. This package was set directly on birch logs in the masonry stove, which was then fired. Seven was the number of logs believed to make the best salt, although in some villages the magical number was six—one log set aside on each of the six Sundays of the long Lenten fast to make "Sunday firewood" for the salt. By the time the logs burned down, the salt mixture had baked into a stonelike mass. Whether with six or seven logs, the making of black salt represents a confluence of superstition and faith, with prayer enhancing the fire's magical properties.

Superstitions aside, black salt can be made in several ways. The original method called for mixing salt with the sediment from kvass—itself made from leftover bread—which ensured that no bit of bread went to waste.

When kvass was no longer regularly made at home, Russians began using rye bread instead, moistening the bread with water before mixing it with the salt. Even more of a shortcut is the use of moistened rye flour, though salt made this way doesn't attain the complex flavor of other bread salts.

The Kostroma region north of Moscow is said to have produced the most extraordinary Thursday salt, thanks to the addition of chopped cabbage leaves. Russians in the Far North added seaweed for iodine and flavor, while monks throughout Russia seasoned their salt mixture with herbs and spices before charring. Because the baking process concentrates minerals rather than creating ash, you can create different nutritional as well as flavor profiles. Think of black salt as an opportunity for creativity, and use it as you would any other seasoned finishing salt. I like it not only Russian style, with shaved frozen salmon, but also on any dish that asks for a burst of intensity, such as carpaccio or steamed or grilled vegetables.

Alexandra's Sweet and Sour Cucumbers

"Мамины" кисло-сладкие огурцы

This recipe is a gift from Alexandra Kuzovnikova, who puts up countless jars of preserves at her family's dacha near the White Sea. I met Alexandra through her daughter, Luba, the artistic director of Pikene på Broen, a Norwegian art collective that promotes cultural exchange in the Arctic. My husband and I spent a long August day with Alexandra and her husband, Yuri, during pickling season. It didn't feel wrong to adhere to traditional gender roles. While the guys worked together to rebuild the *banya* (bathhouse), Alexandra and I happily labored in the kitchen, making vegetable soup, fish pies and berry pies, and these flavorful pickles.

Alexandra's pickles have a forceful personality, thanks to the 6 percent vinegar she uses. Standard vinegar in the United States contains only 5 percent acetic acid (6 percent is sold for cleaning!). But even our gentler vinegar yields excellent pickles. It just takes a little longer for the flavors to develop properly. Patience not being my foremost virtue, I opened a jar after only three weeks to discover too subtle a taste. So with the other jar, I waited. After two months, the pickles were still crisp, and the extra time makes the flavor absolutely zing.

Alexandra adds tannic cherry and black currant leaves to keep the pickles crisp, along with marigold petals for their antibacterial properties. She takes a moment to scald each leaf or petal before putting it in the jar. These steps may seem involved, but they're actually relaxing. After all, the dacha is more than a house or a plot of land. It's a state of mind.

I've provided quantities for a 1-quart jar, but this recipe is easy to scale up, depending on how many pickles you'd like to make.

Makes 1 quart

10 to 12 small pickling cucumbers (each about 4 inches long)

3 seed heads of fresh dill (see Note)

4 small black currant leaves

8 cherry leaves

1 very large horseradish leaf, spine removed and leaf torn into 3-inch pieces, or three ¼-inch slices of peeled fresh horseradish root

3 sprigs tarragon

4 large garlic cloves, peeled and cut in half

6 or 7 allspice berries

3 or 4 marigold petals (calendula)

1½ cups water (approximately)

1 tablespoon salt

1 tablespoon sugar

2½ tablespoons apple cider vinegar (5 percent acidity)

Use a 1-quart wide-mouth canning jar. Sterilize the jar in boiling water.

Scrub the cucumbers well and leave them to soak in cold water for 2 to 4 hours to firm up.

When ready to make the pickles, bring a kettle of water to a boil and have a small bowl ready. Place 2 dill heads in the bowl and pour a little boiling water over them to scald and remove any debris. Place the dill heads in the

continued

bottom of the sterilized jar. Repeat the process with a portion of the remaining greens: separately scald 2 black currant leaves, 4 cherry leaves, half of the torn horseradish leaves, and 2 sprigs of the tarragon, dropping each ingredient in turn into the jar. Add 2 of the halved garlic cloves (four pieces) and all of the allspice berries.

Drain the soaked cucumbers and slice off the ends. Pack the cucumbers tightly in the jar, stem-ends down. (If you have only large cucumbers, you can cut them in half lengthwise so that they fit better.) Fill any remaining space on top with cucumbers that you've cut in half crosswise; they can be laid down horizontally so that the jar is tightly packed.

Top the cucumbers with the remaining seasonings, scalding each one in turn: 1 dill head, 2 black currant leaves, 4 cherry leaves, the remaining horseradish leaves, 1 sprig of tarragon, and the marigold petals. Add the remaining 2 garlic cloves.

Bring the water to a boil in a small saucepan, then pour it over the packed cucumbers. Let stand for 5 minutes, then carefully strain the water back into the saucepan. Stir in the salt and sugar and again bring to a boil, stirring to dissolve the solids. When the water boils, pour it over the cucumbers. There should be just enough room to add the vinegar, letting it come to the very top of the jar.

Seal the jar tightly and turn it upside down on a dish towel. Wrap in flannel or another heavy cloth until completely cool.

Store the pickles in a cold cellar or in the refrigerator. They will be ready to eat in 1½ to 2 months. The opened jar of pickles will keep in the refrigerator for several weeks.

Note
Seed heads are the stage after the yellow flowers have turned to tiny brown seeds.

Dandelion Blossom Syrup

Мёд из одуванчиков

I have to admit, before tasting this syrup I had a bad attitude toward dandelions. I can't get rid of them. The yellow blossoms overrun our lawn every spring, their cheerful beauty lasting only a week before their seeds float off into my gardens, where I have to literally root them out. But then, in the northern Russian village of Oshevensk, I tasted this syrup. The old woman who taught me how to make it insisted that I pick exactly 350 blossoms. I could have picked 10,000. But that would make too much syrup.

The Russians call this thick syrup "honey." Be sure to use blossoms that are ecologically clean. Just nip the blossoms from the stems with your fingers—it's fine to leave the sepal attached. This syrup is very sweet. You can cut it with a bit more lemon juice but don't use too much or it will mask the lovely dandelion flavor.

Serve dandelion syrup on pancakes or Russian blini or use it to sweeten oatmeal. I like it best over tart strawberries and yogurt, though in Oshevensk it was presented very simply, like preserves, with tea.

Makes three 8-ounce jars

350 dandelion blossoms

6 cups cold water

4 cups turbinado sugar

Juice of 1 large lemon (or more, to taste)

Rinse the dandelion blossoms in cold water. Turn them out onto paper towels and let drain for a minute to encourage any bugs to escape. Pick through the blossoms to make sure there are no blades of grass among them.

Place the blossoms in a large saucepan with the water. Cook at a slow boil, covered, over low heat for 1 hour.

Strain the liquid through a fine-mesh sieve into a clean saucepan, pressing down on the blossoms to extract all of the juice. You will have 4 cups of juice. Stir in the sugar and bring the liquid to a boil, continuing to stir until the sugar dissolves. Cook, uncovered, over low heat for 1 hour and 15 minutes, then add the lemon juice and cook for 15 minutes more, until the syrup is viscous and a drop on a saucer holds its shape. Pour into sterilized jars and seal. Store in the refrigerator. It will keep almost indefinitely.

Pear and Carrot Relish

Варенье из груш и моркови

This sweet-tart relish will surprise your guests, who will have a hard time guessing what it's made of. The relish is cooked just long enough for the carrots and pears to absorb the flavor of honey without losing all of their crispness. It's equally good served with roast meat for dinner or with afternoon tea, in the Russian style.

Makes five 8-ounce jars

2 pounds carrots, peeled

1¼ cups honey

½ cup freshly squeezed lemon juice

1 cinnamon stick

2 pounds Bartlett pears, firm but not hard

Grate the carrots on the large holes of a box grater and place in a large shallow saucepan. Add the honey, lemon juice, and cinnamon stick. Peel and core the pears, then chop them into ½-inch dice. As you dice each pear, stir it into the carrot mixture so that the pears don't turn brown.

Bring the mixture to a boil and cook over medium heat for about 30 minutes, stirring occasionally, until most of the liquid has evaporated. Be careful not to let the mixture scorch.

Ladle the relish into sterilized jars and seal. Once cooled, the relish can be stored in the refrigerator for up to a month. For longer keeping, process the jars for 10 minutes in a hot-water bath, according to the manufacturer's instructions.

Strawberry-Cranberry Preserves

Клубничное варенье с клюквой

Historically, Russians preserved fruit in honey, a practice likely introduced from Byzantium. Russian-style preserves are whole fruits suspended in syrup, similar to Greek spoon sweets. They're most often enjoyed with tea, when they're served in small decorative dishes called *rozetki*. Nineteenth-century cookbooks offered recipes for making preserves with honey as well as with the newly available sugar, but sugar eventually displaced honey because it was cheaper. That's too bad, since honey lends a lovely floral note to the preserves, whereas sugar is merely sweet.

Because strawberries are low in pectin, I've added a few cranberries to help the preserves set, but this isn't a thick jam for spreading on toast. It's meant to be syrupy, savored by the spoonful or stirred into hot tea. Or try it with ice cream or yogurt.

Makes two 8-ounce jars

4 cups strawberries, preferably small ones

½ cup cranberries, fresh or frozen

¾ cup mild honey

2 tablespoons freshly squeezed lemon juice

Hull the strawberries and cut any large ones in half or in quarters. Place them along with the cranberries in a large shallow saucepan. Add the honey and lemon juice and bring to a boil. Cook over medium heat until the syrup is thick enough to coat the back of a spoon, 20 to 25 minutes. (You can test it by dropping a bit of syrup on a plate that has chilled beforehand in the freezer. If the syrup holds its shape, the preserves are ready.)

Ladle the preserves into sterilized jars and seal. Turn the jars upside down to cool, so that the fruit doesn't settle on the bottom of the jars. Once cooled, the preserves can be stored in the refrigerator for several weeks. For longer keeping, process the jars for 5 minutes in a hot-water bath, according to manufacturer's instructions.

AN ABUNDANCE OF HONEY

Russia's dense forests were even denser in the past, providing an excellent habitat for bears. So feared were these animals that the Russians avoided naming them directly, lest they call forth the evil eye. Instead they called them *medved'* or "honey-eater," an image that evokes a benign Winnie-the-Pooh-like creature. Lingering fear gradually led the Russians to appropriate the bear as a cultural symbol, thereby diminishing its power. By the late twentieth century, the bear was completely domesticated as Misha ("Mike"), the adorable mascot of the 1980 Moscow Olympics.

Early travelers to Russia wrote of "great pools" and "lakes" of honey in Russia's forests, warning that the trees housed so many swarms of wild bees that passage could be dangerous. Such immense wild hives gave rise to legend. One oft-repeated story told of a man who accidentally fell into a honey-filled hive and was unable to extricate himself. He languished there for two days until a bear appeared. When the bear climbed into the hive to feast on the sweet honey, the man grabbed his tail and shouted, at which the startled bear bolted from the hive, pulling the man out along with him.

So abundant was wild honey that, along with beeswax, it became one of Russia's most valuable exports, rivaled only by fur. The economic importance of these goods was roughly equivalent to that of oil or gas today, and at the height of Russian honey production in the mid-nineteenth century, the yield reached 24 million poods a year. Considering that 1 pood equals 36 pounds, that's an awful lot of sweet stuff. Most honey by this time was produced by domestic beekeeping, since the expanses of forest had greatly diminished, and with them the wild hives. The invention in 1814 of a collapsible frame that sectioned off hives increased yields exponentially—now beekeepers could retrieve honey without killing bees, as had been standard practice.

Honey remained the quintessential Russian sweetener well into the nineteenth century, even after beet sugar became affordable, since many cooks preferred the nuanced flavor honey imparts to traditional preserves. It was also a crucial ingredient in baked goods such as gingerbread, originally known as "honey cake" or "honey bread," and served as the basis for several of Russia's most beloved beverages, including mead, whose name is a homonym for the word *honey*. Raw honey was mixed with tart berry juice—especially raspberry, lingonberry, or cherry—and then allowed to ferment naturally before being sealed in oak barrels, where the mead was aged for at least five years, and ideally fifteen or twenty. Those who had the means flavored their honey wine with imported spices, like cinnamon and cloves.

Early Russians also drank a beverage called *perevar*, a mixture of honey and beer, considered so valuable that peasants could use it as payment to landowners in exchange for cultivating crops on their land. There was also *syta*, a simple mix of water and honey, which was either drunk plain or used to sweeten dishes such as wheat berry porridge. Sometimes the water and honey were boiled together with herbs or spices; other recipes called for pouring warm water over honeycombs to free the honey and then straining out the wax before serving the drink chilled. And we can't forget *sbiten'*, the hot spiced honey drink sold by street hawkers from samovar-like urns (see page 46). *Sbiten'* provided the ultimate warming touch on cold winter days.

Natural honey is still prized by Russians both for its taste and its nutritive properties. Moscow's VDNKh—the Exhibition of the Achievements of the National Economy, a Soviet relic that has become a sort of amusement park—maintains an entire pavilion devoted to beekeeping, complete with museum. Most Russian cities sponsor seasonal honey markets where consumers can choose from a huge array of flavors and styles. And an annual honey festival is celebrated throughout Russia on August 14. Traditionally on this day, honey is collected from the hives and brought to the church for blessing, and all sorts of honey-rich breads and desserts are prepared to enjoy along with mead. I happened to be in Murmansk for one of these annual festivals. A large pavilion on the outskirts of the city accommodated honey vendors from far and wide, many representing monasteries and convents. I happily wandered from stand to stand, tasting dozens of different varieties, assured in the knowledge that I was fortifying my immune system. Though I couldn't stuff my luggage with as much liquid gold as I would have liked, I did succumb to some rare angelica honey, as well as honey mixed with royal jelly to give my system an extra boost.

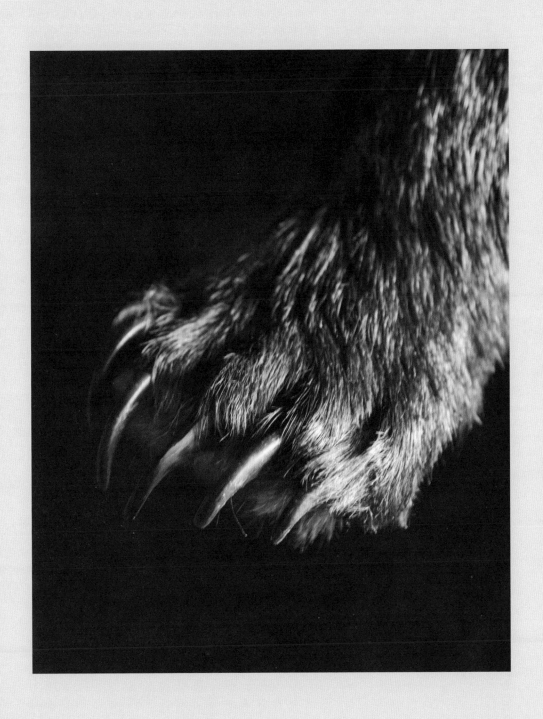

Sugared Red Currants

Красная смородина с сахаром

By now you've probably detected the leitmotif of berries in Russian cooking. Red currants, black currants, cranberries, cloudberries, lingonberries, sea buckthorn—Russians love them all. One of the ways Russians stay healthy in winter is by consuming tart berries that they've stirred with sugar for long keeping. To keep the vitamins intact, they don't subject the berries to any heat, which also keeps the fruit flavor lively and bright.

This recipe can easily be doubled or tripled or quadrupled, and you can substitute other tart berries for the red currants. Serve the preserves in a tiny bowl with tea, as a garnish for cake, or as a topping for porridge, yogurt, or ice cream. Most often I eat them straight from the jar.

Makes about 1 cup

6 ounces red currants

⅓ cup sugar

Rinse the currants well and leave them to dry on paper towels for 20 to 30 minutes. While they're drying, sterilize a 1-pint jar.

Transfer the berries to a medium bowl and gently stir in the sugar, taking care not to crush the berries, then spoon the mixture into the prepared jar and close tightly. Let the currants sit for a few hours, turning the jar occasionally to help the sugar dissolve. They can be left at room temperature for several days or stored for more than a month in the refrigerator.

Note
The yield amounts to less than a full pint, but a 1-pint jar allows room to stir the berries with the sugar before the sugar dissolves.

Black Currant Sauce

Соус из чёрной смородины

The rich color and tart flavor of this deep-purple sauce add a lovely counterpoint to honey cake and sweetened curd cheese. If you want a silky-smooth sauce, you can put it through a sieve, but I like the texture—and extra vitamins—that the tiny bits of currant add.

Makes about 1 cup

2 cups black currants (thawed if frozen)

7 to 8 tablespoons confectioners' sugar

⅓ cup plus 2 teaspoons cold water

½ teaspoon potato starch

1 tablespoon unsalted butter

Puree the currants in a blender. You will have about ¾ cup.

Transfer the puree to a small saucepan. Stir in the sugar and ⅓ cup water. Bring the mixture just to a boil over medium heat.

Dissolve the potato starch in the remaining 2 teaspoons water and stir into the berry mixture. Bring just to a boil again. The mixture will thicken slightly. Remove from the heat and stir in the butter.

Cool to room temperature before serving. The sauce keeps for a week in the refrigerator in an airtight jar.

Hot Cranberry Sauce

Клюквенный взвар

Unlike the chilled and jellied American version, Russian cranberry sauce, or *vzvar,* is served hot like gravy, its garnet hue gorgeous against a pale slice of turkey. It's also lovely over roast pork. With no fat and only a subtle note of honey, this old-style sauce was originally meant to mitigate the oiliness of rich meats, like swan or goose, but its very restraint makes it feel contemporary today.

Makes about 2 cups

3½ cups cranberries (one 12-ounce bag)

1½ cups water

1 cinnamon stick

1 tablespoon rye flour

¼ cup honey

Pinch of salt

Freshly ground black pepper

Add the cranberries, water, and cinnamon stick to a medium saucepan and bring to a boil. Cook over medium heat for 5 minutes, until all the skins have burst. Remove the cinnamon stick from the pan. Put the berries through a food mill to extract the juice; discard the pulp.

Place the rye flour in a small bowl and stir in a few tablespoons of the hot puree to make a slurry, making sure that all the flour dissolves. Transfer the remaining puree to a saucepan and whisk in the slurry, followed by the honey, salt, and a few grindings of pepper. Bring the sauce to a boil and simmer for just a couple of minutes.

The sauce will keep for several weeks in the refrigerator in an airtight container. Serve hot or warm.

Note

Although this sauce can be prepared à la minute, it tastes even better after the flavors have melded overnight.

Horseradish Sauce and Petals

Соус и лепестки из хрена

I came up with this recipe as a way of embellishing the tender brisket left over from making a big pot of borscht (see page 156). I didn't want to eat plain boiled beef, so I decided to jazz it up with horseradish. Even though Russians enjoy scant sunlight in winter and historically have had little access to citrus fruits, horseradish saved them from scurvy, thanks to its high content of vitamin C. Peter the Great considered this potent root so important to his nation's health that he issued a famous edict commanding each inn to keep an astonishing 15,000 liters of horseradish vodka on hand during winter, to invigorate travelers and help prevent seasonal colds. (He also had an ulterior motive: vodka was heavily taxed and thus helped keep government coffers full.)

The grated apple softens the horseradish's fiery bite and makes the sauce hard to resist. I like a bit of texture, so I whisk in the sour cream by hand, but you can create a finer consistency by adding the sour cream and salt to the mixture and continuing to pulse the blender.

To finish the dish, I like to make horseradish petals for garnish, as I learned to do from Svetlana Kozeiko, the chef at Tsarskaya Okhota (The Royal Hunt) in Murmansk. Marinated with beets, they are magenta in color, a brilliant complement to the pale horseradish sauce. Just be sure to prepare them ahead of time so that they'll absorb sufficient color. Any leftover petals can be tucked into a sandwich.

Makes about 1 cup

Petals

1 beet, peeled and finely chopped

1 large apple, peeled, cored, and finely chopped

2 tablespoons honey

2 tablespoons balsamic vinegar

2 tablespoons hot water

6-ounce knob fresh horseradish root, peeled

Horseradish Sauce

½ cup grated fresh horseradish root (from one peeled 3-inch piece, about 1½ ounces)

1 sweet-tart apple, such as Gala, peeled and grated

½ cup boiling water

1 tablespoon apple cider vinegar

¼ cup sour cream

¼ teaspoon salt

To make the petals, first make a marinade by placing all the ingredients except the horse-radish in a blender. Process on high speed until pureed (adding a little more water if necessary to make the marinade pourable). Transfer to a small bowl.

Using a mandoline, slice the horseradish root into very thin, nearly transparent rounds. Drop the horseradish slices into the marinade and stir to coat them well. Cover the bowl and refrigerate for at least 6 hours. (The mixture will keep for a week in the refrigerator.)

To make the horseradish sauce, place the horseradish and apple in a blender. Add the boiling water and vinegar and puree until smooth. Transfer the mixture to a bowl and whisk in the sour cream and salt. The sauce can be served right away or held, tightly covered, for several days in the refrigerator.

To serve, remove the horseradish slices from the marinade and pinch them into slightly rounded petals.

2

FERMENTS

Cultured Butter with Whitefish Roe

Икорное масло

I adore whitefish roe, especially in the dark days of winter when its sunny eggs brighten anything from blini to cream cheese–slathered bagels. These tiny beads have a mild flavor and subtle crunch that pair well with the tang and creaminess of cultured butter. I like to spread this compound butter on black bread or Barley-Rye Cakes (page 203) and have more than once been known to spoon some straight into my mouth—it's that tasty. Leftover butter keeps well for a few days in the refrigerator.

Makes about ½ cup

4 tablespoons cultured butter (see page 78), at room temperature

2 tablespoons whitefish roe

In a small bowl, use a wooden spoon to cream the butter just long enough to make an even mass. Gently stir the whitefish roe into the butter, being careful not to break the eggs. The roe needn't be fully incorporated—streaks or swirls make it more decorative. Serve immediately.

Homemade Sour Cream and Cultured Butter

Домашняя сметана и чухонское масло

Cultured butter is made from sour cream. You can leave fresh, unpasteurized cream to sour on its own overnight, but adding a little kefir speeds up the process and imparts a desirable tang. Both the sour cream and butter will be truly fabulous if you can find raw milk from Jersey cows, whose milk is extra creamy.

Makes about 2 cups

1 gallon raw milk

2 tablespoons plain whole-milk kefir

Salt

First, separate the cream if it hasn't already risen to the top of the milk. Pour the milk into a shallow pan and let it stand in the refrigerator for 24 hours, until the cream rises to the top. Skim the cream off into a bowl. (Alternatively, if you have a jar with a spigot, you can pour the milk into the jar, wait until the cream rises to the top, and then drain the milk through the spigot.) You should end up with 2 cups of heavy cream.

Place the cream in a small pot over medium heat and heat the cream to lukewarm, 105°F, then stir in the kefir. Leave the cream in a warm spot on the counter, covered with a cloth, until thickened, about 8 hours. The sour cream is now ready for use.

If you wish to make cultured butter, beat the sour cream on high speed with a hand mixer for 6 to 8 minutes, until clumps form. Gather the clumps with your hands and press into a ball, leaving any milky residue on the bottom of the bowl. Transfer the ball to a bowl of ice water and knead lightly to firm up, then squeeze out all the water. Wash the butter once more in a bath of clean ice water and again squeeze out any remaining water. Add salt to taste and pack into a crock or jar. Store in the refrigerator, where it will keep for a week.

Homemade Farmer's Cheese
Творог

The Russian kitchen is unimaginable without *tvorog*, a kind of soft, tangy cottage cheese made from soured milk. It's eaten plain for breakfast or drizzled with honey and topped with berries for an afternoon snack. Known to us as farmer's cheese, *tvorog* is essential for making some of Russia's most distinctive dishes: *syrniki* (cheese pancakes), *paskha* (the pyramid-shaped cheesecake made for Easter), *vatrushki* (open-faced pies), and *blinchiki* (crêpelike pancakes).

The traditional way to make *tvorog* is simply to let fresh, unpasteurized milk sour overnight and then heat it gently until curds form. This process yields a soft, slightly sweet cheese from the natural sugars in milk. But it's unpredictable, as the curdling time can vary from batch to batch and sometimes takes hours. Like many Russians, I prefer to add a little boost of kefir to sour the milk and ensure the rapid formation of curds. Kefir also lends a sour tang that I love.

Be sure to save the whey that drains from the curds. It keeps for a good week in the refrigerator and makes a tender dough that has hints of sour, just right for enveloping Russian "pickle" pies (see page 115).

Makes about 1¾ pounds

2 quarts raw milk

½ cup plain whole-milk kefir

Mix the milk and kefir in a heatproof bowl and let stand in a warm place, covered with cheesecloth or a dish towel, for 24 hours. Remove the cloth and place the bowl in a large pot. Pour enough water around the bowl to come almost all the way up the sides. Heat the water over high heat but turn to a low simmer as soon as bubbles begin to form. Cook the milk mixture, without stirring, until tiny bubbles appear on the surface and curds begin to form. This will take about 12 minutes. Remove the pot from the heat and allow the milk to cool to room temperature, about 1 hour.

Line a strainer with a double layer of cheesecloth and set it over a large bowl. Drain the milk through the cheesecloth and let sit for 3 to 4 hours, until the curds are firm. Transfer the curds to a storage container and refrigerate for up to a week. Transfer the whey to a clean jar and store in the refrigerator for another purpose.

Note

If you're making *tvorog* in a very warm kitchen, you may find that the milk curdles naturally overnight. In that case, there's no need to heat it—simply turn the thickened milk into a cheesecloth-lined strainer and let it drain for a few hours, as directed above.

Baked Cultured Milk

Варенец

The rich cultured milk known as *varenets* is one of the glories of the Russian kitchen. Baked slowly in the Russian stove, the milk turns pale gold as it caramelizes, though the addition of sour cream keeps it from being overly sweet. *Varenets* is considered a humble dish, prepared to keep milk from spoiling, but it's so seductive that well-to-do families adopted it, too. Fancy cooks carefully lifted off the skin that formed during baking to use in desserts such as Guriev kasha, a lavish semolina pudding.

Varenets changed my life. Oh so many years ago, when I had a job interview at Williams College (where I ended up teaching for thirty-four years), I was grilled about my dissertation and critical theory—the sorts of things you'd expect for an academic position. But then came a question that floored me, from a professor whose aristocratic family had escaped Russia after the revolution. What, he wanted to know, was *varenets*? He'd heard about it all his life but never tasted it. I'm convinced that my successful answer clinched the job for me.

Baked milk makes a lovely parfait with fresh berries or Black Currant Sauce (page 70). Or you can use it in place of yogurt in baking.

Serves 6

1 quart raw milk

3 tablespoons live-culture sour cream or plain yogurt

Preheat the oven to 300°F. Have ready a 1-quart ovenproof casserole, preferably an earthenware bean pot.

In a medium saucepan, heat the milk over low heat just until tiny bubbles begin to appear on the surface. Transfer the milk to the casserole and place it in the oven. After 1 hour, stir the skin that has formed on the surface into the milk. Bake for another hour and stir the skin into the milk once again. Bake for 1 hour more. The milk needs to bake for 3 hours or until it is reduced in volume by one-third. Remove the pot from the oven and, with a slotted spatula, carefully remove the skin from the top of the milk and transfer it to a plate. Set aside.

Let the milk cool to lukewarm, around 105°F, which will take about an hour. While the milk is cooling, prepare six 4-ounce jars by placing 1½ teaspoons sour cream or yogurt in each jar. Divide the lukewarm milk among the jars and close them tightly. Set the jars in a warm place to thicken, 6 to 8 hours or up to overnight, depending on the room temperature. Chill in the refrigerator before serving. Place a little of the reserved skin on top of each jar.

Fermented Oatmeal

Заквашенная овсянка

Oats were a mainstay of the early Slavs: they fed oats to their horses and ate oats themselves. So I started to play with Russia's oldest oatmeal dish, made simply by soaking oats till they start to ferment and then heating the strained, thickened water once it's poured off. In Russian, this is known as *kisel'*, from the word for "sour." This kind of grain-based *kisel'*, or gruel, was the food of the peasantry for hundreds of years; often they had little more.

I really wanted to convey this essential taste of Russia while making it seductive for contemporary American palates. First I tried going the savory route, adding salt and poppy seeds and crumbled rye bread. Then I veered to the sweet, adding honey and jam and dried and fresh berries. Alas, no amount of doctoring made me fall in love with the stuff. So I decided to focus on the lightly fermented oats and turn them into porridge. Eureka! Here's an oatmeal that I unabashedly love—at once chewy and creamy, with an alluring, sour tang. If you become as hooked on it as I am, you can set aside a little bit of the uncooked fermented oats to use as a starter for each subsequent batch, as you would when making sourdough bread. I often brighten the porridge with dried blueberries or cranberries.

Serves 4

1 pound whole oats (groats)

2-inch chunk of any preservative-free bread, including crust

⅛ teaspoon salt

Place the oats in a medium bowl and pour water over them to cover. Leave to soak for 24 hours.

A couple of hours before the next step, bring 3 cups water to a boil. Remove from the heat and leave to cool to room temperature.

Pour the oats and their liquid into a colander; rinse and drain well. Transfer the oats to the bowl of a food processor and grind until they are broken up into pieces somewhat larger than cracked wheat. Place them in a clean bowl and pour the cooled water over them. Set the chunk of bread on top and cover the bowl with a dish towel. Leave at room temperature for 48 hours, until bubbles start to appear and the oats give off an appealingly sour smell.

Pour the oats and the liquid into a medium saucepan, add the salt, and bring to a boil. Turn the heat to low and cook the oats slowly, over low heat, stirring occasionally, until creamy, about 10 minutes. Serve hot.

Note

The oatmeal thickens quickly on standing. To reheat, simply add water or milk and simmer gently until heated through.

Half-Sour Dill Pickles
Малосольные огурцы

Intensely flavored pickles hold a special place in my heart, but I sometimes long for a fresher taste. Enter half-sour dills—small cucumbers that are brined for just a few days before eating. They retain the satisfying crunch of fresh cucumbers, with just enough tang to lend interest. Enjoy them plain as a snack, as a chaser for vodka, or sliced onto open-faced sandwiches spread with pâté. Save the brine to make soups or braises . . . or use it, as my grandmother did, as a facial. She swore that pickle brine kept her skin nearly wrinkle free.

The horseradish and black currant leaves called for below contain tannins that help keep the pickles crisp, and they add complexity of flavor. But if you can't find them, don't worry. The pickles will still be fantastic.

Makes approximately 2 quarts

2 pounds small, thin pickling cucumbers (each about 4 inches long)

1 large horseradish leaf, spine removed and leaf torn in half

2 large flowering dill crowns

2 black currant leaves

1 teaspoon black peppercorns

4 garlic cloves, peeled

6 cups water

3 tablespoons salt

1 large bay leaf

Scrub the cucumbers well and soak them in cold water for 2 to 4 hours to firm up. Cut off both ends of each cucumber. (Removing the ends keeps the pickles from softening.)

Sterilize a 3-quart earthenware crock. Rinse the leaves and dill well.

Place a half horseradish leaf on the bottom of the crock, then top with a horizontal layer of cucumbers. Add 1 dill crown, 1 black currant leaf, ½ teaspoon of the peppercorns, and 2 garlic cloves, then layer with a second round of cucumbers. Top with the remaining dill crown, currant leaf, peppercorns, and garlic and cover it all with the remaining piece of horseradish leaf.

In a large saucepan, heat the water with the salt and the bay leaf, stirring to dissolve the salt. Do not let the water boil. Pour the salted water into the crock and place a plate on top of the horseradish leaf. Set a heavy weight on the plate to keep the cucumbers submerged in the brine. Cover the crock loosely with cheesecloth and set on a warm countertop to ferment.

The cucumbers will be ready in 2 to 3 days, depending on how big they are and how salty you like them. The longer you leave them, the saltier they will become. When they've achieved your desired degree of saltiness, transfer them, along with the brine, to a half-gallon jar. Cover the jar tightly and store in the refrigerator. Within 2 weeks, the half-sour pickles will have turned to fully brined pickles, which are also delicious.

FERMENTATION

If there's one thing Russians love, it's the taste of sour. When I mention that to people, I see noses begin to wrinkle. Unless you're talking about candy Sour Patch Kids, *sour* isn't always a positive attribute for food in the English language. But it is in Russian. One of Russia's most ancient dishes is *kisel'*, whose name comes from the word *kislyi*, or "sour." This pudding, originally made from the slightly fermented liquid left over from soaking grains, is appreciated for its tart taste, even in its contemporary incarnation as a fruit pudding. So central was the pudding to Russian life that its production was concentrated in a region of medieval Moscow known as the Kisel' Settlement, and several Moscow streets still bear the name *kisel'*.

For Russian peasants, sourness was the essential element in all food and drink. There is the classic Russian soup, *shchi*, which is made from sauerkraut, and ingredients such as whey, kefir, and pickle brine are often used as souring agents in other soups. The most beloved Russian apple is the Antonovka, prized for its acidity. The Antonovka's tartness is intensified by *mochenie*, a Russian method of fermentation that involves soaking fruit in a light brine, a process that produces a gentler conserve than salting or pickling does. Russians make a wide range of cultured dairy products not only to preserve milk but also to satisfy their craving for the taste of sour.

And let's not forget about kombucha, which the Russians have been drinking for hundreds of years. When I first visited the Soviet Union in the 1970s, many families kept a 3-liter jar fermenting on their windowsills, considering the fizzy drink not just healthful but also a homegrown answer to the sweet carbonated beverages of the West, such as Pepsi, which had only just begun distribution in the USSR and was still nearly impossible to find. Russian kombucha wasn't—and still isn't—as sweet as the commercially produced American versions, and it is sometimes flavored with herbs and berries, such as black currant, sea buckthorn, and juniper. Thanks to the current trendiness of kombucha, the once-mundane "tea fungus" (as it's called in Russian) has new cachet, especially when it uses locally grown tea from Krasnodar, in Russia's south.

The drink most original to Russia is kvass, an effervescent, mildly alcoholic beverage whose name derives from the linguistic root *–kvas*, which means "to sour or ferment." When made from grain, kvass resembles beer without hops, but it can also be made from fermented fruits or vegetables. Russian monasteries were famous for the many varieties of fruit kvass that they produced, including cranberry, raspberry, pear, wild strawberry, lingonberry, and mountain ash. "Even bad kvass is better than water," as the saying goes, and the Soviet years bore out that pronouncement. Kvass became an industrial product, sold in bright-yellow tanker trucks with red stencils proclaiming *KBAC!* These trucks were a common summer sight in parks and on street corners, where people would line up to pay a few kopecks for a glass poured from a tap. These glasses were only cursorily rinsed before being handed to the next person in line, though no one ever seemed to get sick. This Soviet product was only remotely related to the traditional Russian "red" kvass, made by slowly steaming malted grains, flour, and water in the Russian stove until the mixture takes on a deep, rich color and flavor. To make "white" kvass, the same ingredients are left to ferment without heating in the stove. The spectrum of flavors from red to white is wide. Where red kvass is often flavored with hearty aromatics, like mint and St. John's wort, white kvass is much more subtle, its artistry evident in such varieties as violet, made from steeped violet roots, raisins, and dried apples. Russians also made the oddly named *kislye shchi* (literally, "sour cabbage soup") from malted grains. This fizzy kvass graced the fine tables of the nobility until the 1917 revolution.

Fermentation goes far beyond beverages, of course. For Russians, the word *pickle* has nothing to do with vinegar. True pickles are the result of the lactic acid fermentation that occurs when cucumbers are layered with garlic and herbs in a salt brine. Mushrooms treated the same way are another highlight of the Russian *zakuska*, or appetizer, table. Nothing goes better with vodka than these naturally fermented foods, which themselves are complemented by a slice of sourdough rye bread. If there's a secular trinity in Russia, this is it, and all three elements rely on fermentation: vodka, pickles, and bread.

And then there are all the cultured dairy products, each of which undergoes a specific process of fermentation that varies from subtle to intense, but all of which result in a tangy product from the originally sweet milk. *Tvorog* is farmer's cheese made by gently heating soured milk until curds form. *Prostokvasha*, whose name translates as "simply soured," is eaten as we eat yogurt. It's made by letting raw milk sour and thicken naturally; adding a crust of sourdough black bread to the milk accelerates the process. *Varenets* and *ryazhenka* are similarly cultured, but both have a distinctively rich taste, since they're prepared from milk that has been slowly baked until its sugars caramelize. These two dairy products are nearly identical, though *ryazhenka* contains additional cream—a true gilding of the lily. Kefir originated in the North Caucasus and, like kombucha, is made from a "mother" consisting of microbes and yeasts. And we can't forget *smetana*, sour cream, without which the Russian kitchen is unimaginable.

In our fermentation-mad moment, when new "discoveries" are announced daily, it's worth remembering that the Russians have been fermenting their food and drink for centuries. The peasants may not have understood the chemistry of lactic acid fermentation, but they knew their sour. And their insistence on soured food reveals that they were well attuned to the health benefits of what we now call probiotics.

Brined Tomatoes

Мочёные помидоры

When the great poet Alexander Pushkin lay dying after a duel, he begged for brined cloudberries—his last wish and last words. It was February, and even in his mortally wounded state, he knew that the berries wouldn't be fresh but preserved, and perhaps, like many of his compatriots, he preferred them this way. No wonder. Preserving fruits and berries in brine gives them the slightly sour flavor that Russians love. Lingonberries taste good this way, too (see page 177), and it's fun to experiment with different fruits, such as watermelon and apples, the classic preparation (see page 90). Tomatoes are also piquant when brined.

This recipe yields ever-so-slightly-sweet tomatoes. I like to use small ones, which absorb flavor faster, but as long as they're firm, you can use any tomatoes on hand. And if you don't have horseradish or currant leaves, just toss in some celery or extra dill. Serve these tomatoes as part of a *zakuska* spread, or as an accompaniment to roast meat. They're so tasty that I often just pop one into my mouth for a snack.

Makes about 2 pounds

2 pounds firm campari or cocktail tomatoes, each 1½ inches in diameter

8 cups water

¼ cup salt

¼ cup honey

4 large garlic cloves, peeled and smashed

1 tablespoon allspice berries

¼ teaspoon black peppercorns

2 bay leaves

3 whole cloves

5 horseradish leaves

6 black currant leaves

3 stalks of dill, including the flowering heads

Rinse the tomatoes and remove their stems.

In a medium saucepan, bring 2 cups of the water to a boil with the salt, honey, garlic, allspice, peppercorns, bay leaves, and cloves. Simmer just long enough to dissolve the salt, then remove from the heat and allow the brine to cool.

Sterilize a 1-gallon jar. Mix the cooled brine with the remaining 6 cups water. Place a couple of horseradish leaves and black currant leaves on the bottom of the jar with a stalk of the dill, then add a layer of tomatoes. Continue layering the tomatoes, leaves, and herbs. Pour the brine over all. To keep the tomatoes submerged, fill a small resealable plastic bag with water and place it on top of them. Cover the jar with cheesecloth secured with a rubber band and leave the tomatoes to ferment at room temperature for 3 to 4 days. Skim off any foam that forms. When the tomatoes have fermented to your liking, transfer them to the refrigerator, where they'll keep for weeks.

Note

Fermentation time depends on the ambient temperature. If you like a bit of effervescence, leave the tomatoes to ferment unrefrigerated even longer. Their skins will split, but they'll still be irresistible.

Brined Apples

Мочёные яблоки

These apples are preserved by one of Russia's oldest methods, variously translated as soaking or steeping or sousing. But none of these words captures the beauty of the apples after they've fermented in a light brine. The Russians favor the fragrant late-fall Anotovka apple, the very mention of which causes them to swoon, so redolent is this variety with sensory (and literary) associations. Here, in place of the beloved antonovki, I've substituted Ashmead's Kernel, a small, firm yellow apple that keeps well.

This recipe takes patience, not so much in preparation as in awaiting the outcome. The timing depends largely on room temperature. If your house is as cool as ours, the apples will take longer to ferment. I waited three months for the first ecstatic bite. The texture was crisp, the flavor slightly winey, with a hint of effervescence. After five months, the flavor was full-blown and exciting; the apples were still crisp to the bite but with wrinkled peels. As with other ferments, keep tasting and testing. Transfer the apples to the refrigerator or other cold storage when you feel that their flavor is right.

Though the cherry or black currant leaves provide tannins to help keep the apples crisp, they aren't crucial. Do, however, be sure not to use chemically treated water.

Sliced brined apples make an excellent garnish for all sorts of meats, and they shine in a pickle array. I also like to serve them with cheese instead of cornichons—an unexpected but harmonious marriage.

Makes 5 pounds

5 quarts filtered or spring water

½ cup rye flour

¼ cup cold water

1 cup raw honey

2 tablespoons salt

5 pounds small unblemished apples (15 to 20), preferably Ashmead's Kernel

12 cherry or black currant leaves, or a mixture of both

3 large sprigs mint

In a large kettle, bring the filtered water to a boil. Meanwhile, in a small bowl, mix the rye flour with the cold water to make a paste. As soon as the water boils, turn off the heat. Stir about 1 cup of the boiling water into the flour paste to make a slurry, then stir this mixture into the boiled water, along with the honey and salt. Mix well to dissolve. Leave the brine to cool to room temperature, which may take several hours.

Rinse the apples well. Place half of the cherry leaves on the bottom of a 10-quart crock. Carefully layer the apples on their sides, tucking the mint sprigs among them. Cover the apples with the remaining cherry leaves and pour the cooled brine over them. Spread a layer of cheesecloth over the apples, then set a plate on top of the cheesecloth. Put a heavy weight, such as a nonreactive bowl filled with water, on top of the plate to keep the apples submerged.

Leave the apples at room temperature until they actively begin to ferment, 5 to 6 days. Skim off any foam that appears on the top. After fermentation has begun, move the crock to a cool, dark place, checking the apples periodically to make sure they are completely submerged and topping them off with a little more brine as necessary. Start tasting after 3 to 4 weeks. Once the apples have reached the desired level of fermentation, transfer them to the refrigerator for storage, where they will keep for several months in a sealed container.

Kvass

Хлебной квас

Kvass is one of Russia's oldest and most basic drinks, traditionally made from nothing more than stale black bread, water, honey, and sometimes a little yeast, which are left to ferment into a lightly alcoholic, refreshing drink. The linguistic root -kvas means "ferment" or "sour," and the drink's flavor is as elementally Russian as you can get. Kvass offers a great canvas for experimentation, since you can use different types of bread, honey, spices, and other ingredients to create interesting flavors. Monasteries were once famous for the fruit kvasses they prepared from black currants, cranberries, raspberries, and pears. Kvass can be made with malt instead of bread, or with vegetables such as beets. Both bread kvass and beet kvass in turn make excellent bases for soup.

I like to make kvass with coriander-scented Borodinsky rye (see Sources), with its hint of caramel. Regular rye bread works well, too, especially if you add coriander or caraway to enliven the taste. Contemporary Russians tend to use sugar instead of pricier honey to feed the yeast, but I love floral notes and often seek out raspberry honey for its suggestion of fruit. I usually cut the sweetness of the kvass with a little lemon juice, but you can adjust that to your liking, too.

Makes about 2 quarts

1 pound preservative-free rye bread

2 to 4 tablespoons dried mint or lemon balm

1 teaspoon cracked coriander seed

3 quarts water (enough to cover the bread)

1⅛ teaspoons active dry yeast (½ package)

¼ cup mild honey

1 to 2 tablespoons freshly squeezed lemon juice

5 raisins

Preheat the oven to 300°F. Cut the bread into 1-inch chunks and place on a rimmed baking sheet. Bake for 30 to 45 minutes, until dry to the touch, tossing every 15 minutes. Place the bread in a 5-quart ceramic crock along with the mint and the coriander seed.

Heat the water in a large stockpot until a few bubbles rise to the surface; don't bring it to a full boil. Pour the hot water over the bread, using a blunt knife or spatula to push the bread down so that it is completely covered by the water. Drape a clean dish towel over the crock and leave the mixture to sit at room temperature for 24 hours.

The next day, line a sieve with cheesecloth and strain the liquid into a large measuring cup, pressing down on the solids with a spoon. You should have 2 quarts of liquid. If you have less, wrap the solids in another layer of cheesecloth and squeeze hard with your hands to extract the last bit of liquid through the strainer. (You can save these bread solids to enrich your next batch of kvass or use some of them to make the black salt on page 54. Otherwise, they make great compost.)

Transfer the liquid to a 1-gallon glass jar. Whisk in the yeast, honey, and lemon juice to mix well. Cover the jar loosely with a cloth and leave the liquid to ferment at room temperature, stirring occasionally. The mixture will start to foam after as little as 3 hours. Some people like to bottle the kvass after anywhere from 6 to 12 hours. However, the longer the kvass ferments, the less sweet it becomes, so I prefer to leave it for a full 24 hours. The best rule is to taste the kvass as it evolves.

When the kvass has fermented to your liking, scald two 750-ml swing-top stoppered bottles, plus one smaller bottle that holds roughly a pint. Drop 2 raisins into each large bottle and 1 raisin in the small bottle. Pour in the kvass, filling the bottles no more than two-thirds full. Seal the tops and leave the kvass at room temperature to ferment some more. The amount of time for this fermentation depends on room temperature, but typically the kvass will be ready to refrigerate after 6 to 8 hours. It's a good idea to carefully open the bottles a few times to let excess gas escape, so you don't have a wild eruption of foam when you open a fully carbonated bottle. You can gauge when the kvass is ready to chill from the raisins, which will rise to the top of the bottles.

Transfer the bottles to the refrigerator, which will slow down the fermentation process. Use the kvass within 3 to 4 days, before it begins to turn too sour. And remember to open the bottles carefully.

Sparkling Kvass

Кислые щи

When I first read *Dead Souls* in English, there was a line that made no sense to me. Nikolai Gogol's hero Chichikov ends his day with "a portion of cold veal, a bottle of pickles, and a sound sleep." A bottle of pickles as a sleep tonic—surely that was a mistranslation! I hoped the original Russian would enlighten me, but what I discovered confounded me even more. Chichikov imbibes *kislye shchi*—which translates literally as "sour cabbage soup."

It turns out that *kislye shchi* is not soup but a sparkling malt beverage, the first cousin of kvass. If kvass was the drink of the people, then the aristocracy enjoyed its fizzier version, drinking it like champagne at their elegant dinners and sipping it at the theater between acts. Researching this beverage led me down several rabbit holes. For instance, in the sixteenth-century *Domostroi*, a book of household management, I discovered a recipe for Arctic char swimming in the drink—a precursor to Russia's beloved cold fish soup *botvinia*. I also learned that *kislye shchi* was excellent for marinating and braising game, and for brining apples and berries. But nowhere could I find a modern recipe for the drink itself, which disappeared after the revolution, along with the aristocracy. The few old recipes I unearthed used antiquated measures amounting to nearly a hundred pounds of malt, enough to intoxicate a regiment.

I finally adapted a recipe from a cookbook by Maksim Syrnikov, experimenting with the flour and malt proportions and adding rye flour to intensify the flavor and sour cherry juice to brighten it. You can adjust the flavors yourself by playing with different proportions of flours, or by substituting barley flour for rye. The kitchen smells fantastic as the beverage ferments on the countertop. *Kislye shchi* is admittedly a bit unpredictable, with a profile that changes each time you make it and a highly variable fermentation time. But if you like sour beer, be sure to give this old-fashioned Russian beverage a try.

Makes about 2 quarts

1 cup crushed barley malt

1 cup crushed rye malt

⅓ cup all-purpose flour

⅓ cup rye flour

⅓ cup buckwheat flour

3 quarts cold water

¾ ounce fresh compressed yeast (about ⅓ of a cake)

1 tablespoon lukewarm water

2 tablespoons mild honey

½ cup unsweetened sour cherry juice

9 raisins

Place the barley and rye malts along with the three types of flour in a large bowl. Bring 1 quart of the cold water to a boil and stir it into the dry ingredients, mixing well. Cover the bowl with a clean dish towel and let sit for 3 hours. Bring the remaining 2 quarts cold water to a boil and add it to the grains. Cover the bowl with a dish towel and leave the mixture to soak at room temperature for 24 hours.

Strain the mixture through a fine-mesh sieve into a large bowl. You should have 2 quarts.

In a small bowl, mash the yeast with the warm water. Stir in the honey. Let the mixture sit for about 5 minutes until bubbles start to form, then add the yeast mixture and the cherry juice to the strained liquid and stir well. Cover the bowl and leave to ferment at room temperature until the mixture is nice and foamy and has a pleasantly sour taste. This will take anywhere from 15 to 48 hours, depending on the ambient temperature of the room.

Scald three 750-ml swing-top stoppered bottles. Stir the fermented liquid well and pour it into the bottles. Don't fill them more than three-quarters full. Drop 3 raisins into each bottle and seal. Let the bottles stand at room temperature for 12 to 24 hours, until the kislye shchi is nicely carbonated. (You can test it by carefully opening the bottles to see how much gas is released.) Transfer to the refrigerator. The drink will be ready in 7 to 10 days. If, after chilling, the drink doesn't seem quite fizzy enough, remove the bottles from the refrigerator and leave them at room temperature to jump-start fermentation. Test them periodically till they reach the degree of carbonation you like. Store in the refrigerator for up to a week.

LAVISH HOSPITALITY

Hospitality is so central to Russian culture that they name it twice. The straightforward word *gostepriimstvo* is like our version of hospitality and means simply "the reception of guests." The more common and more evocative expression is *khlebosol'stvo*, which derives from the words for "bread" (*khleb*) and "salt" (*sol'*). A traditional Russian welcome was the presentation of a large round loaf, milled from the finest flour, often with an indentation to hold a small dish of salt. Thus Russian hospitality means offering the basic staff of life, along with a bit of luxury (salt was once pricey).

The Russian Orthodox Church has historically held that guests are sacred. By receiving them well, the people also served God. Even the poorest households provided sustenance to friends, acquaintances, and strangers alike. As you'd imagine, the level of hospitality became more lavish when the tsar was involved. If foreign guests begged off from a royal banquet, the medieval custom of *podacha*, or "presentation," ensured that their portions were delivered to them in a grand display of the tsar's largesse. In a peculiarly Russian form of street theater, these presentations could occur up to several times a day, with hundreds of men filing through Moscow's narrow alleyways bearing food and drink for all the honored, absent guests.

For Russians, the impulse to indulge is both deeply gracious and often madcap. Stories abound of profligate nineteenth-century aristocrats such as Count Musin-Pushkin, who spent more than 100,000 rubles a year on the pleasures of his table, raising his turkeys on truffles and his calves on cream. Even amidst the deprivations of the Soviet era, ordinary Russians turned themselves inside out to obtain delicacies for guests and for special occasions. Foreign travelers to Russia (myself included) have consistently commented upon what appears to us as immoderation. Yet such excess is neither ostentatious nor uncommon. Instead it reveals a norm: expansive generosity coupled with fatalism about life. Russians have a tremendous capacity to celebrate the moment, since they're aware that darker days inevitably lie ahead.

The urge to bestow upon guests the very best food and drink available, to share the riches of one's home, no matter how meager, is a national trait that endures despite wars and political upheavals wreaking havoc on the

Russians' ability to sustain themselves, let alone others. Which is why in 1998, when the economy crashed and inflation skyrocketed, the Russian sense of cultural identity was genuinely shaken. Ordinary people couldn't entertain. It was difficult to witness the pain of my friends who couldn't fete me as they felt they should, and no amount of protestation on my part could appease their despair. It wasn't just a question of not being able to provide a proper meal; it was all that that meal represented, hospitality going to the very core of what it means to be Russian.

Beet Kvass

Свекольный квас

This fermented beet juice is a gorgeous shade of ruby. I use it to make borscht and a cold summer soup (see pages 156 and 166, respectively) or drink it as a tonic for its healthful properties—something Russians have been doing for centuries.

Makes 2 quarts

2 quarts water

4 pounds beets, greens removed

Bring the water to a boil in a large pot, then remove from the heat and allow it to cool to lukewarm, about 105°F.

While the water is cooling, scrub the beets, peel them, and cut into 2-inch cubes. Place the cubes in a 1-gallon crock. Pour enough of the warm water over the beets to cover them. Cover the crock loosely with a lid and leave the beets undisturbed for several days at room temperature.

After a few days, lift the lid and skim off any foam. The fermenting process is active, so don't be alarmed to find mold—it's harmless. Repeat this process every few days or skim the fermenting liquid daily to remove any hint of incipient mold.

The kvass will be ready in 2 weeks. It will be a deep red, almost purple, color and will taste appealingly sour. Skim any remaining foam or mold from the top of the liquid, then strain through a double layer of cheesecloth into a clean container. Store the kvass in the refrigerator for up to 3 months or, if desired, freeze for long keeping.

Note

A quicker though less flavorful kvass can by made by grating the beets instead of leaving them in chunks. Follow the procedure above, pouring warm water over the grated beets. Cover the crock and leave it in a warm place. This kvass will be ready in 3 to 4 days.

If you find that the kvass has soured too much for your liking, you can cheat by stirring in a little superfine sugar to taste.

Raspberry Kvass

Малиновый квас

This refreshing drink, with its subtle raspberry flavor and pale rose hue, tastes like summer. Unlike other types of kvass that require longer fermenting, this one is quickly prepared, taking only twenty-four hours from berry patch to mouth. Try drinking fruit kvass in place of lemonade for fewer calories and a probiotic boost.

Makes 1 gallon

1 quart raspberries

4 quarts water

½ cup mild honey

1 teaspoon instant yeast

12 raisins

Pour the raspberries into a large stockpot and crush them with a potato masher. Add the water and bring to a rolling boil, then immediately remove the pot from the heat. Cool the liquid to lukewarm, about 105°F. This will take several hours.

Strain the raspberries through a double layer of cheesecloth into a 1-gallon jar. Discard the berries. Stir the honey into the warm liquid.

In a small bowl, dissolve the yeast in 2 tablespoons of the raspberry water. When it foams, add it to the jar containing the rest of the liquid. Cover the jar with cheesecloth (fruit flies can't resist this fermenting kvass!) and leave at room temperature for 12 hours or overnight.

Scald four 750-ml swing-top stoppered bottles. Drop 3 raisins into each bottle and divide the kvass among the bottles. Seal and leave the kvass to ferment at room temperature for 6 hours. Transfer to the refrigerator. This kvass keeps for several weeks. Serve well chilled.

ZAKUSKI

Zakuski are savory "little bites" meant to whet the appetite. That may sound like nothing more than a Russian version of appetizers, but a real *zakuska* course is more like having dinner before dinner. Woe to the uninitiated who fill up on these starters, only to discover that they're but a prelude to the main meal!

Zakuski are most often smoked, pickled, and cured. Naturally, fish tops the list: hot- and cold-smoked sturgeon; smoked whitefish; salmon salted, smoked, and poached whole in aspic; herring pickled in vinegar, swimming in sour cream, or enlivened with mustard and dill; marinated smelts or sardines; sprats in oil. More-extravagant tables once featured crayfish and oysters, too. Roasted and cured meats also make an appearance: ham, tongue, roast beef, pork loin, smoked duck or goose breast, and all sorts of sausages and pâtés. Shimmery meat aspic is accompanied by searingly hot horseradish or mustard. Aged cheeses complement the meats, as do a variety of salads and pickles, either salted, brined, or preserved with vinegar. Beets, berries, cabbage, green tomatoes, olives, mushrooms, and peppers add color and piquancy to the spread. The small hand pies called *pirozhki* are a relatively modern addition to the table. And caviar goes without saying, whether from sturgeon, salmon, whitefish, or pike.

Speaking of caviar, vodka (caviar's natural pairing) is also central to any *zakuska* spread. Indeed, in Vladimir Dal's magisterial dictionary of the Russian language, *zakuska* is tellingly defined as "vodka with pickles and other foods." Icy-cold vodka, glistening in its glass carafe, promises immediate refreshment. After all, salt and smoke make you thirsty!

These days, *zakuski* are usually served at the table as the opening course of the meal, but in tsarist days, wealthy homes boasted a separate *zakuska* table, and often a separate room where the *zakuski* were served. This practice of providing a cold buffet of foods that would keep for hours began in the late seventeenth century and proved well suited to the habits of the Russian gentry, especially those in residence on their country estates. Because visitors had to deal with bad roads and inclement weather, they would often arrive late and famished. With a *zakuska* table set and ready at a moment's notice, guests could refresh themselves immediately upon arrival. The rise of restaurants in the early nineteenth century extended these formal *zakuska* tables to the public. When in Tolstoy's *Anna Karenina* Oblonsky takes Levin to Saint Petersburg's fashionable restaurant Angleterre, he heads first for the buffet to down some vodka with fish before sitting down for the meal. At home, you can achieve the same bedazzling effect by setting out all the *zakuski* before guests are seated. No minimalism is allowed! Dishes should appear cheek by jowl, with nary a space in between.

Such variety and abundance enable freedom of choice, which is a large part of the *zakuska* table's appeal. Guests are not limited to one, two, or even seven appetizers. And compared to the Swedish *smörgåsbord* (to which it's related), the *zakuska* table is more freewheeling. A classical *smörgåsbord* dictates five "tours" in a prescribed order, with the diner bringing each helping back to her seat before getting up for more. In Russia, the classic *zakuska* table encourages grazing—you choose something and consume it standing up before reaching for the next delicacy.

Russian cookbooks from the nineteenth century devote considerable space to the specifics of setting a formal *zakuska* table, including diagrams to ensure that it's properly laid. The table, covered with a sparkling white tablecloth, must be positioned well away from the wall so that guests can have easy access on all sides. Small serving plates of *zakuski* are set around its perimeter, repeating every so often so that guests don't have to stand in line to reach a single large platter. Other plates hold thinly sliced breads of different colors—rye, wheat, and marbled, as well as small buns; near them is set the very best butter, often molded into fanciful shapes. Cloth napkins are artistically folded into triangles and laid in rows at the corners of the table, with the napkin points facing in different directions to create a geometric pattern. Pride of place in the center of the table is given to cut-glass carafes of several different flavored vodkas, with shot glasses radiating out around them.

Nowadays you'll encounter a formal *zakuska* table only at banquets or on special occasions such as weddings. But even a more casual *zakuska* spread, with all the dishes set out on the dining table around which guests are seated, is an astonishing sight. In Soviet times, hordes of guests managed to crowd around kitchen tables in tiny apartments. Squeezing elbow to elbow heightened the intimacy of the meal and the intensity of conversation. Vodka flowed, plates were piled high, and Russians came together in a kind of social sacrament, grateful for the delicacies and for the good companionship, to which they always raised a heartfelt toast.

ZAKUSKI

Because Russian aristocrats had plenty of serfs to do their bidding, it was easy enough to keep an ample *zakuska* table ready for guests at all times. Especially on their country estates, where they could maintain huge larders, the Russians delighted in serving an array of pickles so abundant that it often verged on the fantastical. Yet it's possible to create a lavish *zakuska* spread without preparing for it months ahead or slaving for hours. To complement homemade dishes, you can quickly put together *buterbrody*—small, open-faced sandwiches with various toppings, such as black bread spread with a little farmer's cheese or ricotta and layered with finely chopped radishes and dill, or white toast points topped with a simple crab salad. And because Russians at home and abroad always embellish their tables with store-bought items, you shouldn't feel shy about serving prepared foods. Following are some suggestions to welcome your guests in style, all readily available in Russian delis or online. Just don't forget to offer an array of flavored vodkas with the food!

See page 307 of the index for a list of all the recipes that can be served as *zakuski*.

FISH

Fresh: boiled shrimp

Pickled: herring, herring in sour cream, oysters

Oil-packed: sardines, sprats

Hot- or cold-smoked: sturgeon, salmon, mackerel, whitefish

CAVIAR

Black or gray: osetra, paddlefish, bowfin

Red or orange: salmon, trout

Yellow: whitefish

COLD CUTS

Ham: smoked or boiled

Sausages: cocktail, dry salami, liverwurst, smoked hunter's

Pâté

Tongue

Cured pork belly (*salo*)

PICKLES

Beets

Eggplant caviar

Gherkins, kosher-style dills

Marinated mushrooms

Olives

Sauerkraut

CHEESE

Emmental

Gouda

Havarti

BREAD

Black: Borodinsky rye, pumpernickel

White: Kaiser roll

Crisp: mini bread rings, multigrain rusks

3

PIES, PANCAKES, AND DUMPLINGS

Russian Hand Pies

Пирожки

Russian *pirozhki*—not to be confused with the boiled Polish dumplings called pierogi—are made with enriched dough that's either baked or fried. The dough can enclose an almost endless variety of fillings, from savory to sweet. One of the great satisfactions of Soviet life was the freshly fried *pirozhki* you could buy on the street. Filled with ground beef, they were steaming hot and dripping with so much oil that the cheap gray paper holding them couldn't absorb it. Sometimes, when resourceful vendors ran out of that wrapping, they'd substitute strips of paper from old-fashioned adding machines, which only contributed to the pies' allure. Today it's still possible to buy *pirozhki* from kiosks, but more often, Russians pop into cafés that specialize in a wide range of pies large and small, where they can savor them in a warm space at leisure.

Despite my nostalgia, I never fry *pirozhki*. Instead I use this supple yeast dough to bake lovely, soft pies with a piquant filling.

Makes 24 small pies

Dough

1 package active dry yeast (2¼ teaspoons)

2 tablespoons sugar

1 cup lukewarm whole milk

3¼ cups flour

Heaping ½ teaspoon salt

8 tablespoons melted unsalted butter

2 eggs, lightly beaten

Sauerkraut and Dried Mushroom Filling

¼ ounce dried mushrooms (about ⅓ cup)

3 medium onions, finely chopped

1 small carrot, peeled and grated

3 tablespoons cold-pressed sunflower oil

2 cups rinsed and drained sauerkraut

2 teaspoons sugar

½ teaspoon salt

¼ teaspoon caraway seed

Freshly ground black pepper

1 tablespoon salted butter

2 hard-boiled eggs, minced

2 egg yolks

To make the dough, mix together the yeast, ½ teaspoon of the sugar, and ½ cup each of the warm milk and flour. Stir well. Cover the bowl with a dish towel and let the mixture sit for 30 minutes until bubbly and puffy.

Stir the remaining sugar and milk into the bowl along with the salt, melted butter, and lightly beaten eggs. Mix in the remaining flour to make a very soft and slightly sticky dough. Turn the dough out onto a floured surface and knead lightly for a few minutes until it forms a smooth mass, being careful not to incorporate too much extra flour. Grease a large bowl and place the dough in it, then turn the dough over to grease the top. Cover the bowl with a dish towel and leave the dough to rise in a warm place until doubled in size, about 1 hour.

continued

Russian Hand Pies, continued

While the dough is rising, make the filling. Soak the mushrooms in warm water for 30 minutes to soften. In a large skillet, sauté the onions and carrot in the oil until softened, 8 to 10 minutes. Drain the mushrooms and chop them finely. (You should have about ¼ cup.) Add the mushrooms to the onion mixture along with the sauerkraut, sugar, salt, caraway, and plenty of pepper. Cook, covered, over low heat for 10 minutes. Stir in the butter and the minced hard-boiled eggs. Remove the pan from the heat.

Line two large baking sheets with parchment paper. Punch down the risen dough and divide it into four pieces. (Each piece will weigh about 8 ounces.) Work with one piece at a time; leave the others in the bowl, covered with the dish towel, so that they don't dry out. Divide each quarter of dough into six equal pieces. On a lightly floured surface, roll or pat out the pieces of dough into 3½-inch rounds.

Place 2 tablespoons of the filling in the center of each round, then bring the two sides of the dough together at the top. Starting at one end of the pie, pinch the edges together between your thumb and forefinger. To make decorative pleats, bring the lower edge of the dough up and press it into the inside of the adjacent dough. Make another pinch and press the dough down into the adjacent lower edge. Move back and forth along the pie in this manner to make a decorative, tightly sealed seam. Once all the pies are sealed and shaped, cover them with a dish towel and allow to rise for 20 minutes.

While the pies are rising, preheat the oven to 350°F. Stir the egg yolks together in a small bowl and brush the pies all over with this glaze. Bake the pies for 20 minutes, until golden, and serve hot.

Little Fish Pies

Расстегаи

These charming "unbuttoned" pies, a classic accompaniment to clear fish soup, were all the rage in nineteenth-century Russia. Their name comes from the verb *rasstegnut'*, which means "to come undone," because the pies' fanciful shape, with filling exposed, makes them look as though they've popped open from baking. Though *rasstegai* were once saucer-size—Moscow tavern servers competed in slicing them deftly at the table—today's pies are small enough to be consumed in a couple of bites.

The secret of excellent *rasstegai* lies in their moistness. If you're serving them with the fish soup *ukha* (page 153), pour a little of the broth into the opening of each pie after baking. Otherwise, reserve the broth from poaching the salmon and use a little of that. The most exquisite pies are topped with fatty burbot liver, an ingredient difficult to find in the United States. Here I substitute smoked trout—perhaps not quite as succulent but still delightful thanks to the slight smokiness it imparts.

Makes 16 small pies

Dough

1 package active dry yeast (2¼ teaspoons)

¼ cup lukewarm water

1 cup lukewarm whole milk

2 tablespoons melted unsalted butter

2 egg yolks

1½ teaspoons salt

3½ cups flour

Filling

½ cup fish stock

¾ pound salmon fillet

3 tablespoons unsalted butter

1 medium onion, minced

¾ teaspoon salt

Freshly ground black pepper

2 ounces smoked trout

1 egg yolk

1 teaspoon cold water

4 teaspoons unsalted butter

To make the dough, dissolve the yeast in the warm water. Stir in the warm milk, butter, egg yolks, and salt. Mix in the flour to make a soft dough. Turn the dough out onto a lightly floured surface and knead until smooth and elastic, being careful not to incorporate too much more flour. The dough will be slightly sticky. Place the dough in a greased bowl and turn it over once to grease the top. Cover the bowl with a dish towel and leave the dough to rise in a warm place until doubled in bulk, 1½ hours.

While the dough is rising, make the filling. Pour the fish stock into a small skillet and bring to a boil. Add the salmon fillet, skin-side up, and immediately lower the heat to a simmer. Poach the fish, covered, until barely done, about 6 minutes, being careful not to overcook it. Lift the fish from the pan with a slotted spatula and transfer to a bowl, reserving the stock. Allow the salmon to cool slightly, then remove the skin and flake the fish finely with a fork.

Melt the 3 tablespoons butter in a small saucepan. Add the onion and sauté over low heat until golden, about 6 minutes. Add the buttery onions

continued

to the flaked salmon, mixing well. Season the mixture with the salt and pepper.

Line two large baking sheets with parchment paper. Punch down the risen dough and divide it in half. Roll out one ball of dough into a 10-inch round. With a cookie cutter, cut out four 4-inch rounds. Knead the scraps of dough together and roll them out again, cutting out four more rounds. Place a heaping tablespoon of the salmon filling on each round, leaving a 1-inch border around the edges and mounding it higher in the center. Top the filling with a 1-inch-square piece of smoked trout. (You'll have some trout left over.)

Now shape the pies. Bring the two sides of dough together at the top. Starting at one end of the pie, pinch the edges together between your thumb and forefinger. To make decorative pleats, bring the lower edge of the dough up and press it into the inside of the adjacent dough. Make another pinch and press the dough down into the adjacent lower edge to make a decorative, tightly sealed seam. Stop pleating just before you reach the middle of the pie. Leave a 1-inch gap, then begin pinching and pleating again to finish sealing the pie to the right of the hole. Slightly flare the dough around the hole and gently elongate the edges of each pie into a boat shape. Place the pies on one of the baking sheets, then repeat the rolling, filling, pleating, and shaping with the remaining ball of dough.

Preheat the oven to 375°F. While it preheats, cover the pies with a dish towel and leave them to rise until slightly puffy, about 25 minutes. Mix the egg yolk with the cold water and brush the pies with this wash. Place ¼ teaspoon of butter in the opening of each pie, on top of the trout.

Bake the pies for 20 minutes, until golden. Pour ½ teaspoon of the reserved fish stock into each opening. Serve hot.

"Pickle" Pies

Пирожки с начинкой из свежих огурцов

These little pies don't contain any pickles at all—they just seem to. I was playing around with ingredients one day and decided to make a filling with cucumbers, which we tend to forget are very tasty when cooked. I wrapped them in a tender dough containing whey left over from making farmer's cheese, and the slightly sour note of the whey, along with the filling's fresh dill and salt, reminded me of brined pickles. (If you don't have any whey on hand, kefir makes an excellent substitute.) Though these pies keep well at room temperature, they are nothing short of divine when warm.

Makes 36 small pies

Dough

1¼ cups whey (see Homemade Farmer's Cheese, page 79) or plain whole-milk kefir

1 package active dry yeast (2¼ teaspoons)

1 teaspoon sugar

½ cup (1 stick) melted unsalted butter, cooled to lukewarm

2 teaspoons salt

4 to 4½ cups flour

Filling

1 pound cucumbers (about 2 medium)

1½ teaspoons salt

2 hard-boiled eggs

2 tablespoons softened unsalted butter

2 tablespoons minced fresh dill

Freshly ground black pepper

2 egg yolks

Heat the whey until just lukewarm. In a medium bowl, stir together the yeast, sugar, and ¼ cup of the whey until the yeast dissolves. Let sit 5 minutes until bubbles form, then stir in the butter, salt, and enough flour to make a soft dough. Turn out onto a floured board and knead for 10 minutes. Shape into a ball and place in a large greased bowl, turning it over once to grease the top. Cover and let rise until doubled in size, about 1½ hours.

While the dough is rising, make the filling. Trim and peel the cucumbers. Cut them in half lengthwise and, with a small spoon, scrape out the seeds, then dice. Place the cucumbers in a strainer over a bowl and mix in 1 teaspoon of the salt. Let drain for 1 hour.

Dice the hard-boiled eggs and mix them with the salted drained cucumbers in a medium bowl. Break off bits of the butter and stir into the cucumbers along with the remaining ½ teaspoon salt, the dill, and pepper to taste.

Line two large baking sheets with parchment paper. Punch down the risen dough and divide it in half. Divide each half into 18 equal pieces. On a lightly floured surface, roll or pat out the pieces of dough into 3-inch rounds.

Place a tablespoon of the filling in the center of each round, being careful to avoid any liquid that's accumulated in the bottom of the bowl. Bring two sides of the dough together at the top and pinch firmly to seal. Gently shape the pies into elongated ovals and place them seam-side down on the baking sheets. Cover the pies with a dish towel and allow to rise for 20 minutes.

While the pies are rising, preheat the oven to 375°F. Stir the egg yolks together in a small bowl and brush the pies with this glaze. Bake for 25 minutes, until golden. Serve warm.

AN ABUNDANCE OF PIES

I fell in love with Russian pies before I ever tasted one. As a sophomore in college, I was reading Chekhov's story "The Siren" when I came across this line: "The *kulebyaka* should be appetizing, shameless in its nakedness, a temptation to sin." What siren was this, that beckoned so wantonly? I had to find out. I soon discovered that *kulebyaka* is a multilayered fish pie, only one of the many glorious pies that characterize Russian cuisine. I also discovered that Russian literature is replete with references to pies, from Chekhovs, dripping butter like tears, to Gogols, a four-cornered *kulebyaka* luscious enough to make "a dead man's mouth water."

Russian pies come in all sorts of shapes and sizes, with a near-endless variety of fillings. Because they symbolize well-being, they're considered celebratory, though talented cooks also make magic by enclosing leftovers in dough. The pinnacle of Russian pies might be the *kurnik*, a large domed creation that's light-years away from a homey chicken potpie. Half a foot tall and layered with chicken, mushrooms, and rice, it's traditional for weddings. Before the revolution, there was even Pie Day, the third day after the wedding ceremony, when brides were expected to show off their baking prowess and thereby demonstrate fitness for marriage.

A pie's success—and magnificence—depends on the harmonious conjunction of several elements: filling, dough, shape, and cooking method. I could write a small book enumerating all the possible fillings and the inventiveness with which Russians use them, from a spare and simple pie stuffed with chopped cabbage and onions to a cholesterol-rich extravaganza layered inside with crêpelike *blinchiki,* farmer's cheese, hard-boiled eggs, and butter. The diversity of fish pies alone is astounding, from a silken mousseline filling in a puff-pastry envelope to a sturdy bread crust wrapped around a whole zander. Sweet fillings include berries, stone fruits, and apples, not to mention farmer's cheese and jam.

Pie dough can be made from either rye or wheat flour or a mixture of the two and can range in texture from a quick, short dough made with sour cream to a yeast dough that's either crusty and lean or soft and enriched. Flaky pastry and puff pastry can also be used. The art lies in choosing a dough that will complement the filling, both in flavor and texture. The proportion of dough to filling also varies considerably from pie to pie, and from region to region. In the Russian North, where fresh fish abounds, fish pies contain much more filling than crust; in Russia's interior, the ratio is often reversed. The filling and dough determine the shape of the pie, whether it's round, oval, triangular, square, rectangular, boat-shaped, or domed. Pies are baked open-faced, latticed, or enclosed, in shapes large and small. Small pies—*pirozhki*—are a genre unto themselves, within which many different styles appear. Though large Russian pies are always baked, small ones can also be pan fried or deep fried.

Even the most basic *pirozhki* are often sealed by means of decorative pleating that reveals the Russian love of ornamentation. Special-occasion pies are a marvel, their crusts covered with scraps of dough cut into leaves, flowers, and other organic or geometric forms to create a bas-relief. Inventive bakers sometimes use two different kinds of dough for decoration, making intricate patterns of white wheat and dark rye dough on the top of the pie. For a golden sheen, the crust is usually glazed with an egg wash before baking.

In the tsarist past, pies constituted a separate course at luxurious dinners, when they were served between the fish and the roast. In the nineteenth century, small pies also began to be offered as accompaniments to soup, and by the twentieth century, they'd become a fixture on the *zakuska* table as well. And of course, teatime is unthinkable without a sweet pie, a genuine expression of hospitality. As the Russian saying goes, "The beauty of a house lies not in its walls, but in its pies."

Vatrushki

Ватрушки

Proust had his madeleines. I have *vatrushki*. A single bite of these tender buns carries me back to Soviet times, when they were one of the few foods I could reliably buy fresh. I frequented a bakery in Moscow's Arbat district, not far from the American embassy. The aroma of baking bread wafting into the air conveyed all the comfort that was lacking in my everyday life, and I made a detour for the buns several times a week.

Vatrushki taste best when freshly baked. They're served for breakfast and tea, and for a snack any time. A filling of farmer's cheese is classic, but in summertime, the pies are often filled with fresh berries, especially lingonberries in the North. You can enjoy a fruit filling year-round by substituting thick jam or a combination of jam and dried berries.

Makes 12 small pies

Dough

½ cup lukewarm whole milk

4 tablespoons melted unsalted butter

1 tablespoon sugar

1 egg, lightly beaten

Rounded 1 teaspoon instant yeast

½ teaspoon vanilla extract

¼ teaspoon salt

1¾ cups flour

Filling

2 cups (1 pound) farmer's cheese, homemade (page 79) or store-bought

1 egg, lightly beaten

2 tablespoons sour cream

2 tablespoons sugar

1 teaspoon flour

½ teaspoon vanilla extract

Pinch of salt

1 egg yolk

To make the dough, in a large bowl, mix together the milk, butter, sugar, egg, yeast, vanilla, and salt. Beat in the flour to form a soft and rather sticky dough. Turn the dough out onto a floured surface and knead lightly for a few minutes until smooth and supple, being careful not to incorporate too much extra flour. Grease a large bowl and place the dough in it, then turn the dough over to grease the top. Cover the bowl with a dish towel and leave the dough to rise in a warm place until doubled in bulk, about 1 hour.

While the dough is rising, make the filling. In a bowl, mix together the farmer's cheese, egg, sour cream, sugar, flour, vanilla, and salt.

Line a baking sheet with parchment paper. Punch down the risen dough and, with your hand, shape it into a 12-inch cylinder. Cut the dough into 12 equal pieces. Gently pat out each piece of dough right on the baking sheet into a 4-inch round. Cover the rounds with a dish towel and leave to rise for 25 minutes, until slightly puffy.

With the bottom of a 2-inch shot glass or jar, make a depression in each round of dough. Fill each depression with about 2 tablespoons of the filling. (If you want the pie to look professionally made, smooth the top of the filling. I usually leave it as is for a rustic look.)

continued

Preheat the oven to 400°F. Lightly beat the egg yolk and brush it over the edges of the dough. Bake for about 12 minutes, until the filling is puffed and the buns are golden. Transfer to wire racks to cool, then serve.

Note

You can bake any leftover filling in a small buttered casserole dish until firm, about 15 minutes, and eat it like a pudding.

Variations

For a summertime blueberry filling, stir together 3 cups fresh blueberries, 4½ tablespoons sugar, 1½ tablespoons potato starch, and ⅛ teaspoon salt.

In wintertime, mix 1 cup thick blueberry preserves with ½ cup freeze-dried blueberries.

Drop about 2 tablespoons of either filling into each bun depression and bake as directed.

Puff Pies
Наливные шаньги

These buttery pies, a specialty of the Russian North, are especially popular in the Arkhangelsk region. They are made with a liquid yeasted batter similar to that used for blini, but the resemblance ends there. The yeast and the sour cream filling work splendidly together to give these little pies a subtly sour tang. In texture they resemble a spongy brioche—the Russian kissing cousin of *galettes bressanes*. Like brioche, puff pies taste best when fresh, for breakfast or afternoon tea.

Makes 8 small pies

Batter

2 cups flour

1 package active dry yeast (2¼ teaspoons)

1 tablespoon sugar

½ teaspoon salt

1 cup lukewarm whole milk

2 eggs, lightly beaten

Filling

⅓ cup sour cream

4 tablespoons melted unsalted butter

3 tablespoons flour

Anson Mills toasted oat flour, for garnish (optional)

To make the batter, in a medium bowl, mix together the flour, yeast, sugar, and salt. Stir together the milk and eggs and gradually whisk into the flour mixture to make a batter the consistency of pancake batter. Cover the bowl and let rise in a warm place for 1 hour, until the batter is bubbly.

Prepare the filling by whisking together the sour cream, butter, and flour.

Preheat the oven to 400°F. Grease eight 4-inch tart pans (preferably with removable bottoms) and place them on a baking sheet. (If your pans don't have removable bottoms, it's best to grease them with nonstick baking spray for easy release.)

Ladle the batter into the tart pans, filling them half full. Place a generous tablespoon of filling in the center of each one.

Bake for 20 to 25 minutes, until puffed and nicely browned. Let the pies cool in their pans for 5 minutes, then carefully remove the sides or invert the pans to release. (You may need to go around the fluted edges with the tip of a sharp knife.) Sprinkle each pie with a little toasted oat flour, if desired. Serve warm or at room temperature.

Note

If the sour cream filling firms up before the batter has risen, just heat it in the microwave for 20 seconds to make it spoonable again.

Coulibiac

Кулебяка

Kulebyaka, a large, oval fish pie, is one of Russia's grandest creations, adopted into French cuisine as coulibiac. Craig Claiborne, writing in the *New York Times* in 1976, called it

> . . . the world's greatest dish. . . . It is no mere trifle, no ordinary pâté, something to be dabbled with while awaiting a second course or a third or a fourth. A coulibiac is a celestial creation, manna for the culinary gods and a main course unto itself. I'm not at all convinced that anything should precede such a sublime invention, except perhaps a spoonful or two of caviar. And I am less convinced that anything should follow it. Who can improve on paradisiacal bliss?

Hyperbole aside, Claiborne recognized brilliance when he tasted it, and to dazzle guests, I sometimes make a classic *kulebyaka*. That usually involves an entire day in the kitchen. First I prepare a yeast dough and let it rise. Next I make a batch of *blinchiki* (thin pancakes), poach a salmon fillet, and sauté a sturgeon steak. I boil a portion of buckwheat or rice before sautéing mushrooms and onions and seasoning them with parsley and dill. I hard-boil and thinly slice a few eggs. If I'm lucky (which I rarely am these days), I add *viziga*, the dried, gelatinous backbone of sturgeon, which helps bind everything together. *Viziga* adds another layer of complexity to both the pie and its preparation, since it must first be reconstituted by boiling. When I was testing *kulebyaka* for my first Russian cookbook, I could easily find *viziga* in the Russian stores that lined Clement Street in San Francisco. No longer. Not only have the old Russian stores disappeared, but Caspian sturgeon is now endangered, and even in Moscow it's difficult to find the backbone. When I did an Internet search for "Where to buy viziga," Google responded, "Did you mean 'Where to buy Viagra'?" How times have changed.

At any rate, with or without *viziga*, when all of the pie's components are ready, I roll out the dough and layer it with *blinchiki*, salmon, sturgeon, buckwheat, mushrooms, hard-boiled eggs, and vegetables. Grand as this pie is, it still doesn't quite compare with the legendary *kulebyaka* served at Testov's Tavern in Moscow in the nineteenth century, which had twelve different layers separated by thin pancakes, beginning with burbot liver and ending with bone marrow.

The recipe I offer here is much simpler and smaller, and it doesn't take an entire day to prepare. This pie is more rustic than the Frenchified coulibiac, but because it's less rich, you can enjoy more of it, which to me is a definite boon. Its simplicity makes it no less stunning or succulent.

continued

Serves 10 to 12

Filling

4 tablespoons
unsalted butter

1 medium onion, diced

6 ounces mushrooms,
trimmed and diced

1¾ teaspoons salt

Freshly ground
black pepper

1 cup fish stock

1 pound salmon fillet,
in two pieces

½ pound halibut fillet

3 hard-boiled eggs, diced

¼ cup minced fresh dill

2 tablespoons minced
fresh parsley

Dough

2½ cups flour

1¼ teaspoons salt

1¼ teaspoons baking soda

1 teaspoon sugar

1 egg

1¼ cups sour cream

2 egg yolks

2 teaspoons whole milk

To make the filling, melt the butter in a large skillet. Add the onion and mushrooms and sauté until they are soft and the liquid has evaporated, about 8 minutes. Season with ½ teaspoon of the salt and some pepper, then transfer to a bowl and set aside.

Pour the fish stock into the skillet and bring to a boil. Add the salmon and halibut fillets, skin-side up, and immediately lower the heat to a simmer. Poach the fillets, covered, until barely done, about 8 minutes. Be careful not to overcook them. Transfer to a bowl. Allow the fillets to cool slightly, then remove the skin and flake the fish finely with a fork. Season it with another ½ teaspoon salt and more pepper, then stir it into the mushroom mixture. Add the hard-boiled eggs, dill, and parsley. The filling should be moist but not wet. Stir in the remaining ¾ teaspoon salt and more pepper.

To make the dough, mix together the flour, salt, baking soda, and sugar in a medium bowl. In another bowl, stir together the egg and the sour cream, then mix in the flour mixture. The dough will be sticky. Turn it out onto a floured board and knead for a minute with well-floured hands, being careful not to incorporate more flour than necessary.

Preheat the oven to 375°F. Line a baking sheet with parchment paper. Divide the dough in two, with one piece slightly larger than the other. Pull off a generous lump of dough from the larger piece for decoration.

On a floured surface, roll the smaller piece into an oval 16 inches long and 6 inches wide. Transfer it to the baking sheet. Mound the filling over the dough to within 1 inch of the edges. Roll out the second piece of dough and lay it over the filling. With a sharp knife, trim the edges into an even oval, reserving the scraps of dough. Pinch the edges to seal and make a decorative border around the pie. Lightly beat the egg yolks with the milk and brush the pie with half the mixture.

Use the reserved dough and trimmed scraps to decorate the pie. I like to make a fish-bone pattern that runs the length of the pie. I press the reserved dough together with the scraps and roll it out into a strip about 14 inches long and 2 inches wide, then make notches along both sides to resemble the vertebrae of a spine. Lay the strip along the center of the pie, then brush the pie with the remaining egg wash.

Bake for 40 to 45 minutes, until the crust is nicely browned. Serve at room temperature.

Chicken Pie
Курник

This dramatic pie, filled with shredded chicken and hard-boiled eggs, was traditionally served at weddings to symbolize fertility, though some commentators claim that its domelike shape is meant to recall Monomakh's Cap, one of Russia's great medieval treasures. A skullcap made of gold and ornamented in eight sections with precious jewels, it is the oldest royal crown on display in the Kremlin Armory. Indeed, with its towering golden crust, a *kurnik* does resemble a crown.

Making the pie is an elaborate affair. In some regions of Russia, cooks enclosed a whole chicken, bones and all, in the dough. Even classic variations using boned chicken call for layering it with *blinchiki* (thin pancakes), hard-boiled eggs, mushrooms, onions, and rice. Though I've lightened the recipe here by eliminating the pancake layers, the pie remains time-consuming in its various steps, even if none are technically challenging. This version is still an impressive creation, sure to elicit awe from your guests.

Serves 8 to 10

Dough

3 cups flour

¾ teaspoon salt

1 cup (2 sticks) cold unsalted butter, cut into small pieces

1 egg

¾ cup sour cream

2 tablespoons ice water

Chicken

One 4-pound chicken (including the neck and giblets but not the liver)

6 cups cold water

Handful of parsley sprigs

1 large carrot, peeled

1 onion, peeled and quartered

1 large bay leaf

8 black peppercorns

1 teaspoon salt

1 cup raw basmati rice

2⅓ cups chicken stock (reserved from cooking the chicken)

1 teaspoon salt

2 medium onions, chopped medium-fine

6 tablespoons unsalted butter

1 pound mushrooms, trimmed and sliced ¼ inch thick

Freshly ground black pepper

¼ cup finely chopped fresh parsley

¼ cup sour cream

¼ cup minced fresh dill

4 hard-boiled eggs

1 egg yolk

1 teaspoon cold water

To make the dough, place the flour and salt in the bowl of a food processor. Add the butter and pulse a few times, until the mixture resembles coarse cornmeal. Be careful not to overmix. In a small bowl, beat the egg lightly and stir in the sour cream, then add to the flour mixture along with the ice water. Pulse a few times to mix, then turn the dough out into a bowl and, with your hands, form it into two disks, one slightly larger than the other. Wrap each disk in plastic wrap and chill for at least 1 hour.

To cook the chicken, place the chicken in a large stockpot. Add the water, parsley, carrot, onion, bay leaf, peppercorns, and salt. Bring the water to a boil, skimming any foam that

continued

rises to the surface. Lower the heat and simmer the chicken, covered, for 1½ hours, until the chicken is tender. Strain, reserving the chicken stock. (You'll have more than you need for the filling, so save the rest for another use.)

Remove the skin from the chicken and discard it along with all the vegetables except for the carrot. Separate the meat from the bones and shred it coarsely. Chop the giblets finely. Transfer the chicken to a bowl and set aside. Cut the carrot into ¼-inch slices and set aside.

Soak the rice in cold water to cover for 30 minutes, then drain well. Cook the rice in 1⅓ cups of the reserved chicken stock, along with ½ teaspoon of the salt, until the liquid is just absorbed, about 15 minutes. Remove from the heat and set aside.

In a large skillet over medium-low heat, sauté the onions in 4 tablespoons of the butter until golden, about 8 minutes. Add the remaining 2 tablespoons butter along with the mushrooms, ¼ teaspoon salt, and pepper to taste. Sauté, stirring occasionally, for 5 minutes. Stir in the parsley and the reserved sliced carrot.

In a small saucepan, heat the remaining 1 cup chicken stock. Whisk in the sour cream, dill, and remaining ¼ teaspoon salt. Pour the mixture over the shredded chicken, stirring to coat well. Coarsely chop the eggs and set aside.

Now you're ready to assemble the pie. Preheat the oven to 400°F. Remove the smaller disk of dough from the refrigerator and roll it out on a floured board to ⅛ inch thick. Carefully center the dough in an 8-inch springform pan, easing it into place to cover the sides of the pan. At least 1 inch of dough should overhang the edges.

Spread one-third of the rice onto the dough in a smooth layer. Using a slotted spoon, lift out half of the shredded chicken and spread it over the rice. Top the chicken with half of the hard-boiled eggs, then use the slotted spoon to scoop out half of the vegetable mixture to layer on top of the eggs. Cover the vegetables with half of the remaining rice in an even layer, then repeat the layering with the remaining ingredients, ending with a layer of rice on the top. You'll have three layers of rice and two layers each of chicken, hard-boiled eggs, and vegetables. When the ingredients reach the top of the pan, you'll need to use your hands to mold them into a conical form that is higher in the center than around the sides. The mounded filling will extend a couple of inches above the height of the pan.

Roll out the second disk of dough into a large round ⅛ inch thick. Lay the dough over the pie filling and trim the edges to meet the bottom crust. (You'll have more dough than you need for the pie, but it's nice to have plenty to work with.) Press the edges of the top and bottom crusts together to seal, trimming off any excess dough. To make decorative pleats, choose a starting place anywhere along the edge of the pie and pinch with your thumb and forefinger, bringing the lower edge of the dough up and pressing it into the inside of the adjacent dough. Make another pinch and press the dough down into the adjacent lower edge, continuing in this fashion all the way around the pie, making rising and falling pleats until the pie is completely sealed. Tuck in these pleats so that they don't hang over the edge of the pan; otherwise you'll have a hard time removing the pie once it's baked. With a sharp knife, cut a 1-inch hole in the center of the top crust to allow steam to escape.

Beat the egg yolk with the cold water and brush the dough all over with three-fourths of this egg wash. Use the scraps of leftover dough to decorate the pie. I like to cut out 8 small strips of dough, twist them into spirals, and set them on the pie so that they radiate out from the center hole to the base, creating eight sections that recall Monomakh's Cap. Within each section, I often set a small dot of dough like a precious jewel. Brush the decorations with the rest of the egg wash.

Bake for 50 to 60 minutes, until the crust is golden. Check the pie after about half an hour to make sure the top isn't getting too dark. If it is, loosely tent the whole pie with aluminum foil.

Allow the pie to cool for 20 minutes before removing the sides of the springform pan and digging in.

Scallion Pie

Пирог с зелёным луком и яйцом

I'm so addicted to Russian pies that it's hard to choose a favorite. For sheer drama, the classic chicken pie *kurnik* wins the award. For comfort I turn to *vatrushki*, open-faced curd-cheese pies. My go-to pies in summer are bursting with berries, but when the weather turns cool, this scallion pie tops my list. If you've never had pie made with rye dough, you're in for a treat. The scent of rye wafting through the house as the pie bakes is divine, and the flavor is savory, hearty, and utterly satisfying. I've based this dough on one made by Murmansk chef Svetlana Kozeiko, who always adds a touch of sugar to tenderize the dough.

Serves 10 to 12

Filling

8 tablespoons unsalted butter

8 large scallions, trimmed and finely chopped, including green tops

4 hard-boiled eggs, finely chopped

1 cup minced fresh parsley

⅓ cup minced fresh dill

¼ cup sour cream

2 teaspoons salt

Freshly ground black pepper

Dough

2½ cups rye flour

1¼ teaspoons baking soda

1 teaspoon salt

1 teaspoon sugar

1 egg

1¼ cups sour cream

2 egg yolks

2 teaspoons whole milk

To make the filling, melt the butter in a large skillet. Add the scallions and sauté over medium-low heat for 4 to 5 minutes, until softened but not browned. Remove from the heat and stir in the remaining ingredients. Season with black pepper. Set the filling aside while you prepare the dough.

To make the dough, mix together the flour, baking soda, salt, and sugar in a medium bowl. In another bowl, stir together the egg and sour cream and add to the flour mixture. The dough will be sticky. Turn it out onto a floured board and knead for a minute with well-floured hands, being careful not to incorporate more flour than necessary. A little miracle occurs as you work this dough: it suddenly turns supple and pliable. You'll want to knead on, but don't, or the dough will toughen.

Preheat the oven to 375°F. Line a baking sheet with parchment paper. Divide the dough in half. On a floured surface, roll one piece out to a 10-inch round and transfer it to the baking sheet. Spread the filling over the dough to within 1 inch of the edge. Roll out the second piece of dough to a round slightly larger than the first and lay it over the filling. With a sharp knife, trim the edges into an even round, then crimp and turn them under to seal. Use the trimmed scraps of dough to make decorative shapes to adorn the pie.

Lightly beat the egg yolks with the milk and brush the pie with half the mixture. Arrange the decorations on top of the pie, then brush again with the remaining glaze. Bake for 40 to 45 minutes, until the crust is nicely browned. Serve at room temperature.

Blini

Блины половинные

Yeast-raised pancakes are one of Russia's most beloved foods. Thicker than crêpes but less dense than flapjacks, they're wonderfully porous, perfect for soaking up butter. Many different types of blini exist, but I like this version with half buckwheat and half all-purpose flour best. It used to be easy enough to find good buckwheat flour in health-food stores, but with the soaring popularity of gluten-free foods (which buckwheat naturally is), manufacturers have been refining buckwheat flour until it is almost as white as wheat flour—and in the process destroying its distinctive taste. So you'll want to look for buckwheat flour ground from whole groats (see Sources). If you can't find that, you can finely grind some whole roasted buckwheat groats in a coffee grinder and either use a full cup of that flour for a hearty taste or mix it with pale buckwheat flour for a somewhat subtler flavor.

Don't worry too much about the recipe's timing. The batter is very forgiving and can be left to rise for a few hours without harm. Also, don't fret about the first pancake you make, which rarely turns out well. As the Russians say, "The first pancake's a lump." You'll quickly get the hang of it.

These blini can be topped with any of the classic accompaniments (see page 136), but I find them so good on their own that I usually just add melted butter and a sprinkling of *tolokno*, toasted oat flour.

Makes 24, serves 4 to 6

1 package active dry yeast (2¼ teaspoons)

1 teaspoon sugar

2¾ cups lukewarm whole milk

4 tablespoons unsalted butter, melted

1 cup buckwheat flour

1 cup all-purpose flour

Generous ½ teaspoon salt

3 eggs, separated

Vegetable oil, for the pan

Melted butter and Anson Mills toasted oat flour, for garnish (optional)

In a large bowl, dissolve the yeast and sugar in ¼ cup of the warm milk and stir until the yeast dissolves and begins to foam. Stir in the remaining milk, the butter, both flours, salt, and egg yolks. Whisk well by hand until no lumps remain, or beat with an electric mixer for a minute or two. Cover the bowl and leave the mixture to rise in a warm place until doubled in volume, about 1 hour.

Beat the egg whites until stiff but not dry and fold them into the batter. Let the batter rest for 30 minutes more.

Heat an 8-inch cast-iron crêpe pan over medium heat and brush the surface with vegetable oil. When the pan is hot, test the consistency of the batter by pouring a little out onto the pan—it should pour easily enough to swirl over the surface of the pan. (If it's too thick, gently fold in a little more warm milk.)

continued

Pour 3 to 4 tablespoons of batter onto the pan. Pick up the pan and swirl it so that the batter forms a thin, even round, 5 to 6 inches in diameter. Cook over medium heat until bubbles appear on the surface, about 1 minute. Flip the pancake with a spatula and cook on the other side just until faintly colored, another 30 seconds or so. Turn the pancake out onto a plate and repeat with the remaining batter, adding more oil to the pan as needed.

Blini are best served hot from the pan, and ideally each person is served a stack of three. If they must be kept for later, pile them in a deep dish, brushing each one with butter, and cover the top of the dish with a linen towel. You could also cover the dish with aluminum foil and keep the blini warm in a 200°F oven.

Note

If you want to make small, appetizer-size blini to serve American-style, use just a tablespoon of batter for each pancake. Small blini are most easily made in a Swedish *plättpanna* that has seven indentations. This recipe will make about 40 mini blini.

Pink Blini

Розовые блины

These pancakes are drop-dead gorgeous, their deep-pink hue enhanced by the rosy tones of gooseberry-apple compote. The great Russian poet Alexander Pushkin adored these blini, if we're to believe his friend Alexandra Smirnova-Rosset, who recalled in her memoirs that he would eat thirty pancakes at one go, to no ill effect, gulping down some water in between each one. Pushkin also adored gooseberry jam and kept a jar on his desk for dipping into. Here, in the poet's honor, I've paired gooseberry compote with the blini, and added a dollop of sour cream for good measure. If, like Pushkin, you invite guests to share these pancakes for a brunch or a light supper, you'll have friends for life.

Makes about 20 blini, serves 4 to 6

2 cups flour

1 teaspoon salt

4 eggs, separated

1½ cups full-fat buttermilk

½ cup beet juice

2 tablespoons water

2 tablespoons melted unsalted butter, plus more for greasing the pan

Gooseberry-Apple Compote (facing page), for garnish

Sour cream, for garnish

Mix together the flour and salt in a medium bowl. In another bowl, lightly beat the egg yolks, then stir in the buttermilk, beet juice, water, and butter to make a thin pancake batter. Beat the egg whites until stiff but not dry and fold them into the batter.

Preheat the oven to 175°F. Grease an 8-inch cast-iron crêpe pan with a little butter. Pour about ¼ cup of batter into the pan and swirl the pan so that the batter forms a thin, even round, 5 to 6 inches in diameter. Cook over medium heat until bubbles appear on the surface, 1 to 2 minutes. Flip the pancake and cook on the other side just until faintly browned, another minute or so. Turn the pancake out onto a plate and repeat with the remaining batter, greasing the pan again if necessary. Stack the pancakes on a plate to keep warm in the oven until you've finished making them all.

Serve the pancakes topped with some compote and a generous dollop of sour cream.

GOOSEBERRY-APPLE COMPOTE

Варенье из крыжовника с яблоками

Makes about 2 pints

1 pound pink
gooseberries, fresh
or frozen

1 pound tart apples,
such as Granny Smith,
peeled, cored, and cut
into ½-inch cubes

¾ cup sugar

½ vanilla bean

Place the gooseberries and apples in a medium saucepan along with the sugar. Slit the vanilla bean and scrape the seeds into the pan, then toss in the pod. Bring to a boil and cook over medium-low heat for 10 minutes. Cool the compote before removing the vanilla pod. The compote keeps well in the refrigerator for a couple of weeks when stored in an airtight jar. Serve at room temperature or lightly chilled.

BLINI

We may be most familiar with blini as bite-size vehicles for caviar or smoked salmon at fancy cocktail receptions, but real Russian blini are something quite different: saucer-size, with lacy edges and the robust flavor of buckwheat. "Plump as the shoulders of a merchant's daughter" is how the great Russian writer Anton Chekhov described these classic pancakes. Blini are one of Russia's most ancient dishes, dating back to pre-Christian times, when they were baked on hot stones at the vernal equinox. Shaped into rounds in the image of the sun, they beckoned its return after the long, dark months of winter.

When Russia embraced Christianity, the Orthodox Church wisely allowed blini to morph into the premier symbol of indulgence during Maslenitsa, the Butter Festival preceding Lent, giving blessing to excess and encouraging feasting on rich foods that would soon be proscribed. Unlike pre-Lenten Shrove Tuesday or Fastnacht—both single days marked by eating pancakes or doughnuts—Russia's Butter Festival lasts for an entire week. Each day was designated for a different way of sharing pancakes, as a means of solidifying familial relations. For instance, on Wednesday, mothers-in-law invited their sons-in-law for blini to demonstrate their approval, while on Friday the sons-in-law were expected to reciprocate and thereby demonstrate mutual affection.

Blini are so embedded in the national psyche that Russian dream books are filled with interpretations of the blini you might see in your sleep. If they're lacy and plump, they signal well-being and abundance; if they appear burned, your unconscious mind is anticipating trouble ahead.

Not all blini are alike, though each is delicious in its own way. They can be made with all buckwheat or all white flour or a mixture of the two. Originally, blini were baked in a very hot oven rather than being cooked on a stovetop. In the northern village of Bestuzhevo, I learned how to bake blini the traditional way, in a Russian masonry stove so hot that coals still glowed at the back of the oven. Made with yellow split-pea powder, these pancakes were extraordinary, golden and crisp, truly in the image of the sun.

Blini variations include quick blini, a modern invention made with baking soda instead of yeast, and sometimes with additions such as scallions or ham stirred into the batter. Thin *blinchiki* are basically crêpes, with no leavening. Russians like to stack them into a kind of torte called a *blinchatyi pirog*, layering them with fillings either savory or sweet. When rolled and filled with farmer's cheese or jam and then fried in butter, *blinchiki* become what we know as blintzes. Yeast-raised blini are usually rolled as well.

As for blini accompaniments, butter is mandatory. It keeps the pancakes from sticking together when they're piled into a stack, and they benefit from an extra drizzle of melted butter at the table, too. Some blini aficionados top the butter with sour cream, while others (like me) prefer caviar (as pictured on page 131), but sour cream and caviar should never be mixed together. The American practice of piling blini with sour cream, caviar, chopped hard-boiled egg, onion, herring, and more is an affront to the Russian pancakes. Chekhov cautions against such excess in his sketch "On Human Frailty," where the gluttonous hero, Podtykin, can't resist piling one accompaniment after another onto the blini he's served. After a dose of hot butter, he spreads them with caviar, a choice that seems momentarily fine, until he can't resist pouring sour cream over all the empty spaces not covered by caviar. He continues with a garnish of oily salmon, a sprat, and finally a sardine. After rolling up the blini together, Podtykin takes a shot of vodka and, with mouth wide open, is poised to enjoy his creation when he suddenly succumbs to a stroke.

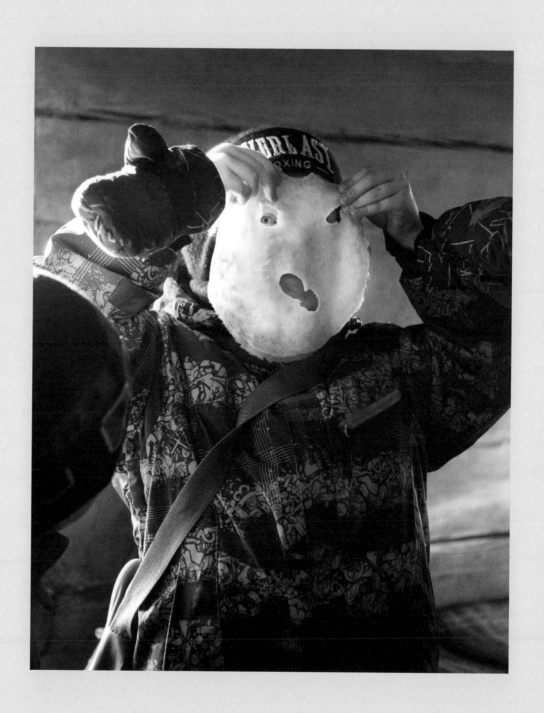

Farmer's Cheese Pancakes

Сырники

In the wide world of pancakes—a world I enter into whenever I can—these classic Russian *syrniki* rank at the top. It's not just their tangy-sweet flavor that keeps me coming back. It's also their emotional resonance. In Soviet times, *syrniki* were a mainstay of my diet, offering a quick hit of protein and an always-reliable meal. Over the years, I tasted my way through hundreds of pancakes. This recipe makes them the way I like them—tender rather than firm, and not too sweet.

Since the batter doesn't contain much flour, its consistency will depend on the type of farmer's cheese you use. I tend to like a slightly sticky batter to ensure that the pancakes turn out moist, so if the farmer's cheese seems dry, I often add a tablespoon or two of heavy cream to the batter. Even when the batter's sticky, you shouldn't have trouble shaping the pancakes if you flour your hands well and use a light touch. Make sure to cook the *syrniki* as soon as you make them, while the batter is still cold. Otherwise they might lose their shape. You can also shape the patties ahead of time, dust them with flour, and keep them chilled until you're ready to fry them. A 12-inch skillet accommodates about half the batter. If you want to make all the pancakes at once, use two skillets, adding enough butter and oil for both.

Makes 12 pancakes, serves 4

2 egg yolks

2 cups (1 pound) tvorog or farmer's cheese, homemade (page 79) or store-bought

Scant ½ cup sugar

¾ cup flour

½ teaspoon baking powder

Pinch of salt

A tablespoon or two of heavy cream (optional)

2 tablespoons unsalted butter

2 tablespoons vegetable oil

Sour cream, for garnish

In a medium bowl, beat the egg yolks into the farmer's cheese, then stir in the sugar. Mix together ½ cup of the flour, the baking powder, and the salt and add to the cheese mixture. If the mixture seems dry, add a little heavy cream.

Place the butter and oil over medium-low heat in a large nonstick skillet and melt the butter.

Sprinkle the remaining ¼ cup flour onto a plate and dust your hands with some flour, too. With your hands or a spoon, scoop out about 2 table-spoons of the batter and set the mound on the floured plate. Use your hands to gently shape it into a round patty about 2 inches in diameter and coat it lightly on all sides with flour. Repeat with the remaining batter.

Carefully transfer the patties to the pan and cook them slowly until the undersides are browned, about 3 minutes. Turn with a spatula and cook until the other sides are browned, 3 to 4 minutes more. Serve immediately, with sour cream.

Pumpkin Pancakes

Оладьи с тыквой

In the United States, we tend to think of pancakes as breakfast fare, but in Russia they're more often eaten for supper. *Olad'i*—plump pancakes fried in oil—are quick to prepare, since they're not raised with yeast like traditional blini. Grated summer squash is a frequent addition; in winter, pumpkin is used. I often substitute winter squash for its more reliable flavor and texture. But don't expect dry, fluffy pancakes. These cook up crisp on the outside and moist and creamy within. A dollop of sour cream elevates these pancakes to a meal for company.

Makes about 16 pancakes, serves 4

½ cup flour

½ teaspoon baking soda

¼ teaspoon salt

1 cup whole-milk kefir

1 egg, lightly beaten

½ pound pumpkin or winter squash, peeled, seeded, and shredded in a food processor or on the large holes of a box grater (packed 2 cups)

1 large scallion, finely chopped

4 tablespoons sunflower oil for frying, plus more as needed

Sour cream, for garnish (optional)

In a medium bowl, mix together the flour, baking soda, and salt. In a small bowl, stir the kefir into the egg and pour this liquid into the dry ingredients, stirring with a fork just until a batter forms. Be careful not to over-mix. Stir in the pumpkin and scallion.

Heat the oil in a 12-inch skillet. Using a 2-tablespoon measure, drop the batter into the oil, gently shaping it into rounds with the back of the spoon. The pancakes will swell to 3 inches in diameter, so you can cook eight at a time. Fry the pancakes over medium heat for 4 minutes, until bubbles appear on the surface and the undersides are brown. Flip the pancakes over with a spatula and cook for another 4 minutes until they are cooked through. Transfer the pancakes to a plate and keep warm. Repeat with the remaining batter. Serve hot and pass the sour cream, if desired.

Pelmeni, or Siberian Dumplings

Пельмени

Russians prepare these addictive dumplings in large quantities, both to consume immediately and to freeze for future use. During the deep Russian winter, *pelmeni* can be simply buried in the snow, or hung in a bag outside an apartment window, where they keep for months on end, ready to boil up at a moment's notice—making them the ultimate fast slow food. Siberians swear by a garnish of mustard and vinegar: just place a spoonful of strong Russian-style mustard on the edge of the plate and mix it with vinegar to taste before stirring this sauce through the dumplings. Muscovites prefer a milder topping, slathering butter and sour cream on the *pelmeni* in lavish amounts.

Making these delectable dumplings involves a couple of secrets. First, use an old-fashioned meat grinder instead of buying packaged ground beef and pork or grinding the meat in a food processor. A manual grinder's blade doesn't compress the meat the way that machine grinding does. Second, simmer the *pelmeni* rather than boiling them to ensure that the dough doesn't toughen.

Makes about 168 dumplings, serves 6 to 8

Dough

2½ cups flour

1 teaspoon salt

2 eggs

6 tablespoons warm water

Filling

¾ pound well-marbled rib-eye steak

¾ pound pork loin, including fat

1 large onion

1¼ teaspoons salt

½ teaspoon freshly ground black pepper

¼ cup ice water

Garnishes

Melted unsalted butter

Sour cream

Russian-Style Mustard (page 247)

Cider vinegar

To make the dough, mix together the flour and salt in a medium bowl. Make a well in the center and add the eggs and warm water. Stir with a fork until the mixture holds together, then turn out onto a floured surface and knead for about 5 minutes. Form the dough into a ball and place the inverted mixing bowl over it. Let stand at room temperature for 1 hour.

To make the filling, put the steak and pork through a manual meat grinder, using the large die, then chill the meat before grinding it a second time through the plate with the small die. Grind the onion through this finer plate, too. Stir in the salt, pepper, and ice water. If you're not planning to use the filling right away, store it in the refrigerator.

Divide the dough into four pieces. Working with one piece at a time, roll the dough out onto a floured board into a 12-inch round, as thin as possible (¹⁄₁₆ inch thick or less). Using a 2-inch cookie cutter or the rim of a glass, cut out about 32 rounds. Place a teaspoon of the filling on each round. Bring one edge of the round over to meet the other and seal the edges to form a half-moon. Then bring the two pointed edges together in the center of the half-moon along its straight edge, lifting them slightly to form a tortellini-like dumpling. Make sure that the edges are securely pressed together. As each ball is formed, place it on a clean dish towel.

Repeat with the remaining pieces of dough. Then press all the dough scraps together, knead gently, and roll out into another thin round. If you're not going to cook the pelmeni right away, cover them with a dish towel.

When ready to serve, bring a large kettle of salted water to a boil. Lower the heat to a simmer and drop the pelmeni into the water, making sure not to crowd them. Simmer for 3 to 5 minutes, just until they rise to the surface.

Use a slotted spoon to transfer the pelmeni from the water to a warm serving dish and pour melted butter over them. Repeat with the remaining dumplings. Serve with sour cream or with Russian-Style Mustard and cider vinegar.

Variations

To serve the pelmeni in chicken soup, cook them as directed. When they're done, add a generous number of dumplings to each portion of hot soup and top with a dollop of sour cream and some minced dill.

Cold leftover pelmeni can be fried in butter until crisp and golden.

Note

To freeze pelmeni for future use, let them dry slightly on the dish towel, then transfer to a baking sheet, arranging them so that they don't touch. Place the sheet in the freezer. When the dumplings are frozen, slide them into a resealable bag for storage. They will keep in the freezer for up to 6 months. To serve, drop the frozen dumplings directly into simmering salted water and cook until they rise to the surface.

TRANS-SIBERIAN TALES

In 1983, after ten months in Moscow, my husband and I traveled to Beijing on the Trans-Siberian Railway, a trip that we paid for by selling our winter coats and three pairs of jeans on the black market. Our Russian friends knew that food would be scarce on the train, so they saw us off with a parting gift, a willow basket with an embroidered linen cloth concealing the real gift inside: roast chicken, cabbage-stuffed *pirozhki* (hand pies), hard-boiled eggs, and an apple pie large enough to last us through four time zones. Even as the sun rose earlier and earlier on our eastward progression, the train remained on Moscow time, making the journey even more dreamlike.

We soon discovered why no food could be had on the train: at every stop, the kitchen staff madly, illegally, sold provisions out of the caboose. Anticipating this hungry situation, another dear friend of ours had arranged for *her* dear friend to meet us at the Krasnoyarsk station, a tricky proposition since Krasnoyarsk was at that time off-limits to foreigners. Kalashnikov-wielding guards made sure that we didn't stray beyond the platform's perimeter. We scanned the crowd, trying to identify our contact with our friend's words in mind: "Look for the Soviet Marilyn Monroe!" And sure enough, there she was: a buxom blonde in a tight black dress and stiletto heels—materializing out of nowhere and nearly smothering us in her glad embrace. "You are friends of Marianna! You are my friends!" She handed us a basket, kissed us three times on both cheeks, and then disappeared. Was this a dream? Luckily we had material proof that it was not. As the train pulled out of the station, we opened the basket and swooned. Inside were *pelmeni*, Siberian dumplings, still hot and swimming in rich chicken broth. Garlicky salted cucumbers and a bottle of cedar nut–infused vodka rounded out our meal.

We traveled on for four more days across Russia's vast steppe, passing through the Gobi Desert. The train ground to a halt at one o'clock in the morning just across the Mongolian border with China. It had stopped to change the wheel chassis, which had to be done by hand in order for the train to continue on China's standard-gauge tracks—an emblematic moment of two socialist systems being out of sync. We were brusquely awakened and commanded to go to the dining car, which seemed odd, since the kitchen had been out of everything on the menu for a good 5,000 miles. But we obeyed. It turned out that the dining car was a Chinese one, on another track, giving us new cause for worry. Being deeply familiar with Soviet ineptitude and indifference, we were convinced that we'd be hooked up to the wrong train and find ourselves heading back to Moscow. But our suspicions lifted as the train pulled into the floodlit station of Erenhot and a brass band struck up. The scene was surreal—a Chinese oompah band dressed in gold-corded uniforms on the edge of the desert in the middle of the night. As if on cue, a smiling waiter appeared, brandishing a large platter of stir-fried pork atop a tangle of dark green shoots. Garlic scapes, our first bite of fresh greens in ten long months! We had left the deprivations of Soviet life behind.

Dumplings with Mushrooms and Buckwheat

Кундюмы

This fascinating, largely forgotten dish calls for baking dumplings and then steaming them, a method perfectly suited to the Russian masonry stove with its great capability for slow cooking (see page 243). Everyone who has tasted these dumplings agrees that they're both unusual and delicious, but in Russia there's disagreement about how the original *kundiumy* were made. Although some older recipes call for hard-boiled eggs, I like the intensity of dried mushrooms and greens, with only a little buckwheat to bind.

Authenticity is elusive, if not unattainable. But no matter. These dumplings are enticing, with a texture that's simultaneously chewy and tender. The flavors are very adult, thanks to the potent dried mushrooms, so I often add a dollop of sour cream to soften the effect. If you really want to throw authenticity to the wind, you can simply bake these dumplings without steaming them. They make a great appetizer, like baked wontons, with a crisp, light dough.

Makes about 60 dumplings, serves 4 to 6

Dough

2 cups flour

½ teaspoon salt

¾ cup boiling water

4 tablespoons sunflower or other vegetable oil

Filling

½ ounce dried mushrooms

2 cups warm water

½ bunch (¼ pound) sorrel or mustard greens

¼ cup uncooked buckwheat groats

¾ cup cold water

Salt

1 medium onion, minced

3 tablespoons sunflower or other vegetable oil

2 tablespoons minced fresh dill

Freshly ground black pepper

2 large bay leaves

5 black peppercorns

3 large garlic cloves, minced

Salt

1 tablespoon minced fresh parsley

Sour cream, for garnish (optional)

To make the dough, place the flour and salt in a medium bowl and pour on the boiling water. Quickly add the oil and stir briskly till the dough holds together. Knead the dough a few times in the bowl with your hands, then cover the bowl and leave the dough to rest for at least 20 minutes and up to 1 hour.

While the dough rests, make the filling. Reconstitute the dried mushrooms by soaking them in the warm water for 30 minutes. Drain the mushrooms, reserving the water, and mince them. While the mushrooms are soaking, remove any coarse stems from the greens

continued

and rinse them well. Place them in a large pot and steam them, using the water clinging to the leaves, for 5 minutes. Squeeze all the liquid out and chop the greens finely. You should have about ½ cup. Set aside.

Place the buckwheat in a small saucepan with the cold water and a little salt. Simmer over low heat until the water is absorbed and the buckwheat is tender, about 15 minutes. Measure out ½ cup and set aside.

In a large skillet, sauté the onion in the oil over low heat until golden, about 8 minutes. Stir in the mushrooms, the greens, the ½ cup cooked buckwheat, a generous ½ teaspoon salt, the dill, and pepper to taste. Taste the filling for seasoning and set aside.

Preheat the oven to 350°F. Line two large baking sheets with parchment paper. Divide the dough into two balls. Leave one ball in the bowl, covered, while you work with the other. On a generously floured surface, roll out the dough into a very thin 12 by 16-inch rectangle, about 1/16 inch thick. Cut the dough into 2-inch squares. Place 1 teaspoon of the filling on each square. Bring one edge of the square diagonally over the filling to form a triangle. Pinch the edges tightly to seal. (You'll want to flour your hands well, as the dough is sticky.) With your fingers, twist and turn the sealed edges to make decorative pleats. As each dumpling is made, place it on the prepared baking sheet. Repeat with the second ball of dough.

Bake the dumplings for 18 minutes, until they are dry and just beginning to take on color.

While the dumplings are baking, bring the reserved mushroom water to a boil with the bay leaves, peppercorns, garlic, and ¼ teaspoon salt. Simmer, covered, for 10 minutes. Transfer the dumplings to a shallow 2-quart ovenproof baking dish, arranging them in two layers. Pour on the hot mushroom broth. Cover the dish tightly with aluminum foil and return the dumplings to the oven to steam for 15 minutes. They will absorb almost all of the mushroom broth.

Serve the dumplings hot, sprinkled with the parsley. Offer sour cream on the side, if desired.

4

SOUPS

Dried Mushroom and Barley Soup

Суп из сушёных грибов

No matter the season or my location, a spoonful of this delightfully earthy soup transports me to the Russian forests in autumn. It tastes slightly different each time I make it, depending on the mushrooms I use. I especially like a combination of porcini—the mushroom the Russians prize most—and bronze boletes.

Serves 4 to 6

1¾ ounces dried wild mushrooms (such as porcini, bronze boletes, black trumpets, morels, or oyster mushrooms)

8 cups water

2 large onions, chopped

2 large carrots, peeled and sliced into ½-inch rounds

2 tablespoons sunflower or other vegetable oil

2 large garlic cloves, minced

2½ teaspoons salt

Freshly ground black pepper

1 large boiling potato, scrubbed but unpeeled, then cut into ½-inch cubes

2 bay leaves

½ cup pearl barley

1 teaspoon freshly squeezed lemon juice

Snipped fresh dill, for garnish

Finely chopped scallions, for garnish

Sour cream, for garnish (optional)

Soak the dried mushrooms in the water for 30 minutes. Meanwhile, in a large stockpot, sauté the onions and carrots in the oil over medium-low heat until the onions turn pale gold in color, about 15 minutes.

When the mushrooms have finished soaking, use a slotted spoon to transfer them to a cutting board, reserving the soaking liquid. Chop the mushrooms coarsely and add them to the onions and carrots along with the garlic. Season with the salt and some pepper and cook the mixture a few minutes more.

To capture any residual dirt from the mushrooms, pour the reserved soaking water through a fine-mesh sieve into the stockpot. Stir in the potato, bay leaves, and barley. Bring the soup to a boil, then lower the heat and simmer, covered, for about 1 hour, or until the barley is tender.

Just before serving, stir in the lemon juice. Taste for seasoning. (I usually add some generous grinds of pepper for a bit of a bite.) Ladle the soup into bowls and garnish with dill and scallions. Top with a dollop of sour cream, if desired.

Pomor-Style Fish Soup

Уха поморская

Russians so love the clear fish broth known as *ukha* that they place it in a separate category of its own, distinct from other soups. This version is named after the Pomors, the inhabitants of the White Sea coast in Russia's Far North. *Ukha* is the quintessential Russian fisherman's soup, traditionally prepared by simmering the catch of the day over a fire made right on the riverbank. Some campfire connoisseurs even immerse a hot birch log from the fire into the soup to lend a smoky flavor. At the other end of the social spectrum, wealthy nineteenth-century Francophiles served *ukha* at their stylish dinners, adding a splash of champagne to the broth at the table.

Regional variations abound. So-called black *ukha* is made from bottom-feeders, like carp, while sturgeon results in "red" (i.e., beautiful) soup. White *ukha* is made from perch or pike. In the North, the broth is often made from ocean fish, like cod and halibut. True Pomor-style *ukha* includes cod liver for richness, though I substitute more readily available halibut cheeks here. I also add saffron and lemon, which turn the broth golden and reflect the influence of trade to Arkhangelsk from points east and west. This is an elegant, delicate soup.

Serves 8

1 small salmon head, tail, and spine (1½ pounds)

8 cups cold water

1 small carrot, peeled

1 small onion, quartered

1 bay leaf

6 black peppercorns

1¾ teaspoons salt

1 medium onion, halved vertically, then sliced horizontally ⅛ inch thick

⅛ teaspoon saffron threads

Freshly ground black pepper

1 pound cod fillet, skin removed, cut into 1½-inch pieces

1 pound halibut fillet, skin removed, cut into 1½-inch pieces

1 pound halibut cheeks, halved if large

¼ cup minced fresh dill

8 lemon slices

Remove the gills from the salmon head. Place it and the other fish parts in a large stockpot with the water. Add the carrot, quartered onion, bay leaf, peppercorns, and salt and simmer, partially covered, for 30 minutes, to make a light broth, skimming any foam that rises to the surface. Strain the broth through a fine-mesh sieve and return it to a clean stockpot. Discard the fish pieces, vegetables, and spices.

Add the sliced onion to the pot and simmer, uncovered, for 10 minutes. Meanwhile, in a small bowl, steep the saffron in a couple table-spoons of the broth, then stir it into the pot with some pepper. Add the cod and all the halibut, cover the pot, and return to a simmer. Remove the lid and simmer the soup for 5 minutes more, until the fish is barely done. Stir in the dill and let the soup stand for 5 minutes, covered.

To serve, place a lemon slice in each bowl and ladle soup over it.

Note
The broth can be made in advance. Finish the soup just before serving.

Savory Fish Soup
Рыбная солянка

During my years in the Soviet Union, I virtually lived on *solyanka*, one of the few dishes reliably available at restaurants, cafeterias, and cafés. These days when I'm in Russia, even with many dishes on offer, I still gravitate to this piquant soup with its medley of fresh and cured ingredients. *Solyanka* can be made with either meat or fish—it's the mix of ingredients that makes the soup exciting. It should always include a good dose of the sour and salty, from sauerkraut, dill pickles, salted mushrooms, or brined apples. After olives and capers were introduced to Russia, they became a very welcome addition.

Serves 8 to 10

1 salmon head (1½ to 2 pounds)

8 cups cold water, plus more as needed

2 small carrots, peeled, one whole, the other cut into ¼-inch slices

1 small onion, peeled and quartered

1 bay leaf

6 black peppercorns

1¾ teaspoons salt

3 tablespoons unsalted butter

1 large onion, finely chopped

8 white mushrooms, sliced ¼ inch thick

¼ cup sauerkraut

½ cup pickle brine (from Half-Sour Dill Pickles [page 83], Alexandra's Sweet and Sour Cucumbers [page 57], or commercially fermented pickles such as Bubbies)

1 cup chopped sour dill pickles

2 tablespoons capers

⅓ cup pitted Kalamata olives, coarsely chopped

3 ounces smoked salmon, cut into 1-inch pieces

1 pound cod fillet, skin removed, cut into 1½-inch pieces

1 pound halibut fillet, skin removed, cut into 1½-inch pieces

1 pound salmon, skin removed, cut into 1½-inch pieces

Remove the gills from the salmon head. Place the head and the water in a large stockpot with the whole carrot, the quartered onion, the bay leaf, peppercorns, and salt. Simmer for 30 minutes, partially covered, skimming any foam that rises to the surface. Strain the broth through a fine-mesh sieve into a large heatproof measuring cup. Add enough water to top off the broth so that you have 8 cups. Discard the fish head, vegetables, and spices.

Melt the butter in a large stockpot. Add the chopped onion, sliced carrot, and mushrooms. Sauté the vegetables over low heat until softened, 12 to 15 minutes. While they're cooking, pour boiling water over the sauerkraut to scald it, then drain. Stir the sauerkraut into the sautéed vegetables, then pour in the fish broth and the pickle brine. Add the pickles, capers, olives, and smoked salmon. Bring the soup to a boil. Drop in the cod, halibut, and salmon pieces. Simmer, uncovered, until the fish is barely done, about 5 minutes. Serve hot.

Borscht

Борщ

How many bowls of borscht have I consumed in my life? I'd need hundreds of fingers to count them. Borscht comes in seemingly endless varieties, some made with beef, others pork, many vegetarian. An acidic ingredient such as vinegar, tart apples, lemon juice, or tomatoes should always be added to balance the beets' natural sweetness—or you can use some beet kvass to make the stock. A dollop of sour cream in the bowl adds a crowning touch.

There are nearly as many techniques for preparing borscht as there are ingredients, and each cook swears by her own method. The beets can be grated, finely chopped, or cut into large chunks; they can be used raw, roasted, or boiled. Sometimes borscht makes do without beets at all, as in the green version made with sorrel. The recipe here is typical of Russian-Jewish style, marrying the sour and the sweet. I use a generous amount of vegetables in relation to broth, and simmer the shredded beets, carrots, and cabbage for only twenty minutes to ensure that the vegetables don't overcook and the soup keeps its bright color. I also use chicken stock to mitigate the richness of the beef. If you happen to have beet kvass on hand and want the sweet-sour flavor to be less pronounced, you can substitute that. The color will be even more brilliantly garnet-hued.

Serves 8

Beef Broth

3 pounds beef brisket, trimmed of excess fat

1 teaspoon salt

6 cups water

1 onion, peeled and halved lengthwise, with stem ends intact

1 carrot, scrubbed

1 bay leaf

10 black peppercorns

1 medium head of white cabbage (about 2 pounds)

4 large beets (2 pounds)

1 carrot

2 tablespoons unsalted butter

1 large onion, finely chopped

3 large garlic cloves, finely chopped

2 quarts chicken stock or Beet Kvass (page 99)

3 tablespoons red wine vinegar

6 tablespoons freshly squeezed lemon juice

6 tablespoons sugar

1½ teaspoons salt

Freshly ground black pepper

Sour cream, for garnish

Snipped fresh dill, for garnish

To make the beef broth, place the brisket in a large stockpot and sprinkle it with the salt. Add the water, halved onion, carrot, bay leaf, and peppercorns. Bring to a boil, then turn the heat to very low and simmer, covered, for 2 hours.

While the broth is simmering, remove any tough outer leaves from the cabbage, core it, and shred on the grating disk of a food processor or the large holes of a hand grater. Peel the beets and carrot and grate them as well. Set aside.

In a medium skillet, melt the butter. Add the chopped onion and garlic and sauté until golden, about 10 minutes. Set aside.

After the broth has simmered for 2 hours, remove the onion and carrot with a slotted spoon and discard. Add the chicken stock to the pot and continue to simmer the brisket for 1 hour more, or until it is tender. Remove the meat from the broth and set aside on a cutting board.

Add the sautéed onion and garlic and the shredded cabbage, beets, and carrot to the soup. Simmer, covered, for 20 minutes.

While the soup is simmering, slice the brisket thinly, against the grain.

Season the soup with the vinegar, lemon juice, sugar, salt, and plenty of pepper. Taste for seasoning.

To serve, place a slice or two of brisket in the bottom of each soup bowl and ladle the borscht over it. Top with a generous dollop of sour cream and some freshly snipped dill.

Notes

If you don't plan to serve the soup right away, leave the brisket whole and return it to the pot while the soup cools. When ready to serve, remove the brisket and follow the directions for slicing it while you reheat the soup.

Borscht will keep for several days in the refrigerator. In fact, Russians claim it tastes best after three days. If the soup has been sitting in the refrigerator, taste it for seasoning after reheating, since chilling can flatten the taste. More salt will perk it right up.

Any extra brisket makes an easy second course or a meal in itself when served with Horseradish Sauce (page 72).

Classic Cabbage Soup

Суточные щи

All Russians, north and south, rich and poor, enjoy cabbage soup, or *shchi*, and the many varieties they've devised reflect not only preferences in taste but also geography and affluence. "Empty" cabbage soup is, not surprisingly, meatless, while "rich" is loaded with meat. "Lazy" cabbage soup, made with fresh cabbage, signals a lack of time and womanpower to prepare the sauerkraut for a proper *shchi*. The classic cabbage soup offered here, loaded with sauerkraut and beef, is rich in both senses of the word. Its Russian name, meaning "24-hour," comes from the fact that it takes nearly that long to make this soup from start to finish, though you don't have to stand over the pot the whole time.

I adapted this recipe from Maksim Syrnikov's *Russian Home Cooking*. Syrnikov has made it his mission to gather endangered recipes likely to be lost along with the last generation of women who learned pre-revolutionary methods of cooking. "24-hour" cabbage soup involves several necessary steps. First, sauerkraut is slowly braised in the oven and then frozen before being added to the broth. Until freezers became widespread—and even today in some rustic households—Russians deposited the simmering pot of sauerkraut outside to flash freeze in the snow. Imagine the house filled with enticing smells and then having to wait twenty-four hours for supper! This soup calls for forbearance, but your patience is amply rewarded with a layered and complexly flavored soup.

You don't have to make the sauerkraut from scratch—it's fine to use a good deli brand as long as you follow the instructions on the next page for stewing and freezing. Or, in expectation of soup season, you can keep braised sauerkraut and beef broth at hand in the freezer. That way you can make the cabbage soup at a moment's notice, even when there's no snow outside.

The classic accompaniments to all sorts of *shchi* are Steamed Buckwheat and Buckwheat Croutons (pages 200 and 210, respectively).

continued

Serves 6 to 8

Stewed Sauerkraut

3 cups finely shredded sauerkraut, with brine

1 large onion, peeled

4 tablespoons melted unsalted butter

2 tablespoons flour

Broth

2 pounds beef chuck roast

2 to 3 pounds beef bones

10 cups cold water

1 onion

2 carrots, trimmed

1 leek, cut in half crosswise

2 bay leaves

4 parsley sprigs

8 black peppercorns

1 teaspoon salt

3 large garlic cloves, minced

2 tablespoons minced fresh dill

2 tablespoons finely chopped scallions

First, prepare the sauerkraut. Preheat the oven to 400°F. Strain the sauerkraut, reserving ¼ cup of the brine. Chop the onion finely. Place the sauerkraut and onion in a 10-inch cast-iron pan along with the butter and sauerkraut brine. Bake for 10 minutes, then turn the heat to 250°F and stew, uncovered, for 3 hours, until the sauerkraut has turned a russet brown, checking occasionally to make sure it hasn't dried out. If it seems dry, add a couple tablespoons more brine or water. Once the sauerkraut has turned brown, remove the pan from the oven and stir in the flour. Allow the mixture to cool to room temperature, transfer it to a storage container or resealable bag, and freeze for at least 24 hours, or until needed. Thaw before using.

To make the broth, place the beef and beef bones in a large stockpot with the cold water. Bring to a boil, skimming off any foam that rises to the surface. Add the onion, carrots, leek, bay leaves, parsley, peppercorns, and salt. Lower the heat and simmer, partially covered, for 3 hours, until the meat is tender and the broth flavorful.

Remove the beef from the broth and set aside. Strain the broth, discarding the vegetables, herbs, and bones. You should have 6 cups of broth. (You can proceed directly to the next step to finish the soup, but at this point, I like to cool the broth and return to the soup the next day. More forbearance! This waiting time develops the flavor and allows me to skim the fat.)

Cut the meat into ½-inch cubes, discarding any fat or gristle. Stir the meat into the broth along with the thawed sauerkraut and simmer, covered, for 30 minutes. Add the garlic, dill, and scallions. Let the soup stand, covered, for 15 minutes before serving.

Rassolnik

Рассольник

Russian soups are marvelous in their variety and innovation. Almost every time I make one, I feel like declaring, "*This* one's the ultimate!" Although cabbage soup may be the most Russian of Russian soups, this rich, sour dill pickle soup is a major competitor. Please don't be put off by the kidney in the ingredient list. The flavor of kidneys is quite mild and mainly adds lushness to the broth. The most important element here—the one that elevates the soup from ordinary to divine—is the souring agent. Be sure to use lacto-fermented pickles and brine, not vinegar-based ones.

Serves 8

1 veal kidney
(about 1 pound)

1 cup whole milk

4 tablespoons
unsalted butter

1 large carrot, peeled
and julienned

2 medium onions, halved
vertically, then sliced
horizontally into ¼-inch
half-moons

2 medium boiling
potatoes, peeled and
cut into ½-inch cubes

1¼ teaspoons salt

Freshly ground
black pepper

1 tablespoon flour

8 cups beef stock

3 large sour dill pickles,
seeds scraped out,
julienned

1 large bay leaf

¼ cup uncooked
pearl barley

2 tablespoons pickle
brine (from Half-
Sour Dill Pickles
[page 83], Alexandra's
Sweet and Sour
Cucumbers [page 57], or
commercially fermented
pickles such as Bubbies)

Sour cream, for garnish
(optional)

With a sharp knife, slice through the length of the kidney's lobes to separate it into two parts. Remove all the membrane and fat. Soak the kidney halves in the milk for 1 hour.

While the kidney is soaking, prepare the vegetables. Melt 3 tablespoons of the butter in a large stockpot and sauté the carrot, onions, and potatoes over low heat for 10 minutes, stirring occasionally, until softened. Season the vegetables with ¾ teaspoon of the salt and pepper to taste.

Rinse the kidney halves and pat dry, then slice them crosswise into ½-inch pieces. Place the kidney slices in a bowl and toss with the flour and the remaining ½ teaspoon salt. In a small frying pan, melt the remaining 1 tablespoon butter and cook the kidney slices briefly over high heat until they are just barely brown, 3 to 4 minutes.

With a slotted spoon, transfer the kidney to the stockpot with the vegetables, discarding any liquid left in the skillet. Add the stock and pickles. Bring the soup to a boil, skimming off the foam that rises to the surface. Lower the heat. When the foam subsides, stir in the bay leaf and barley. Cover the pot and simmer the soup for 45 minutes.

Stir in the pickle brine. Serve the soup hot, with a dollop of sour cream, if desired.

A TALE OF
TWO SOUPS

In his painting *An Englishman in Moscow*, Kazimir Malevich, the founder of the artistic avant-garde movement called Suprematism, captures the confusion foreigners feel when confronted with unfamiliar sights and an indecipherable alphabet. Fragments of urban life are jumbled in seemingly random disorder—a sword slashing a ladder, a church superimposed on a fish. Seeing the fish-church juxtaposition always carries me back to my own first encounter with the Cyrillic alphabet, specifically with the twenty-seventh letter, Щ. Transliterated as *shch*, it encompasses in a single letter and sound what it takes four Roman letters to represent. I remember, on my very first day of Russian 101, the professor teaching us to pronounce *shch* by making us repeat "Fish church fish church fish church" over and over, in rapid succession. Try it.

Few of us got the pronunciation right away, and no wonder: "fish church" makes little sense. A better approach would have been to repeat the words *borshch* (борщ) and *shchi* (щи). Not only would they offer linguistic practice, they would also open a window into Russian culinary culture, especially when you make students repeat the aphorism *"Shchi da kasha, pishcha nasha"* ("Cabbage soup and kasha, that's our fare"). Talk about sibilants!

Most Americans consider *borshch*—usually transliterated as *borscht*—distinctively Russian. It's true that the appearance of this garnet beet soup in American life coincided with a massive late-nineteenth-century immigration from Russia. But the immigrants who brought borscht to our tables were not Russians; they were Jews from the Pale of Settlement, an area that stretched along the western edges of the Russian Empire and included much of present-day Ukraine. Borscht is, in fact, the Ukrainian national soup. Russians, by contrast, claim cabbage soup as their own. Both soups have long histories and fierce partisans.

Bulbous garden beets, as we know them, didn't develop until the sixteenth century. Earlier beetroots were long and thin, like carrots. Before cooks made soup from the beetroot, they used the leaves and stalks of a wild plant called *borshchevik*, much as we make nettle soup today. Once the modern beetroot disseminated throughout Europe, Ukrainians began making borscht with the root instead of the leaves. They were rewarded with deeper flavor and a gorgeous color. Several centuries later, when borscht arrived in the United States, it found widespread popularity in Jewish delicatessens. The soup later achieved glamour in the haunts of post-revolutionary White Russian émigrés, like New York City's Russian Tea Room, which served up a clear, elegant variety called *borshchok*.

That potential for elegance elevates borscht into the realm of haute cuisine, and even when carelessly made, it is vibrant to behold. Not so cabbage soup. No garnet or ruby or any other gem color can redeem it when not properly prepared. For years I couldn't shake the vision of the watery *shchi* served in Moscow State University's student cafeteria. The huge room, in the dormitory basement, reeked of overcooked cabbage. Our first visit was nearly our last, but hunger sometimes forced us to descend into that circle of hell.

Over the years, I've tried to overcome this vision from the Soviet era, especially since cabbage soup is so deeply embedded in Russian culture. When I began developing recipes for this book, I knew I had to give *shchi* another chance. But it was only when I discovered the time-honored way of making it with braised sauerkraut that I was surprised, delighted, and then converted. Here is a complex soup, homey enough to provide comfort, yet spectacular enough to please sophisticated guests. And quite apart from its captivating flavor, cabbage soup carries symbolic weight, as the word *shchi* can be traced back to an Old Slavonic word meaning "sustenance."

Both borscht and *shchi*, with their many variations, contain cultural, culinary, and etymological worlds unto themselves. As for their fan bases, in the south of Russia, borscht has the edge, while *shchi* remains more common in the North, with its harsher climate. But then we're faced with a conundrum. The well-loved "green borscht" made with spinach and sorrel is known as "green *shchi*" in the North. Which one to ask for—borscht or *shchi*? Maybe it's pointless to take sides after all.

Cold Vegetable Soup with Kvass or Kefir
Окрошка

Russians have an impressive array of refreshing cold soups. My favorite among them is *okroshka*. The soup's name comes from the Russian verb *kroshit'*, meaning "to mince." *Okroshka* is really a liquid salad, bursting with fresh summer vegetables and herbs that are given a lift with kvass rather than dressing.

This soup lends itself well to improvisation. The basic ingredients almost always include cucumbers, radishes, scallions, and dill, but you can also add tarragon and boiled carrots or beets, along with salted mushrooms for piquancy. The most elemental version of *okroshka* consists simply of minced vegetables over which kvass is poured for a light yet satisfying dish. But many Russians add cooked meat or fish to deepen the flavor and make the soup more substantial.

In Central Asia, kefir is preferred over kvass to create the soup's sour tang. Some cooks also stir a little sparkling water into each bowl to achieve last-minute effervescence. Because it's impossible to make kvass from scratch on the day when you crave *okroshka*, it's fine to use good bottled kvass for this soup, as many time-challenged modern Russians do.

Serves 6 to 8

6 hard-boiled eggs

4 teaspoons prepared mustard, preferably sweet Scandinavian-style

2 teaspoons prepared horseradish

½ teaspoon salt

4 cups Kvass (page 92) or plain whole-milk kefir

4 scallions, thinly sliced

4 radishes, diced

1 cucumber, diced

¼ cup diced dill pickles

½ cup minced fresh dill

¼ cup minced fresh parsley

1 cup diced ham (optional)

2 large potatoes, boiled, peeled, and diced

Remove the yolks from the hard-boiled eggs and finely chop the egg whites. Set the whites aside. In a large bowl, mash the yolks with the mustard, horseradish, and salt, then gradually whisk in the kvass until the mixture is well blended.

Place the scallions, radishes, cucumber, pickles, dill, and parsley in a medium bowl. Bruise them with a pestle until they are slightly broken down, then stir them into the kvass mixture along with the ham (if using). Chill the soup in the refrigerator for at least 2 hours to allow the flavors to blend.

Just before serving, add the potatoes and as much of the minced egg white as you want. Ladle into bowls and serve immediately.

Summer Beet Soup

Летний борщ на свекольном квасе

Once you have kvass on hand, this light soup is a breeze to make, and it couldn't be more refreshing on a hot summer day. Simply chop up some garden vegetables and place a generous portion in each soup bowl, pour the kvass over them, and voilà. Soup's on!

For each serving

2 to 3 tablespoons each diced hard-boiled eggs, diced boiled potatoes, diced cucumbers, sliced scallions, diced radishes, and minced fresh dill

1 to 1½ cups Beet Kvass, (page 99)

Sour cream, for garnish (optional)

Place the chopped up eggs and vegetables in a soup bowl. Pour the kvass over the mixture, garnish with sour cream (if using), and serve.

Note

If you want to make the soup less austere, simply stir in some sour cream. The sour note gets even brighter, and the soup turns luxuriously creamy.

5

SALADS AND VEGETABLES

Twenty-Minute Pickles

Малосольные огурцы за 20 минут

These pickles couldn't be simpler. The recipe comes from Katya Bruyaka, whose small kitchen in Murmansk is a wonderland of homemade distillations and preserves that allow her to throw together fabulous meals on the spur of the moment. When Katya served me these pickles, I worried that she might be using up the last of her precious summer preserves before winter had come to an end. But she just laughed and happily confessed that these pickles can be made quickly any time of the year. Now I make them whenever I crave a quick Russian fix.

Makes ½ pound

3 Persian cucumbers (about 8 ounces), trimmed and sliced lengthwise into quarters

1 large garlic clove, finely chopped

2 tablespoons minced fresh dill (about 3 sprigs, coarse stems removed)

1 tablespoon vodka

¾ teaspoon salt

Place all the ingredients in a small resealable sandwich bag and gently massage to distribute the seasonings evenly. Leave the bag on the counter for 20 minutes, turning it occasionally to bathe the cucumbers in the liquid that forms. The pickles taste best chilled after 20 minutes. They will hold well in the refrigerator for a couple of days.

Lightly Salted Chanterelles

Малосольные лисички

The Russians affectionately call chanterelles "little foxes" for their tawny color. They're often stirred into a skillet with fried potatoes or simmered in a sour cream sauce. But I prefer salting them to bring out their delicate woodsy flavor. The first commandment is to use fresh specimens, as fresh as you can find.

Two days in brine yields a very subtle flavor, so I sprinkle them with a bit of fleur de sel to make them pop. I probably like these mushrooms best after they've brined for a week, but I rarely get to enjoy them that way, since they inevitably disappear much sooner. They make a great chaser for vodka.

Makes 1 quart

8 ounces fresh chanterelles

3 cups water

6 large sprigs dill, including stems

2 large garlic cloves, peeled and thickly sliced

4 allspice berries

½ teaspoon black peppercorns

4½ teaspoons salt

Fleur de sel (optional)

Rinse the chanterelles and pick them over to remove any forest debris. Cut out any bruised or slimy spots.

In a medium saucepan, bring the water to a boil. Drop the chanterelles into the water and immediately lower the heat. Simmer for 10 minutes, then drain, reserving the cooking water.

Meanwhile, sterilize a 1-quart glass jar.

Gather the dill sprigs into a bunch and cut crosswise into four parts. Place a layer of dill in the bottom of the jar, then add a layer of mushrooms and sprinkle with some of the garlic, allspice, and peppercorns. Repeat the layering, ending with dill on top.

Return the cooking water to the saucepan and add the salt. Bring to a boil, stirring until the salt dissolves. Pour this brine into the jar, making sure to cover all the mushrooms and dill. Close the jar tightly.

Leave the chanterelles to sit at room temperature for 2 days, then refrigerate. They will keep for several weeks, but bear in mind that they'll become saltier over time. To serve, just scoop them out of the brine.

Marinated Mushrooms

Грибы маринованные

Marinated mushrooms are always welcome on the *zakuska* table, as they provide a great foil for vodka. This recipe is simple to prepare; you just need to plan a couple of days ahead to give the mushrooms time to absorb the marinade. Feel free to use other types of mushrooms or to mix several varieties to add different notes of flavor and texture.

Makes 1 quart

1 pound cremini mushrooms, trimmed and cut into quarters, or into eighths, if large

1 cup distilled white vinegar

¾ cup water

1 tablespoon salt

1 teaspoon sugar

5 black peppercorns

3 allspice berries

1 large bay leaf

1 small onion, thinly sliced

1 cup coarsely chopped fresh dill

Bring a large pot of water to a boil and add the mushrooms. Allow the water to return to a boil and blanch the mushrooms for 1 minute, then drain.

Meanwhile, sterilize a 1-quart glass jar.

In a medium saucepan, bring the vinegar, ¾ cup water, salt, sugar, peppercorns, allspice, and bay leaf to a boil. Remove this marinade from the heat and let cool to room temperature.

Layer the mushrooms in the jar with the onion and dill, then pour the cooled marinade into the jar. Seal and refrigerate for 2 days before serving. The mushrooms will keep in the refrigerator for several weeks.

Beet Salad

Свекольный салат

Beets are for more than borscht. They also make vivid salads, which the Russians take in various directions, mixing in walnuts and prunes for a touch of the sweet, or onions and garlic for a savory edge. This refreshing version gets a nice kick from horseradish and vinegar, along with tartness from grated apple. The quality of the sunflower oil is crucial here—only a good, nutty oil will bring out the best in the other ingredients. Like borscht, this salad tastes even better on the second day, or even the third.

Serves 4 to 6

1½ pounds beets

1 large carrot

1-inch slice of horseradish

1 tart apple (such as Granny Smith)

¼ cup minced red onion

½ teaspoon salt

Freshly ground black pepper

2 tablespoons cold-pressed sunflower oil

2 tablespoons cider vinegar

2 tablespoons sour cream

Preheat the oven to 425°F. Wrap the beets in aluminum foil and bake until tender, 45 minutes to 1 hour, depending on their size. Let cool.

Peel the beets and put them through the grating disk of a food processor. Peel and grate the carrot, horseradish, and apple. Transfer the grated vegetables and fruit to a medium bowl. Add the onion and season with the salt and pepper. Stir in the oil, vinegar, and sour cream and mix to combine. Chill before serving.

Salted Cabbage

Кислая капуста

This mainstay of the Russian table is a quick version of sauerkraut, crisp and fresh tasting. Unlike classic sauerkraut, which is lacto-fermented for several weeks, salted cabbage is ready in just two to three days. It's a lot easier to make, too. Elena Molokhovets, in her famous nineteenth-century cookbook, *A Gift to Young Housewives*, notes "It has been observed that cabbage which is set to sour at the new moon is firm and squeaks on the teeth. Therefore, if soft cabbage is preferred, it should be set to sour in the last quarter of the moon." Luckily, you don't have to follow this advice, the only imperative being to cut the cabbage properly, as described below. Although you can grate it in a food processor, the texture won't be nearly as good.

I like to dress up this plain salad with a generous drizzle of sunflower oil and a showering of brined lingonberries. You can also add finely chopped green apples for additional tartness.

Serves 12

1 medium head of white cabbage (about 2 pounds)

2 large carrots, peeled

1½ tablespoons salt

Cold-pressed sunflower oil, for drizzling

Brined Lingonberries (facing page), for serving

Remove the coarse outer leaves of the cabbage, then cut the head in half and remove the core. Place the cabbage cut-side down on a board. With a sharp, heavy knife, thinly slice each half diagonally across the grain. Shred the carrots on a box grater, using the large holes. You want the vegetables to be fine enough to absorb salt but not so fine that they feel flimsy.

Transfer the shredded cabbage and carrots to a large bowl and stir in the salt. Knead vigorously with your hands for 3 to 5 minutes until the cabbage begins to release its juices. Place a saucer on the vegetables and top it with a heavy weight. Cover the bowl with cheesecloth and secure it with a rubber band. Let the cabbage sit at room temperature for 2 to 3 days, stirring it once daily, until it is salty enough for your taste. Transfer it to jars and store in the refrigerator, where it will keep for several weeks.

To serve, drizzle the cabbage with oil and top with some drained brined lingonberries.

BRINED LINGONBERRIES

Мочёная брусника

Makes 2 cups

2 cups fresh or frozen lingonberries (about 8 ounces)

3 cups boiling water

3 tablespoons honey

Heaping ¼ teaspoon salt

A few grindings of white pepper

Spoon the lingonberries into a sterilized wide-mouth 1-quart mason jar. In a medium bowl, pour the boiling water over the honey, salt, and white pepper, stirring to dissolve the honey and salt. Leave this brine to cool to room temperature, then pour it over the berries. Cover the jar with cheesecloth, securing it with a rubber band. Let the berries sit at room temperature for 7 to 10 days, until they taste mildly salty. Store in the refrigerator, where they will keep for several months.

PETER THE GREAT IN THE KITCHEN

When Peter the Great came to power in 1689, he set to work transforming Russia from a backward country into a modern nation. Determined to turn the Russian gaze from the East, where it had been directed for centuries, to the West, he built a new city from scratch. Saint Petersburg was to be "a window on Europe" and provide access to the Baltic Sea (no matter that the city was built on a swamp). Peter upturned societal norms, forcing women out of seclusion and commanding men to shave their long beards. He created an imperial navy and introduced goods and practices of all sorts from Western Europe, including new foods and drinks. Peter embraced French, German, and Hungarian wines over the traditional Russian meads and kvass, eventually replacing the elaborate drinking vessels the Russians had used for centuries—the *chasha, charka, kubok,* and *stopa*—with the shot glass (*riumka,* from the German *Römer*) and the goblet (*bokal,* from the French *bocal*).

In the kitchen—in affluent kitchens, at least—the innovations were even more profound. From Holland came the Dutch range, which, unlike the traditional Russian stove, relied on a stovetop (*plita*) rather than an oven. While the Russian poor continued to live meagerly, subsisting on little more than grains and occasional dairy products, the tables of the wealthy were transformed by the use of the stovetop. Quick cooking meant that meat could be butchered into tender French cuts such as filets. The newfangled methods also necessitated new cooking utensils whose names betrayed their foreign origins. Saucepans largely replaced the customary *gorshok,* or earthenware pot, and the traditional cast-iron pot (*chugun*) gave way to the griddle.

Under Peter, wealthy Russians developed a taste for foreign foods for the first time. Peter had invited Europeans to Saint Petersburg to help encourage the arts, and this nonnative population influenced local eating habits, as did returning Russians whom Peter had sent abroad for study. Peter also sought foreign talent. When he hired Johann Velten of Saxony to serve as his private chef, the nobility soon followed suit. Russia's first foreign chefs came primarily from Saxony, Bavaria, and Austria; later in the century, under the influence of the Empress Elizabeth, Peter's Francophile daughter, French chefs came into vogue.

From Holland, Peter imported hard cheeses, which the Russians didn't know how to produce, and he introduced the European method of churning butter. The vocabulary that infiltrated Russian over the course of the eighteenth century reveals influences from the Dutch, German, English, and ultimately French cuisines. Although some preparations, such as sauce, already existed in Russia's culinary repertoire, the new Latinate words superseded the original Slavonic ones. Thus *vzvar*, a traditional sweet-and-sour condiment served with meats, became simply *sous*, while the sweet *zaedki* served after a meal became the more fashionable *desert*. When pineapples were introduced around 1721, the nobility embraced them with particular fervor, and those with enough resources began growing them year-round in hothouses. A nobleman named Zavadovsky chopped and soured the pineapple like cabbage in barrels and used it to make pineapple *shchi* and *borshch*. Zavadovsky is said to have died in poverty, having squandered his entire fortune on the expensive fruit.

The culinary changes wrought during Peter's thirty-six-year reign were so great that by the time his daughter Elizabeth seized the throne in 1741, lemons and oranges were no longer a luxury, and English beer was in greater demand than traditional Russian brews. As the century progressed, more and more European influences came to bear on traditional Russian methods, until by the close of the eighteenth century, food in the homes of the wealthy was unabashedly French. Under foreign influence, Russian cuisine had lost its simple character, causing a degree of backlash in conservative quarters.

How should we understand Peter the Great's culinary reforms today? There's no question that Peter modernized the Russian kitchen—at least for those affluent enough to benefit from the changes he introduced. The masses had neither the means nor the desire to adjust their cooking style, which is why in the countryside today, especially in the North, it's easy to find dishes still being made as they were before Peter's reign. Although cuisines need to absorb new foods and techniques to remain dynamic, and many outside influences have enriched Russian cuisine, there is a new passion for rediscovering the spirit of "real" Russian food. You find it in the dark, sour loaf of rye bread—the quintessential expression of Russian taste—and in the earthy savor of buckwheat and mushrooms steamed slowly in the Russian stove. It lies in the refreshingly sour kvass fermented from black bread, and in the burn of horseradish-infused vodka, as it does in the tang of sour cream and the sweetness of honey. Ultimately, no white *bulka* (from the French *boule*) or elegant cream *sup* (from *soupe*) will entirely win over the Russian heart, tsarist decrees notwithstanding.

Salted Salmon Potato Salad

Картофельный салат с малосольным лососем

Throughout Europe and especially Latin America, *salade russe* or *ensalada rusa* is a familiar dish. This "Russian Salad" is, in its simplest form, a mixture of diced potatoes and vegetables and sometimes meat, dressed with mayonnaise. If that sounds prosaic, the salad's lineage is not. It can be traced back to 1860s Moscow, where the Belgian-French chef Lucien Olivier created a sensation with a stylish salad at his Hermitage restaurant. Olivier presented a pyramid of potatoes with roast hazel hen, partridge, crayfish, veal tongue, and other expensive ingredients doused in a rich mayonnaise sauce. In the aftermath of the Russian Revolution, this fancy salad emigrated with fleeing White Russians and eventually became a fixture on restaurant menus wherever they settled. In the Soviet Union, a more proletarian version survived, without the game and seafood. This "Capital Salad" (*stolichnyi salat*) is still very popular today—a mound of potatoes, boiled carrots, canned peas, and poached chicken, liberally doused with mayonnaise.

I was intent on including potato salad in this book but didn't want to reproduce the same old tsarist or Soviet recipes, so I started to play instead with some basic Russian flavors. The version of Russian Salad that emerged is one that layers potatoes with lightly salted salmon and cucumbers and crowns it all with vivid orange salmon roe. I dress the salad not with mayonnaise but with a honey mustard dressing, olive oil being the only nod to the salad's illustrious French past.

Serves 6

Salted Salmon

2 tablespoons salt

1 pound center-cut salmon fillet, skin on

Honey Mustard Dressing

2 tablespoons mild honey

2 tablespoons whole-grain Dijon mustard

2 tablespoons freshly squeezed lemon juice

⅛ teaspoon salt

Freshly ground black pepper

2 tablespoons mild olive oil

4 medium boiling potatoes (1 pound)

2 Persian cucumbers, sliced ⅛ inch thick

4 tablespoons minced fresh dill

4 to 6 tablespoons salmon roe

Three days before you plan to serve the salad, prepare the salmon. Rub the salt over the surface of the salmon, then place the fish in a resealable plastic bag. Put the bag in the freezer and leave it there for 2 to 3 days. Rinse the salmon well and pat it dry with a paper towel. Slice thinly against the grain. You will have 2 cups.

Boil the potatoes in salted water until a knife pierces them easily but they're still firm, 20 to 30 minutes. Rinse under cold water, drain, and peel. Slice the potatoes ¼ inch thick.

While the potatoes are boiling, make the dressing. Heat the honey in a small saucepan over low heat just until it liquifies, then pour it into a bowl. Add the mustard, lemon juice, salt, and pepper to taste, then gradually whisk in the oil to form an emulsion.

Place one-quarter of the potatoes on a serving platter and drizzle them with 2 tablespoons of the dressing. Top with ½ cup of the salted salmon, one-quarter of the cucumbers, and 1 tablespoon of the dill. Repeat this layering three more times, until you have four layers each of potatoes, dressing, salmon, cucumbers, and dill. Garnish the top of the salad with about 2 tablespoons of the roe. Sprinkle the rest of the roe decoratively around the edges. Serve immediately.

Note

Be sure to think ahead for this recipe, as the salmon needs to freeze for two to three days. The other components can be quickly assembled.

Roasted Radishes with Garlic and Caraway

Запечённая редиска с чесноком и тмином

Russians love radishes, from garden-variety red to pungent black, enjoying them not only fresh but also salted, marinated, or turned into savory preserves. I like simply to roast them. If you've never had cooked radishes before, you'll be delighted. Though they retain some crunch, their flavor mellows, and the muted red of their skin is alluring.

Serves 4 to 6

1 pound large red radishes (about 24)

1 tablespoon sunflower oil

½ teaspoon salt

Freshly ground black pepper

2 tablespoons unsalted butter

1 large garlic clove, minced

½ teaspoon caraway seed

Preheat the oven to 450°F. Trim the tops and tails of the radishes, then cut them in half vertically. Place them in a 10-inch cast-iron skillet and toss with the oil, salt, and pepper to taste. Roast for 20 minutes, until a knife pierces them easily.

While the radishes are roasting, melt the butter in a small skillet over low heat. Stir in the garlic and caraway and cook, stirring, for about 3 minutes, just until the garlic turns golden. Be careful not to let it burn.

Pour the butter over the roasted radishes and transfer them to a serving bowl. Serve hot.

Roasted Cabbage with Sour Cream

Капуста жареная со сметаной

Cabbage, sour cream, and rye bread . . . what flavors could be more Russian? This simple recipe is a standout. Though the dish takes only minutes to assemble, it roasts into a dazzling cabbage rose, with a beguiling, rich taste.

Serves 4

1 medium head of white cabbage (about 2 pounds)

2- to 3-ounce chunk of seeded rye bread

4 tablespoons melted unsalted butter

½ cup sour cream

Salt

Freshly ground black pepper

Preheat the oven to 400°F. Separate 8 leaves from the head of cabbage. Remove the hard core.

Cut the bread into four chunks, removing the crust if it's very hard. (If you're removing the crust, start with 3 ounces of bread.) Place the bread in a food processor and process it briefly into soft, medium-fine crumbs. You should have 1¼ cups of crumbs.

Pour 2 tablespoons of the butter into an 8-inch cast-iron pan. Place a cabbage leaf in the pan, cup-side up. Spread it with 1 tablespoon of the sour cream, then sprinkle on 1 tablespoon of the bread crumbs and season with salt and pepper. Repeat this process with the remaining cabbage leaves, layering them, though not cup upon cup; you don't want the cabbage to be in separate stacks. Sprinkle the last ¼ cup of the bread crumbs over the top. With a sharp knife, make a few slits in the cabbage leaves from the outside of the edges toward the inside, to help them lie a bit flatter.

Drizzle the remaining 2 tablespoons butter over the cabbage. Cover the pan with aluminum foil and roast for 30 minutes. Remove the foil and continue to roast until the cabbage is tender and the edges are charred, about 25 minutes more. Serve the cabbage directly from the pan, cut into quarters, to preserve its rustic, patterned appearance.

Cucumbers in Sour Cream

Огурцы в сметане

This easy salad appears year-round on almost every Russian table, and it's not hard to see why. It brings together several well-loved components: refreshing cucumbers with their satisfying crunch, aromatic dill, and sour cream and vinegar for the right amount of tang. I often add raw leeks for an extra burst of flavor.

Serves 6

1½ pounds cucumbers

1 small leek, white and light green parts only, very thinly sliced crosswise (½ cup)

¼ cup minced fresh dill, plus more for sprinkling

¾ cup sour cream

2 tablespoons cider vinegar, or to taste

2 teaspoons salt

Freshly ground black pepper

If the cucumbers have been waxed, peel them; otherwise, wash them well but leave the peel on. Slice the cucumbers very thin and pat them dry with paper towels.

Place the cucumbers in a bowl with the leek and dill. In a separate bowl, mix together the sour cream, vinegar, salt, and pepper to taste. Stir this mixture into the cucumber mixture. Let stand at room temperature for 30 minutes, then refrigerate for at least 1 hour. Serve sprinkled with dill.

Vegetarian Cabbage Rolls

Вегетарианские голубцы

Stuffed cabbage rolls are endearingly known as "little doves" in Russian for the way they nestle together in the pot like small birds at rest. Most often they're filled with a mixture of ground meat and rice, but here I've devised a lighter version using mushrooms and barley. These cabbage rolls reheat well, so feel free to make them a day or two in advance. Any extra filling makes a great side dish on its own.

Makes about 20 cabbage rolls, serves 4 generously

2 cups vegetable stock or water

¾ cup pearl barley

4 tablespoons sunflower oil

1 tablespoon unsalted butter

1 medium onion, finely chopped

12 ounces mushrooms, trimmed and finely chopped

Salt

Freshly ground black pepper

1 medium carrot, peeled and grated

3 garlic cloves, minced

2 tablespoons minced fresh parsley

2 tablespoons minced fresh dill

1 small head of white cabbage (about 1 pound)

1¼ cups canned or bottled tomato juice

½ cup sour cream

Bring the stock to a boil in a medium saucepan. Add the barley and simmer, covered, until the liquid is absorbed, about 40 minutes. Meanwhile, heat 3 tablespoons of the oil and the butter in a large skillet. Add the onion and mushrooms along with ½ teaspoon salt and pepper to taste. Sauté over medium heat until the liquid evaporates, about 10 minutes. Stir in the carrot and garlic and cook for 1 minute more, then remove the pan from the heat. Stir in the minced herbs.

Stir 2 cups of the cooked barley into the mushroom mixture. Taste for seasoning, adding more salt and pepper if needed. The filling should be highly seasoned.

Bring a large pot of water to a boil. Make deep cuts along all four sides of the cabbage core and drop the whole head into the boiling water, core-side down. Boil for 5 minutes, then transfer to a cutting board with a slotted spoon, reserving the cooking liquid. Carefully peel off the leaves, which should separate easily from the head. If necessary, return the cabbage to the water and boil for another 5 minutes to soften the remaining leaves. Reserve the cooking water.

Place a cabbage leaf on a cutting board cup-side up and trim any hard spots near the core end, for ease of rolling. Place about 2 tablespoons of the filling along the center of the leaf. Tuck up the cored end, fold in one side, then roll and tuck in the other side of the leaf until the filling is completely enclosed. Repeat with the remaining leaves until all of the filling has been used.

continued

Vegetarian Cabbage Rolls, continued

Line the bottom of a 4-quart Dutch oven with any leftover cabbage leaves, or with bits and pieces of cabbage that you've cut away. Drizzle the remaining 1 tablespoon oil over the leaves. Layer the cabbage rolls in the pan, seam-side down, placing them snugly against each other to make sure they hold together. Sprinkle them with ½ teaspoon salt and a liberal amount of pepper.

Mix together the tomato juice, ½ teaspoon salt, and ¾ cup of the reserved cooking water and pour over the cabbage rolls. Cover the pan and bring to a boil, then lower the heat and simmer for 20 minutes. Spread the sour cream over the tops of the rolls and continue simmering for 10 minutes more. Serve warm. The cabbage rolls keep well for several days in the refrigerator. Gently reheat to serve.

Steamed Turnips with Sunflower Oil

Пареная репа с подсолнечным маслом

This old Russian recipe made me a turnip convert. Cultivated since pre-Christian times, turnips are the ur-Russian staple, their antiquity recalled through dozens of folktales and sayings that build their meaning from the humble root. Only with the widespread cultivation of potatoes in the nineteenth century did the popularity of turnips wane.

This is a highly minimalist dish, so the quality of each ingredient is important. Cold-pressed sunflower oil has a golden shimmer and a lovely nutty flavor that offsets the turnips' slight bitterness.

Serves 4 to 6

4 purple-topped turnips (about 1½ pounds)

¾ teaspoon salt

Freshly ground black pepper

6 tablespoons water

Cold-pressed sunflower oil, for drizzling

Preheat the oven to 350°F. Have ready a 2-quart earthenware bean pot with a lid.

Slice the ends off the turnips, peel them, and then slice them horizontally ⅛ inch thick, using a mandoline or the slicing attachment of a food processor.

Place a layer of sliced turnips in the pot. Sprinkle them with some of the salt and grind on some pepper. Continue layering the turnips with salt and pepper until the slices are used up. Add the water to the pot and cover it.

Bake the turnips for 1 hour, until soft. Transfer them to a plate and drizzle generously with oil. Serve immediately.

SOVIET FARE

Many of my earliest impressions of the Soviet Union were smells. The first time I took the bus from Helsinki to Leningrad, it stopped in Vyborg—not, as I thought, for a pit stop, but to allow border guards to scrutinize our documents and search us for contraband. After clearing inspection, I decided to explore the bus depot, a striking functionalist building that had been built when the city still belonged to Finland. Stepping inside, I was overwhelmed by the sour smell of overcooked cabbage emanating from the depot's buffet. It was an intense introduction to Soviet cooking. And things didn't improve from there, at least as far as my nose was concerned.

The Soviet food system wasn't supposed to have turned out that way. Like socialism itself, the food system was based on utopian ideals, though they quickly gave way to more mundane concerns about how to feed an entire nation. One major political platform was women's liberation from domestic chores; early propaganda posters proclaimed, "Down with kitchen slavery!" Communal kitchens and cafeterias were touted as the solution. Visionary architects of the 1920s built "living cells"—one-room apartments where the "kitchen" was a mere hotplate. Proper meals were to be taken along with the apartment block's other residents in a large communal facility. For workplace dining, huge "factory kitchens" were designed by such leading architects as Alexander Rodchenko. One famous factory kitchen in the city of Samara was built in the shape of a hammer and sickle. From the hammer-kitchens, the food was ferried along three conveyer belts for serving in the sickle-cafeterias. But because most of the workers in these kitchens and cafeterias were women, their "liberation" from the kitchen actually entailed much more grueling labor than they had faced at home. Instead of cooking for a small nuclear family, they had to prepare and serve food to a hundred people at a time. Not surprisingly, enforced communal dining didn't last long, and by the mid-1930s, it had largely disappeared.

But public cafeterias survived. No matter where you went, you could find generic state-run cafeterias throughout the Soviet Union. Each offered virtually the same menu of appetizers, soups, main courses, and desserts, and all were as unappetizing as they were inexpensive: lackluster cutlets of unidentifiable meat, gummy potatoes, grayish canned peas, and viscous fruit pudding. But, at least in the larger cities, you could get satisfaction at specialized cafés. For a quick bite, you went to a *zakusochnaya*, where you'd eat standing at a high, round table. For tea (*chai*) you went to a *chainaya*, where the atmosphere was studiously cozy, with curtains and a giant samovar on which perched a large tea cozy in the shape of a plump, smiling babushka. There you could enjoy a glass of tea along with a selection of pastries, from flaky apple hand pies to sponge cake and cookies. For beer (*pivo*) and a more raucous setting, you headed for a *pivnaya*. Though the beer sold on tap was inevitably watery, steamed crayfish were often available. And so it went, for grilled meat, dumplings, blini, and Crimean meat pies. There were also specialized kiosks selling ice cream and doughnuts, two of Soviet Russia's best street foods. My favorite doughnut stand stood adjacent to Moscow's Belarus train station. I would look for steam billowing up in great clouds. There, at a tiny kiosk, a hefty woman spooned hot doughnuts, still dripping with fat, right from the fryer into paper cones, then dusted them with powdered sugar, which immediately clumped. The neon Krispy Kreme outlets in Moscow today don't begin to compare.

If the food in state-run cafeterias was abysmal, grocery shopping was arguably worse, especially since it wasn't optional. The Soviet system practiced centralized industrialized agriculture, to dire effect. Instead of a network of productive small farms supplying the market, everything was grown or raised on enormous state-run farms. If equipment broke down, which it invariably did, there were no spare parts, so seeds didn't get sown on time, and fields weren't harvested when ready. Sometimes the equipment was operating but there was no fuel. Projected yields from the five-year plans became increasingly unattainable, until people just shrugged their shoulders and accepted life in a system where reality itself often seemed unreal. They turned instead to their dachas, or their own garden plots, where they grew the food that gave them pleasure and allowed them to survive, creating a second agricultural system that the government came to rely on. Though potatoes always topped the list, most families also grew onions and garlic; cucumbers and beets; tomatoes; and abundant herbs, especially dill with its tender fronds for sprinkling into soups and stews and its flowering heads for aromatic pickles. Even the most diehard city dwellers preserved their summer bounty, laboring in tiny kitchens to produce gallons of pickles that they stored in odd corners of their apartments, under sofas and beds and in closets.

This activity was crucial, since the state produce stores were nearly empty, with sprouting potatoes, soft onions, wizened carrots, and long lines for anything beyond these most basic of foods. The highly controlled, bureaucratic Soviet system, which guaranteed full employment, made every shopping experience fraught from beginning to end. First you stood in line to get into the store. If you were lucky enough to get inside before the goods disappeared, you approached the counter to place your order. With pounding heart, still somehow distrusting your good fortune, you waited while the saleswoman computed your purchase on an abacus and wrote out a chit. Clutching this precious scrap of paper—material proof of your purchase—you moved to a second line for the cashier, where you paid. The third and final line brought you back to the original counter to pick up what you'd paid for. There the saleswoman scrutinized the chit, made a decisive tear in it, and either shoved the food toward you across the counter or unceremoniously dropped it into your *avos'ka*, a "just-in-case" string bag that everyone carried in purses or pockets. These endless queues, day after day, week after week, were demeaning and exhausting. And yet sometimes a sense of camaraderie arose among those standing in line, a loose community of people who shopped for supper, each with a wealth of experience to share. You could pick up a hint about how to treat a stubborn infection or how to cook the unfamiliar fish that had suddenly materialized at Balaton, the Hungarian frozen-food store.

More privileged workers received special perks from their factories or institutions in a system of incentive based on little more than maintaining an illusion of government largesse. Members of the Writers' Union often received delicacies such as osetra caviar, smoked sturgeon, and *ptich'e moloko*, "bird's milk" candies so light and airy that they were much in demand. Their fantastical name—a quest for the unattainable—spoke volumes. Over time I learned the reality of Soviet life: nothing was available, and yet almost everything could be had. You just had to know how to obtain it.

During one stint in the Soviet Union, when I was a grad student on an American government-sponsored program, I had access to the *diplomaticheskii gastronom*, fondly known as the Dip Gas, a grocery store for diplomats that sold all kinds of coveted Western goods in exchange for hard currency. My husband and I tried not to shop there. We wanted to live like most Muscovites did and, in any case, my student stipend was issued in rubles. And so we subsisted largely on potatoes and onions and cabbage and beets, miraculously transformed in our friends' kitchens into soul-warming borscht and cabbage soup and endlessly satisfying plates of fried potatoes with garlic. And every once in a while, we broke down and trekked across Moscow to the Dip Gas, where we bought bananas and eggs and, in a kind of penance, forced ourselves to walk home through the frigid streets, feeling the emotional weight of our bounty in the string bags that pulled at our shoulders.

Those with rubles to spare could find abundance in Moscow's enchanting farmers' markets, where country dwellers brought their homegrown produce and foraged foods to sell—bosky mushrooms, tiny wild strawberries, lingon-berries and blueberries, gooseberries and currants in shades of red, black, and white. Because the markets were so expensive, I sometimes went just to window-shop, though the vendors' insistence that I taste their cheese or their pickles meant that I might put together a meal. For appetizers, I would head to the corner where pickles were sold, my nose scrunching from the heady smell of fermentation. I ogled cucumbers swimming in salty brine; whole heads of cabbage like stunning pink roses in a bath of beet juice and vinegar; slim Asian eggplants stuffed with carrots and garlic; pickled turnips and beets; salted watermelon floating in vats; sauerkraut brightened with carrots or tarted up with cranberries. Uzbek Koreans sold spicy kimchi and shredded carrot salad. Next came the dairy course: fresh cow's milk with a thick layer of cream on top; and row upon row of farmer's cheese, in textures ranging from soft to firm, silken to grainy. Yogurt and kefir were familiar enough, but with other cultured milk products such as *prostokvasha*, *ryazhenka*, and *varenets* I entered into new territory. My sampling culminated at the fruit stalls manned by vendors from Central Asia, Georgia, and Azerbaijan, who delighted in offering tastes of sweet melons, ruby pomegranates, and aromatic feijoa, which they taught me to grind with sugar for a quick burst of vitamin C. They coaxed me with sultanas and Muscat grapes and tiny dried wild apricots. Piles of green hazel-nuts still in their husks lay next to green walnuts for making preserves. Here, in this friendly place, this gastronomic microcosm of the Soviet Union, the idea of a "brotherhood of all peoples" actually made sense.

It's easy enough to succumb to nostalgia when thinking about those Soviet days, and not only because we had the chance to immerse ourselves in Russian culture and make extraordinary friends. The superhuman efforts required to obtain food meant that even simple meals became feasts and carried special resonance. Everything mattered. But the constant stress of hunting for food and carrying it through the Moscow crowds was exhausting. So, despite our sadness at leaving dear friends behind, we always felt some relief when it was time to go.

Mashed Potatoes and Parsley Root

Пюре из картошки и корни петрушки

Of all the root vegetables and tubers enjoyed in Russia, potatoes are relative upstarts, having been introduced only at the turn of the eighteenth century. Devout peasants were initially reluctant to plant them, despite assurances that potatoes were more reliable than grain. They viewed them with deep suspicion—surely only the fruit of the devil would grow underground and have eyes! It took several imperial edicts and a few riots against forced cultivation before the potato was finally established in the mid-nineteenth century. Then there was no looking back. Not only were potatoes embraced by the populace but they came to symbolize prosperity and self-sufficiency. During the lean Soviet years, when government harvests frequently failed, potatoes became the essential dacha crop, affording people a sense of security that as long as they grew their own potatoes, they wouldn't starve. No wonder potatoes are usually referred to as *kartoshka*, in the affectionate diminutive. They carry emotional as well as nutritional weight.

More often than not, Russians pan-fry potatoes or turn them into a vegetable salad dressed with mayonnaise or sour cream. Potatoes are also mashed, but they take on real character when paired with parsley root, which adds a lovely herbal note. Using sour cream instead of butter and milk lends a subtle tang to the puree, and a nice Russian flair.

Serves 4

6 cups cold water

1 teaspoon salt

¾ pound parsley root, peeled, trimmed, and cut into 2-inch chunks

¾ pound Yukon gold potatoes, peeled, trimmed, and cut into 2-inch chunks

½ cup sour cream (preferably high-fat, see Sources)

In a large saucepan, bring the water and salt to a boil. Drop in the parsley root and boil for 5 minutes. Add the potato chunks and continue to boil, partially covered, until the vegetables are very soft, 20 to 25 minutes. Drain in a colander and return to the pan. Add the sour cream and vigorously mash the vegetables into a smooth puree. Serve immediately.

Potatoes and Mushrooms Baked in a Pot

Грибы с картошкой в горшочке

What a difference a pot makes. The secret to this recipe's deliciousness is the earthenware pot that the potatoes and mushrooms are baked in, which allows them to steam slowly rather than turning them crusty as a shallow pan would do. Called a *gorshok* in Russian, this traditional bulbous pot is similar in shape to American bean pots and, like bean pots, it encourages a slow exchange of flavors.

Russians favor fresh porcini for this dish, but any kind of mushrooms will do. I like to keep things elemental, adding just enough sour cream to help the vegetables steam. But if you want a richer dish, you can use more sour cream as you layer the ingredients or pour on some heavy cream to create a sauce.

Serves 4

2 tablespoons melted unsalted butter

1 pound low-starch potatoes, such as Red Bliss, unpeeled and sliced ¼ inch thick

8 ounces mushrooms, such as porcini, trimmed and sliced ¼ inch thick

1 medium onion, halved vertically, then thinly sliced into half-moons

2 tablespoons minced fresh dill

2 tablespoons minced fresh parsley

Salt

Freshly ground black pepper

¼ cup sour cream, plus more as desired

Preheat the oven to 350°F. Pour 1 tablespoon of the butter into a 2-quart bean pot or casserole. Add a single layer of potatoes; top them first with a layer of mushrooms, then a layer of onion, then a layer of minced herbs. Sprinkle each layer with salt and pepper. Halfway through the layering, add 2 tablespoons of the sour cream. Continue layering the remaining ingredients, ending with potatoes on top. Pour the remaining tablespoon of butter over the potatoes and dab the potatoes with another 2 tablespoons of sour cream.

Cover the pot tightly and bake until the potatoes are tender, about 75 minutes. Give them a good stir before serving.

6

GRAINS

Steamed Buckwheat

Гречневая каша

Kasha, or cooked buckwheat, is the most essential of Russian foods, basic and traditional. The recipe included here is the only one in this book that exactly replicates a recipe I published in *A la Russe* thirty-seven years ago, and the reason is simple: I haven't found anything that improves upon the old-fashioned method of baking buckwheat rather than boiling it on top of the stove, as most contemporary cookbooks recommend. These groats turn out richly flavored and fluffy. Just be sure to use whole roasted groats. (Raw green groats will need to be roasted first; see Note.)

What *has* changed since I published my first Russian cookbook is the awareness of kasha as gluten-free, which has brought it newfound attention. Although we treat buckwheat like a grain, often boiling it like rice or grinding it into flour, it's actually a member of the rhubarb family, native to Central Asia. The edible groat is the fruiting part of the plant, technically known as an achene. Buckwheat's cultivation in Russia has been documented as early as the thirteenth century. Its name ("Greek porridge" or, affectionately, "the Greek one") derives from the active trade with Greek merchants who plied the Black Sea and introduced a number of foodstuffs to Russia. Buckwheat is an amazing crop, so sturdy that it thrives where even hearty grains such as rye struggle. Little surprise, then, that the Russian peasantry called kasha "our dear mother," always there for them in times of need.

Buckwheat can also be a dinner-party savior. If you learn at the last minute that a gluten-free guest is arriving for dinner, you can just pull out the kasha. It's a great accompaniment to meat, and when mixed with mushrooms, onions, and herbs, it becomes a guest-worthy main dish (see facing page).

Serves 4 to 6

1 cup coarse-cut buckwheat groats

Unsalted butter, cut into bits, for greasing the pot, plus 2 tablespoons

½ teaspoon salt

2 cups boiling water

In a large frying pan, toast the groats over medium-high heat for about 5 minutes, stirring often, until the grains begin to turn a darker shade of brown.

Preheat the oven to 350°F. Lightly grease a 1½-quart covered earthenware casserole. Add the groats and the salt. Pour the boiling water over all and dot with the butter. Cover and bake for 20 minutes, until the liquid has evaporated and the groats are fluffy.

Note

To roast raw buckwheat, preheat the oven to 300°F. Spread 1 cup raw groats on a rimmed baking sheet and bake for 35 to 40 minutes, until browned, stirring occasionally, especially toward the end.

SIX WAYS TO SERVE KASHA

Although I love the taste of plain steamed buckwheat, the master recipe can be riffed on in numerous ways. Here are a few of them.

Mushroom Kasha. Mushrooms both complement and intensify the flavor of buckwheat. I sometimes use broth from soaked dried mushrooms in place of boiling water. To make a mushroom broth, soak about 3 ounces dried wild mushrooms in 2¼ cups room-temperature water for 1 hour. Strain the broth into a measuring cup, adding water if necessary to yield 2 cups of liquid. Pour the broth into a saucepan and bring to a boil, then add it to the groats in place of the water along with some of the chopped rehydrated mushrooms.

Kasha with Sautéed Mushrooms. Another way to add mushroom flavor is simply to stir some sautéed mushrooms into the groats before baking.

Kasha with Sautéed Onions. Add sautéed chopped onions to the groats, along with a tablespoon or two of snipped fresh dill, before baking. When you add mushrooms, onions, and herbs to the kasha, you end up with a dish complex enough to serve on its own as a casserole.

Groats Cooked with Egg. If you want a less fluffy porridge, crack 1 egg into a small bowl and whisk lightly. Pour the egg over the groats in the frying pan, stirring well to coat each piece. Cook the groats over medium-high heat for about 5 minutes, until all the moisture from the egg has evaporated. Then proceed as directed in the master recipe.

Buckwheat Porridge. For a creamy consistency, which the Russians like when they serve buckwheat porridge for breakfast, in a large saucepan, boil 1 cup groats with ½ teaspoon salt in 2 cups water over medium heat, uncovered, until the water is absorbed, about 5 minutes. Stir in 2 cups whole milk and simmer the groats, covered, until very soft, about 20 minutes. Serve hot. I sometimes stir dried cranberries or blueberries into the porridge for texture and a hint of sweetness.

Buckwheat Croutons. An excellent use of leftover groats is to make buckwheat croutons (page 210), a classic accompaniment to Borscht.

Barley-Rye Cakes

Ячменно-ржаные хлебцы

These little cakes have a sour tang and a lingering taste of the cabbage leaves they're baked on. They're also charming, with the leaves forming charred lace around the edges. You can serve them as an accompaniment to soup or on their own as an appetizer, either plain or topped with butter. They're especially tasty paired with Cultured Butter with Whitefish Roe (page 76).

Serves 8

1 small head of white cabbage (about 1 pound)

½ cup barley flour

½ cup rye flour

½ teaspoon salt

1 cup full-fat buttermilk

2 tablespoons melted unsalted butter

Preheat the oven to 450°F. Line a baking sheet with parchment paper.

On a cutting board, core the cabbage. Separate seven leaves from the head and cut each one in half along the rib. Slice off any hard bits of core at the bottoms. Place the leaves, cup-side up, on the parchment.

Pour the barley and rye flours into a medium bowl and stir in the salt. Gradually beat in the buttermilk, then stir in the butter. Fill each cabbage leaf with 2 to 3 tablespoons of batter, making sure not to cover the edges of the leaves.

Bake for 20 to 25 minutes, until the cakes are lightly browned and the leaves nicely charred. Serve warm or at room temperature.

Millet Porridge with Pumpkin

Каша пшённая с тыквой

These tiny golden seeds were once an important food crop in Russia, where millet was never displaced by maize, as happened in other parts of the world. Even today, millet porridge is considered one of the healthiest foods for children, and it's a mainstay of Russian kindergarten lunches. Millet deserves a place in our kitchens, too. It pairs beautifully with pumpkin, which enhances its sweetness. Just be sure to use baking pumpkins, not jack-o'-lanterns, whose flesh is watery and flavorless. I especially like millet with kabocha squash, otherwise known as Japanese pumpkin. This recipe uses about half of an average-size pumpkin or squash. You can grate the rest for Pumpkin Pancakes (page 140). This millet porridge radiates gold, and when drizzled with sunflower oil, it actually shimmers, making it especially appealing on a gray winter's day. Serve it with salad for a casual supper or as an accompaniment to roasted meat or stew.

Serves 8

1 cup millet

2 cups water

¼ teaspoon salt

1 tablespoon unsalted butter

1½ pounds sugar pumpkin or kabocha squash, peeled, seeded, and cut into 1-inch cubes

2 cups whole milk

Cold-pressed sunflower oil, for garnish

Freshly ground black pepper

Place the millet in a medium saucepan and toast over medium heat until the seeds turn golden brown and give off a nutty smell, about 4 minutes. They will start to sizzle and dance like popcorn. Stir in the water, salt, and butter. Cover the pan and simmer over low heat until the millet has absorbed all the water, about 20 minutes.

While the millet is cooking, place the pumpkin cubes in another medium saucepan and add the milk. Bring to a boil and cook over low heat, uncovered, until the cubes are soft, stirring occasionally, about 15 minutes. The milk will look curdled and a little skin will have formed. (This step can be done up to an hour ahead of time.)

When the millet is done and the pumpkin is soft, pour the pumpkin mixture into the millet and stir gently, being careful not to break up the pumpkin. Turn out into a serving bowl. Drizzle the porridge with oil and grind pepper liberally over the top. Serve hot.

FOODS FROM THE EAST

After his humiliating retreat from Moscow, Napoleon is claimed to have said, "Scratch a Russian, and you'll find a Tartar." The emperor meant to disparage the Russians by casting them as barbarians partially descended from the Mongol Horde, but the truth is that Tartary—the East—should be thanked for its exquisite contributions to European culture in architecture, the decorative arts, music, and, important for us, cuisine. Staples of the Russian kitchen such as sauerkraut, pickles, dumplings, and tea traveled from China overland along the ancient Silk Road, taking up permanent residence in Russia.

Long before Russia became a unified nation, local populations carried on active trade with Asia along the Great Volga Route that extended all the way from Russia's northwest regions to Baghdad. By the early tenth century, the princes of Kievan Rus' had signed an agreement with Constantinople, the seat of the Byzantine Empire, that opened up even more avenues for trade. In exchange for honey and furs, the Russians imported rice (which, until the mid-nineteenth century, they called "Saracen millet"), spices, and wine. In 1237, the Mongols (aka Tartars) invaded the Russian principalities, and for nearly two hundred years, Russia paid tribute to the Golden Horde. But because the Mongols restored ancient trade routes from China, their domination carried savory benefits. Noodles and cultured milk products such as koumiss—the fermented mare's milk drunk by Turkic nomads (and by Leo Tolstoy in his old age)—were transported along these routes. Most important of all, the Mongols introduced from China the art of fermenting cabbage, forever changing the Russian culinary landscape and palate. Even today, some of the most basic food words in Russian ("noodles," "groceries," and "dried fish") reveal Turkic roots.

A lesser-known trade route was the Astrakhan Highway that stretched 1,800 miles from the city of Astrakhan at the mouth of the Caspian Sea along the high banks of the Volga River and on to Moscow via the great river's tributaries. Peter the Great developed this route into the Astrakhan Post Road; his daughter, the Empress Elizabeth, turned it into an imperial "fruit express" that carried fresh produce from Astrakhan all the way to the Saint Petersburg court in specially equipped carts. During blizzards, villages along the route would "chime the storm" by ringing the church bells so that travelers wouldn't lose their way.

The expansion of Russian trade had begun with Ivan the Terrible, who conquered the Volga region in the mid-sixteenth century. Commerce in spices such as pepper, saffron, cinnamon, and ginger increased, as did trade in rhubarb, which became a lucrative export prized for its medicinal properties. From this region, too, came sweet watermelons from Astrakhan and greater access to the extraordinary sturgeon and caviar of the Caspian Sea. Lemons and dried fruits were also introduced from the East, and Russians have used them deftly ever since. Eastern methods for preserving root vegetables in sugar syrup, including carrots and radishes, became part of the culinary repertoire in affluent homes.

Toward the end of his reign, Ivan also annexed Siberia, an eastward extension that gave Russia land on two continents, Europe and Asia. From this union came various types of boiled dumplings, such as *manty* stuffed with ground lamb. Siberia's beloved *pelmeni*—wonton-like pockets of dough filled with ground meat and onions—arrived somewhat later. Their origins are contested, though they're likely Chinese. Enormous quantities of these dumplings were prepared at the onset of the Siberian winter and kept frozen outdoors, ready for boiling into a quick meal. Tea from the Far East also arrived by way of Siberia, as a seventeenth-century gift to the tsar from the Mongol khan.

Continuing its expansion, the Russian Empire held Central Asia and the Caucasus under its control by the late nineteenth century. Scholars endlessly debate whether the three countries of the Caucasus—Armenia, Azerbaijan, and Georgia—are Asian or European, but there's no question that their culinary traditions have more in common with the Middle East than with Europe. After the 1917 revolution, the Caucasian and Central Asian territories were forcibly turned into Soviet Socialist Republics. What followed was less Marxism than imperialism. Along with Soviet rule came a kind of culinary nationalism in which new, "exotic" foods from the East were adopted into Russian cuisine. Georgian food, in particular, became chic, thanks to sought-after dishes such as chicken *tabaka* (garlicky flattened chicken), *khachapuri* (cheese bread), and *lobio* (herbed kidney beans). Also popular were Uzbek *plov* (rice pilaf) and *lyulya-kebab* (ground lamb kebabs) from Azerbaijan. Vil'iam Pokhlyobkin's famous 1978 cookbook, *The National Cuisines of Our Peoples*, claimed all of these dishes and more as part of the Soviet patrimony. Close reading reveals condescension toward the culinary practices of non-Russian peoples, who remained barbarians at the gate even as their foods were eagerly adopted.

Today, chefs and home cooks throughout Russia make full use of many dishes and techniques adopted from the East. Some of the most exciting pies I tasted were *khychiny* from the North Caucasus: soft, thin rounds of dough stuffed with salty goat cheese, beet greens, and plenty of garlic and then pan-fried on a griddle. The *khychiny* were served on a platter alongside traditional Russian *blinchiki*—crêpelike pancakes filled with fresh goat cheese and rolled into batons before pan-frying and dousing with sour cream. A perfect blend of East and West, occurring not along the ancient trade routes through the south of Russia but in Murmansk—the North—far above the Arctic Circle.

Buckwheat Croutons

Гренки из гречневой каши

If you've ever fried leftover polenta into crisp squares, you'll have an inkling of how appealing leftover kasha can be when given the same treatment. I like these croutons so much that I usually make them from scratch, especially since kasha cooks up quickly on the stove. Russians serve the croutons on a small side plate as an accompaniment to borscht. They are also excellent topped with sautéed wild mushrooms for a casual supper. This recipe is adapted from Pelageya Alexandrova-Ignatieva's classic textbook, *The Practical Foundations of the Culinary Art*, first published in 1899.

Serves 8

1 cup coarse-cut buckwheat groats

2 cups water

½ teaspoon salt

4 tablespoons unsalted butter

½ cup all-purpose or buckwheat flour

1 egg, lightly beaten

¾ cup fine, dry bread crumbs

1 tablespoon sunflower oil

Rinse the buckwheat groats in a colander, then place them in a medium saucepan with the water, salt, and 2 tablespoons of the butter. Bring to a boil, then lower the heat and simmer, covered, for 10 minutes, until tender. Remove the lid and continue to cook the buckwheat, stirring occasionally, until it is thick and firm, another 8 to 10 minutes.

Grease a 10.5 by 7.5-inch rimmed baking sheet. (A 9-inch square pan will also work, but it's easier to cut the buckwheat on a sheet with low rims.) Spoon the cooked buckwheat onto the baking sheet, pressing down with a spatula to smooth the top and form a firm mass about ½ inch thick. Cover with plastic wrap and chill in the refrigerator for at least 6 hours, or overnight.

When you're ready to make the croutons, place the flour, egg, and bread crumbs in three separate shallow bowls. Cut the chilled buckwheat into 12 rectangles. Dredge each piece by dipping it into the flour, egg, and bread crumbs to coat on both sides.

Heat the remaining 2 tablespoons butter and the oil in a large skillet over medium heat until sizzling. Transfer half the croutons to the pan and cook for 3 minutes, until golden, then turn and cook until crisp on the other side, 2 to 3 minutes more. Transfer to a serving plate and keep warm. Cook the remaining croutons the same way (adding a little more butter and oil if necessary). Serve hot.

Note

If you want to make the croutons gluten-free, use buckwheat flour and gluten-free bread crumbs for dredging.

Sprouted Rye Porridge

Ржаная каша

I wanted to include a recipe for Russia's once-beloved "green kasha" in this book. Made from underripe rye berries, this porridge was prized as much for its delicate flavor as for its extravagance. Very few people had the luxury of harvesting grain before it was fully ripe and containing the most nutrients. The rye had to be harvested at the beginning of August when still slightly green, a stage known in English as "yellow ripeness." Modern farming effectively put an end to this specialty crop, which can't be reaped by machine. Still, I didn't want to give up on the essential flavor of rye, so I decided to try sprouting the berries. Success!

While it may seem extreme to call for sprouting your own rye berries, it's actually quite easy. Just keep them warm and damp, and nature will do the rest. The germination time varies with climatic conditions, so you'll need to check the berries daily to observe their progress. In our cold house in winter, they didn't sprout for three whole days, but in the heat and humidity of summer, they were sporting threads within twenty-four hours. Don't be tempted to rush the cooking by boiling the sprouted berries on top of the stove. The secret to the porridge's success is its slow steaming in the oven, replicating the environment of the Russian masonry stove.

Sprouted rye porridge is now one of my favorites, especially since it's so versatile. Drizzled with cream or honey, it's great for a hearty breakfast. Mix it with sautéed onions and mushrooms, and you have a savory side dish for dinner. Or serve it for dessert with yogurt and berries (or, in winter, dried fruits). I also like to steam the berries with milk or whey for a creamier porridge.

Serves 4

1 cup whole rye berries

½ teaspoon salt

Scant 1 cup boiling water

Soak the rye berries in cold water for 2 days, changing the water twice daily. Run a large linen dish towel under cold water and wring it dry. Place the towel on a rimmed baking sheet so that half of it covers the bottom of the sheet. Drain the berries and spread them in a single layer on the towel, then fold over the other half of the towel to cover the berries. Set the pan in a dark place to germinate, periodically using a mist sprayer to keep the towel moist. The berries will take from 1 to 3 days to sprout, depending on the heat and humidity. I like them best when the wispy sprouts are about ½ inch long. Don't expect all the berries to have sprouted.

Preheat the oven to 350°F. Place the sprouted berries and the salt in a 1½-quart earthenware bean pot. Pour on the boiling water, cover, and place the pot in the oven. Steam for 1 hour, until the water has been absorbed.

Serve the porridge hot, at room temperature, or chilled.

Barley Porridge with Almond Milk and Blueberries

Ячменная каша на миндальном молоке

This porridge is another favorite breakfast dish. Its origins lie in the six-week Lenten fast, when the Russian Orthodox Church prohibits all dairy products. In the past, most Russians traditionally went without, but the wealthy enjoyed the means and the womanpower to pound "milk" from almonds and pistachios to replace cow's milk. I often go against the grain and drizzle the porridge with cream, but even without that illicit touch, this dish is so rich and satisfying that you won't miss the milk or dairy.

Serves 4

1 cup pearl barley

2 cups unsweetened almond milk

Pinch of salt

2 tablespoons unsalted butter

1 to 2 tablespoons sugar

¼ cup dried blueberries

Rinse the barley and transfer it to a medium saucepan. Stir in the almond milk and the salt. Bring to a boil, then turn the heat to low and cook, uncovered, until the liquid is absorbed, about 20 minutes.

Stir in the butter, sugar to taste, and the dried blueberries. Cover the pan and allow the porridge to sit, undisturbed, for 30 minutes, until the blueberries are plump. Reheat gently to serve.

Wheat Berry Porridge

Кутья

This wholesome porridge has strong ritual associations with a sweet existence, both on Earth and in the afterlife. Grains symbolize the circle of life and resurrection: Just as seeds rise up from the ground, so the souls of the pious will rise up to eternal life. For this reason *kutya* are always served at Russian Orthodox funeral feasts, and the deceased are recalled with each sweet bite. Folk tradition holds that the porridge must be eaten with a spoon, never a fork. The two-pronged fork, originally introduced from Byzantium, too closely resembled a pitchfork—an abstraction of the devil's horns—and aroused suspicion among the most devout, who also feared that the fork's sharp tines could poke the soul of the deceased instead of helping to send it on a comfortable journey.

Kutya is also traditional for the Christmas Eve feast, which breaks the forty-day Nativity fast when the first evening star appears. Some families used to toss a spoonful of *kutya* up to the ceiling. If the grains stuck, the coming year would be prosperous; if not, things didn't bode well. Luckily, there's enough honey in *kutya* to ensure that a ceiling toss isn't much of a gamble.

Serve this porridge for breakfast or dessert.

Serves 4 to 6

1 cup wheat berries

1½ cups raw whole almonds

2 cups water

½ cup chopped blanched almonds

Butter, for greasing

½ teaspoon salt

3 tablespoons poppy seeds

3 to 4 tablespoons honey

Sour cherry preserves (optional)

Soak the wheat berries overnight in cold water to cover.

The next day, make almond milk by placing the raw almonds in a medium saucepan with the water. Bring to a boil, then remove the pan from the heat and let the almonds steep until the liquid cools to room temperature. Drain the almonds, reserving the liquid. The almonds can be saved for another use (see Notes).

Preheat the oven to 325°F. Toast the chopped almonds until golden, about 8 minutes. Set aside.

Raise the oven temperature to 350°F. Grease a lidded 1½-quart earthenware casserole. Drain the wheat berries, place them in the casserole, and add the salt.

Bring the almond milk to a boil and pour it over the wheat berries. Cover the casserole and bake for 1½ hours, until the wheat has absorbed most of the water and is tender but still a bit chewy.

While the wheat berries are cooking, soak the poppy seeds in warm water for 30 minutes to soften, then drain them and grind finely in a mini food processor.

continued

When the wheat berries are done, stir in the poppy seeds. Add honey to taste, mixing well. Transfer the porridge to a serving dish. Serve slightly warm or at room temperature, sprinkled with the toasted almonds and with sour cherry preserves, if desired.

Notes

Make sure the poppy seeds are very fresh, since stale seeds can taste bitter and slightly rancid after grinding.

Drained, pitted whole Morello cherries in syrup can be used to garnish the *kut'ya* if you don't have sour cherry preserves on hand (see Sources).

The drained whole almonds are excellent when toasted. Spread them on a rimmed baking sheet and toast at 325°F for an hour. They can be tossed with a little salt beforehand, if you like.

7

FISH

Murmansk-Style Cod

Треска по-мурмански

This simple dish is a specialty of the North, where the cold waters yield abundant and exceptionally flavorful fish. All the raw cod needs is a drizzle of nutty sunflower oil to create a perfect balance between *mer* and *terre*.

Serves 4

½ pound sushi-grade cod fillet (or other whitefish, such as halibut), sliced ¼ inch thick

¼ teaspoon fine sea salt

Freshly ground black pepper

1 bay leaf

3 tablespoons cold-pressed sunflower oil

Place the fish in a single layer in a shallow container with a lid. Season with the salt and pepper and tuck in the bay leaf. Drizzle the oil over the fish. Chill for at least 3 hours before serving. This dish keeps well in the refrigerator for a couple of days.

Herring in Mustard-Dill Sauce

Селёдка в горчично-укропном соусе

As Anton Chekhov wrote in his short story "The Siren"

> The best appetizer, if you'd like to know, is herring. Imagine you've eaten a bite of it with onion and mustard sauce. Just imagine! . . . Then, my benefactor, while you're still feeling sparks in your stomach, you must immediately eat some caviar, either plain or, if you prefer, with lemon; and then some radishes with salt, then some more herring. . . .

Look for salt herring fillets at delicatessens and some supermarkets, but be sure to buy good-quality fish that isn't overly salty. The soaking time will depend on your preference and the saltiness of the fillets. Cut off a little piece after about two hours to see if it's to your liking.

Serves 10 to 12

1 pound salt herring fillets

2 cups whole milk

2 tablespoons Dijon mustard

1 tablespoon honey

2 tablespoons distilled white vinegar

½ cup vegetable oil

½ cup snipped fresh dill

Freshly ground black pepper

1 large beet, for garnish (optional)

1 large potato, for garnish (optional)

Dill sprigs, for garnish

Soak the herring fillets in the milk to cover for 3 to 6 hours. Rinse the fillets and pat them dry. Cut the fish on the diagonal into 1-inch pieces. Transfer to a 9 by 13-inch glass baking dish, laying the pieces out in a single layer.

In a small bowl, whisk the mustard and honey together, then add the vinegar. Gradually beat in the oil until an emulsion is formed. Stir in the snipped dill. Season with pepper. Pour the sauce over the sliced herring. Chill for at least 2 hours, but remove the herring from the refrigerator about half an hour before serving so it isn't ice-cold. Transfer to a serving platter and garnish with dill sprigs.

For a more substantial presentation, boil the beet and the potato in separate pots. Peel and slice the vegetables and arrange them decoratively on the platter around the herring. Garnish with dill sprigs.

The herring will keep, tightly covered, for several days in the refrigerator.

Shaved Salmon

Строганина

Stroganina, or shaved frozen fish, is a stunning party dish that needs no advance preparation beyond freezing the fish. Gather your guests around as you shave off paper-thin slices to eat right away. When the cold fish hits the warm tongue, the ice crystals melt with a thrilling tingle.

Stroganina is made in the Russian Arctic with fish that's been freshly pulled from icy waters. The Russians favor *muksun*, a type of whitefish. I substitute salmon. Traditionally *stroganina* was a wintertime dish, served when the fish were at their fattiest and most delicious. The day's catch was simply left to freeze outdoors. But with today's freezers, *stroganina* can be enjoyed year-round, even in summer, when its iciness is especially welcome.

Besides serving the fish ice-cold, it's important to shave it very thinly. The Russians work with whole fish that they hold vertically, using a mandoline or sharp knife to shave off slices from tail down to head. For ease of preparation, I suggest a center-cut fillet of salmon.

Serve the fish on a wooden board covered with parchment paper, which will keep it from thawing as quickly as it would on ceramic or glass. Or, for a dramatic presentation, the day before you plan to serve the *stroganina*, pour water into a shallow freezer-proof bowl or decorative mold and freeze until it becomes a solid disk of ice. Place the bowl on a wooden board or tray and mound the shaved salmon directly on the ice.

Though you can offer plain sea salt with *stroganina*, I like to serve a couple different types of flavored salt for dipping. Monastery Salt and Black Salt are particular favorites. Because *stroganina* is always eaten with the fingers, be sure to have plenty of napkins on hand.

**Serves 8 to 10
as an appetizer**

1-pound center-cut fillet of fatty fish, such as salmon or whitefish, the freshest and highest quality you can find

Plain or flavored salt (see page 52)

With a sharp knife, remove the skin from the fish, being careful to leave the layer of fat between skin and flesh intact. Wrap the fish in plastic wrap and freeze. The fish can be held in the freezer for up to 2 weeks.

When ready to serve, remove the fish from the freezer. Place a piece of parchment paper on a wooden board and have a clean dish towel ready.

You'll need a second cutting board to prepare the fish. Using the dish towel, hold the frozen fish by one edge, with the narrowest side at the top. Place one corner of the fillet against the cutting board to stabilize it, then tip the

continued

fillet slightly. Working from top to bottom, shave the fish at an angle with a mandoline or very sharp knife onto the cutting board. Quickly transfer the frozen slices onto the parchment paper, mounding them loosely in ribbons with a fork. Serve immediately, with salt for dipping.

Return any unused fish to the freezer so that it doesn't thaw. Repeat the shaving process if people want seconds—as they undoubtedly will.

Variation

Though *stroganina* is traditionally made with fish, you can also make it from a frozen fillet of venison, following the method instructions.

CAVIAR

Sturgeon has long been considered the king of fish in Russia. The caviar industry was first developed under Mongol occupation in the thirteenth century, and by the fourteenth century, sturgeon fishing flourished near the southern Russian city of Astrakhan, where the Volga River flows into the Caspian Sea. Grand Prince Yaroslav Vsevolodovich of Novgorod appointed a special sturgeon master to his thirteenth-century court to oversee the fish's procurement, preparation, and serving. Into the eighteenth century, astonishing numbers of sturgeon were caught as they swam upriver to spawn; some accounts claim catches of up to 250 giant belugas an hour.

The Caspian harbors three types of sturgeon. The largest, the beluga, can weigh more than 2,000 pounds, though such specimens are nonexistent today. The beluga's roe—pearl gray in color and subtle in flavor—has historically been the most prized. The osetra sturgeon weighs in at 400 to 600 pounds, with roe that is nutty in flavor and deep gold to gray in hue. The smallest Caspian sturgeon, the sevruga or stellate, weighs a mere 100 pounds; its roe is steel gray to black and much firmer than the beluga's. Many Russians seek out the strong flavor of pressed caviar, or *payusnaya*, made from eggs that have been broken in processing or from very mature eggs that are pressed into a thick, pastelike mass.

To make caviar from wild Caspian sturgeon, the eggs are harvested twice a year when the fish swim upstream to spawn. If harvested too early, the eggs turn out rough and dry, since the sturgeon's fat remains in her belly. If harvested too late, they can be unappealingly soft. Like good wine, wild roe differs in taste from season to season and depends on the skill of a caviar master who understands how to work with the fragile eggs. The roe is ideally extracted from the fish by hand and must be kept cold during processing. Salt is added to lower the temperature at which the eggs will freeze, as well as to help preserve them. The best caviar contains 3 to 4 percent salt and is known as *malossol* ("little salt") in Russian. It should have a fresh marine scent and never a fishy odor or overly salty taste. The eggs should be uniform and unbroken, firm but not hard. One of the great pleasures of eating caviar is to feel the eggs pop against the palate.

The wealthy considered caviar standard fare on the numerous Russian Orthodox fast days when meat and dairy products were proscribed. Whether fasting or not, medieval Russians seasoned their caviar with black pepper, chopped onion, vinegar, and oil. Often they ate it hot. After extracting the fresh roe, they would sprinkle the egg sac with salt and pepper, dust it with flour, fry it (as we do shad roe), and serve it with an onion, cranberry, or saffron sauce. Pressed caviar was sometimes chilled, cut into slices, and drizzled with herb vinegar or mustard sauce. For the Muscovite dish *kal'ia*, pressed caviar was cut into thin rounds and placed in an earthenware pot with chopped onion, black pepper, pickles, pickle brine, and water to steam in the Russian masonry stove. Nineteenth-century culinary fashion called for slicing pressed caviar and serving it in a napkin as "serviette caviar." The ever-practical Elena Molokhovets suggests another use for pressed caviar in her nineteenth-century cookbook, *A Gift to Young Housewives*: substitute one-quarter pound of protein-rich caviar for two egg whites to clarify stock.

By the mid-nineteenth century, the finest sturgeon caviar had become rare enough that it was generally served unadorned. Beluga caviar, with its large pearly grains, was considered the ultimate roe, presented on toast points at fancy dinners or mounded in a pyramid and decorated with lemon wedges, with croutons on the side. To please elite palates, caviar was transported overland in linden barrels from the Caspian Sea to Moscow and Saint Petersburg. For the tsar and other extravagant consumers, live sturgeon were transported in carts, and later in special railway cars with tanks, so that the eggs could be harvested on site for optimal freshness. It was a gilded age.

The caviar trade was highly lucrative, especially when huge belugas were caught. Russia exported a great deal of caviar, even as fish stocks declined. In 1896, Russia exported more than 800,000 pounds of sturgeon caviar (and more than 5 million pounds of salmon caviar), primarily to Europe. As Caspian production fell due to overfishing, a caviar industry arose in the United States, based on the Atlantic sturgeon that swam in the Hudson and the Delaware Rivers. But history repeats itself. Soon these waters, too, were overfished.

Russia's entry into World War I and the chaos of the 1917 revolution and subsequent civil war provided a respite for the sturgeon, whose depleted stocks began to recover. Astrakhan once again found itself at the center of the world caviar trade, now reliant on state-controlled fishing collectives. Recognizing caviar as a ready source of foreign currency, the Soviets in 1920 signed an exclusive agreement with the Petrossian brothers to ship Russian caviar to Paris. Other export agreements soon followed. Despite the massive hydroelectric dam built at Volgograd (Stalingrad), which effectively reduced the sturgeons' spawning grounds by two-thirds, government controls actually helped preserve the sturgeon. But with the demise of the Soviet

Union, the caviar trade became a free-for-all, with illicit profit the sole motive and no thought given to ecological concerns.

Today, due to pollution and poaching, all varieties of Caspian sturgeon are endangered, and the spectacular beluga is nearly extinct. Russia is no longer the world's leading producer of caviar; that honor goes to China. Now entrepreneurs around the world, from Israel and Italy to Uruguay and the United Arab Emirates, are competing to produce roe in their own countries from farm-raised sturgeon. Russians continue to enjoy "caviar" from salmon, burbot, pike, carp, grayling, and Arctic char, though sturgeon roe—especially when fresh and unpasteurized—remains the gold standard. Some connoisseurs convince themselves that they might as well enjoy the last true Caspian caviar before it's gone. As for me, I buy only sustainable roe these days, usually from wild-caught paddlefish, a sturgeon relative that swims in the Mississippi and the Missouri Rivers. It tastes awfully good, but it doesn't feel legendary. I miss the romance of Russian roe.

Baked Fishcakes

Котлеты из рыбы, запечённые в духовке

Though fishcakes are common in many cultures, this two-step method for cooking them is distinctively Russian. First they're sautéed on the stovetop, then they're steamed in the oven. The steaming approximates the moist heat of the Russian masonry stove, yielding handsome, lemony, herb-strewn fishcakes.

Serves 3 to 4

1 medium onion, chopped

1 pound halibut, halibut cheeks, or cod, cut into small pieces

1 small egg, lightly beaten

1¼ teaspoons salt

¾ teaspoon freshly ground black pepper

4 garlic cloves

1 tablespoon plus 1 teaspoon unsalted butter, at room temperature

¾ cup rye flour

2 tablespoons vegetable oil

½ cup finely chopped fresh parsley

½ cup finely chopped fresh dill

8 lemon slices

¼ cup finely chopped scallions

Grate the onion in the bowl of a food processor. Add the fish, egg, 1 teaspoon of the salt, and ½ teaspoon of the pepper. Pulse until ground medium-fine. Transfer the mixture to a bowl and chill in the refrigerator for at least 1 hour.

Peel and smash 2 of the garlic cloves and set aside. Mince the remaining 2 garlic cloves and set them aside, too.

Preheat the oven to 400°F. Cut out a piece of parchment paper large enough to cover a 12-inch skillet and grease it with the 1 teaspoon butter. Mix the rye flour with the remaining ¼ teaspoon each of the salt and pepper and spread on a large plate.

Remove the fish mixture from the refrigerator and pour off any liquid that may have accumulated in the bottom of the bowl. The fish will be very moist, so it helps to moisten your hands with cold water before working with it. Gently shape the fish mixture into 8 round patties, setting each one on the rye flour as soon as it's shaped. Carefully turn the patties to coat both sides well.

Heat the oil, the remaining 1 tablespoon butter, and the 2 smashed garlic cloves over medium heat in a 12-inch cast-iron or other ovenproof skillet. When the butter begins to foam, add the fishcakes. Cook for 4 minutes, periodically sliding a spatula under the cakes to make sure they don't stick. After 4 minutes, turn the fishcakes and turn the heat to medium-low. Cook the second side for an additional 4 minutes.

Remove the pan from the heat and sprinkle the fishcakes with the parsley, dill, and minced garlic. Top with the lemon slices. Lay the parchment paper, buttered-side down, over the fishcakes, pressing down lightly. Cover the pan with an ovenproof lid. (If the pan doesn't have a lid, cover it with tightly sealed aluminum foil.) Bake for 8 minutes. Remove the lid and parchment paper and sprinkle the chopped scallions over the fishcakes. Serve directly from the skillet.

Pickled Smelts

Маринованная корюшка

The first of the Baltic smelts appear in late February, as early harbingers of spring. By the end of April, when the fish have made their way across the Gulf of Finland and down Saint Petersburg's Neva River, the smelts have grown considerably, but they retain the distinctive smell of fresh cucumbers that the Russians love. It's this attribute that makes the local smelts special and distinguishes them from those caught in the White Sea or in the Far East. So beloved are these small fish that devotees risk their lives to catch them when they're at their best, in March and April, just as the ice is beginning to break up. Every year, smelt fishermen are stranded on ice floes. And every year, the fishermen return to the thawing ice, chop holes in it, set up makeshift tents against the fierce wind, and lower their nets into the icy water.

Spring smelts are most often pan-fried in butter, though chic Saint Petersburg restaurants now serve them as ceviche. They're also excellent smoked and marinated. Just don't expect the sweet Scandinavian style of pickled fish. This brine has a bold, vinegary bite.

Serves 10 to 12

1 pound gutted smelts, fresh or frozen

6 cups water

3 tablespoons salt, plus 4 teaspoons

2 cups cider vinegar

¼ cup sugar

2 bay leaves

10 black peppercorns

1 teaspoon dill seed

1 teaspoon brown mustard seed

1 large carrot, peeled and sliced into ¼-inch rounds

1 large onion, halved vertically, then thinly sliced into half-moons

Thaw the smelts if frozen. Make a brine by stirring together 3 cups of the water and the 3 tablespoons salt in a large bowl until the salt dissolves. Drop the smelts into the brine, cover, and refrigerate for 8 hours or overnight.

Rinse and drain the smelts in a colander. In a medium saucepan, bring to a boil the remaining 3 cups water, the vinegar, the remaining 4 teaspoons salt, and the sugar, bay leaves, spices, and carrot. Simmer for 5 minutes, then remove this brine from the heat.

Place a layer of onion in a sterilized 2-quart container, then add a layer of smelts. Continue to layer the onion and smelts, ending with a layer of onion. Pour in the hot brine, seal the jar, and leave to cool to room temperature. Place the pickled smelts in the refrigerator to marinate for at least 12 hours before serving. They taste best when consumed within a week.

FEASTING
AND FASTING

In grad school, I struggled mightily to work my way through the archaic language of the Russian *Primary Chronicle*, which documents the early history of the Eastern Slavs—until I encountered the story of Princess Olga, the first ruler of Kievan Rus' to convert to Christianity. Olga was more than a pious figure. She was also a crafty ruler. I found her story so riveting that I breezed through arcane words and grammatical forms, so eager was I to discover how she'd avenge her husband Igor's death at the hands of the fierce Derevlians. (Think *Game of Thrones*!) Olga conspired to invite her enemies to a funeral feast in Igor's memory. Invoking the best of Russian hospitality, she plied them with vast quantities of mead, and when they were thoroughly drunk, she had them all massacred, five thousand people in all. That was in 945.

Olga's grandson, Grand Prince Vladimir, adopted Christianity for his new nation in 988, to unify the pagan Slavic tribes. But Russia's embrace of Christian practice wasn't immediate. There was still plenty of magical thinking to ease the hunger most of the population felt. One of the most vivid images in Russian fairy tales is that of the *skatert'-samobranka*, a self-spreading tablecloth on which food miraculously appears. All you have to do is unfold it and a lavish feast fans out before your eyes. In a classic tale of Ivan Tsarevich and the Grey Wolf, the self-spreading tablecloth nurtures Ivan as he fulfills his superhuman quests. It also feeds an entire city when he returns, victorious, to claim his bride. Tables set with gold plates and crystal materialize in the city streets. Silk carpets lie at the diners' feet. The food is like none ever tasted before: "*Ukha* [fish soup] like liquid amber, sparkling in large stockpots; huge, fat Volga sterlets seven feet long, on patterned gold plates; *kulebyaka* [fish pie] with a sweet filling; geese with milkcap mushrooms; kasha with sour cream; blini with fresh caviar as large as pearls; hearth-baked pies drowning in butter." And it is all effortless.

Of course, in a land of frequent famine, the tablecloth's magical powers bespeak a poignant utopian dream. Russians have long been subject to forces beyond their control. Invaders, bad weather, and pestilent insects frequently destroyed harvests, while cruel masters and rulers kept the people chronically underfed. In the face of such hardship, the peasantry developed a fatalistic attitude. If the gods are willing, the harvest will be good and our bellies will be full. If not, we'll manage somehow. Perhaps a magical tablecloth will miraculously appear.

The Russian Orthodox Church understood all of this and cannily transformed many existing pagan celebrations, such as those marking the seasons, into religious holidays such as Christmas and Easter. The church also understood the cyclical hunger that afflicted most of the population, and by dividing the religious calendar into feast days and fast days, the church equated paucity with piety. Rather astonishingly, the fast days—requiring varying degrees of abstinence but almost always restricting meat and all other animal products—accounted for roughly 180 days of the year. Thus the Russian peasant diet consisted largely of what we would today consider vegan fare. Most people relied on grains, root vegetables, foraged mushrooms and berries, and occasionally fish.

Russian peasants took fasting seriously. In addition to meatless Wednesdays and Fridays, some also avoided forbidden foods on Mondays as well. These weekly fasting days were supplemented by extended fasts, the most important of which were the great Lenten fast (40 days, plus 1 week of Passion Week preceding Easter), the Nativity or Filippov fast (6 weeks preceding Christmas), the fast of Saints Peter and Paul (beginning in late May or June and lasting from 1 to 6 weeks, depending on when Easter fell); and the fast of the Dormition (2 weeks in August). On the most stringent fast days (Lent and the Dormition fast) even fish and vegetable oils were forbidden. Generally, the poorer the household, the more devoutly it fasted, since meat and dairy products were scarce even on non-fast days. But for the wealthy, fasting didn't necessarily mean deprivation. A mid-seventeenth-century state dinner given on a fast day for the English ambassador presented no less than five hundred dishes, not one made with meat products.

For regular folks, the church calendar compensated for the stringent fasts with numerous feast days to celebrate weddings, funerals, and the name days of saints, which the Russians observed instead of birthdays. (Until the Soviet period, nearly all Russians were named after saints, which is why you encounter so many people with the same name.) Many religious holidays were also considered feast days. During Butter Week (*Maslenitsa*), an extended Mardi Gras or last indulgent gasp before the rigorous Lenten fast, Russians consumed excessive amounts of dairy products, most often in the form of the wonderfully porous pancakes known as *bliny*, designed to soak up plenty of melted butter.

Easter is the most important holiday in the Russian Orthodox year. In Old Russia, the sumptuous Easter table remained set for an entire week to regale the guests who dropped in to exchange Easter greetings. Along with all sorts of other delicacies, three symbolic foods always graced (and continue to grace) the Russian Easter table: colorfully dyed eggs, *kulich* (a tall enriched loaf of bread with a mushrooming crown), and *paskha*, perhaps the most glorious version of cheesecake in any national cuisine. Much of the population scrimped throughout the year in order to extol Christ's rebirth properly. The profusion of dairy products at Easter reflects both the release from Lenten restraint and the ancient association of rebirth and fertility with fresh cheese, like eggs, a symbol of spring.

Brine-Poached Turbot

Палтус, припущенная в рассоле

I love turbot for its buttery texture and because it holds its own with other ingredients. Here the fish gets a gentle bath in pickle brine, which transforms it from an everyday affair into a special occasion. The flavors are both woodsy and elegant, while the presentation is dramatic—a halo of orange and green vegetables enclosing creamy white fish. Pull out your finest platter for this one.

Serves 4

3 tablespoons unsalted butter

1 medium onion, halved lengthwise, then cut crosswise into ⅛-inch slices

1 medium carrot, peeled and grated on the large holes of a box grater

8 ounces mushrooms of any kind (halved if large), trimmed and sliced ¼ inch thick

½ teaspoon salt, plus more for sprinkling

Freshly ground black pepper

2 pounds skinless turbot fillets

1½ cups water

½ cup pickle brine (from Half-Sour Dill Pickles [page 83], Alexandra's Sweet and Sour Cucumbers [page 57], or commercially fermented pickles such as Bubbies)

2 large sour dill pickles, peeled, seeded, and diced (about 1 cup)

1 bay leaf

3 allspice berries

5 black peppercorns

2 tablespoons minced fresh dill, for garnish

2 tablespoons minced fresh chives, for garnish

Melt the butter in a 14-inch skillet over medium heat. Add the onion, carrot, and mushrooms and season them with the salt and pepper. Cook, stirring occasionally, for 8 to 10 minutes, until the vegetables soften.

Sprinkle the turbot fillets on both sides with salt and pepper. Lay the fish over the vegetables in the skillet. Add the water, pickle brine, diced pickles, bay leaf, allspice, and peppercorns. Cover the pan and bring to a simmer. Gently poach the fish for 4 minutes, just until it flakes.

With a large spatula, transfer the fish to a warm serving platter. Scoop out the vegetables with a slotted spoon and arrange them around the fish. Pour some of the broth over the top and garnish with the dill and chives. Serve hot.

Braised Cod with Horseradish

Треска, тушёная с хреном

This method of cooking cod keeps it wonderfully moist. Don't be alarmed at the large amount of horseradish called for—it mellows as it steams, imparting flavor to the fish without overwhelming it. I like to serve this flaky cod dish with mashed or boiled potatoes.

Serves 4

2 pounds cod fillet, cut into four pieces

Salt

Freshly ground black pepper

4 tablespoons unsalted butter

1 to 1½ cups freshly grated horseradish (from a peeled 4- to 6-ounce piece)

4 teaspoons cider vinegar

1 cup fish stock

4 teaspoons fine rye flour

2 tablespoons minced fresh dill

Sprinkle the fish generously on both sides with salt and pepper. Melt 2 tablespoons of the butter in a saucepan large enough to accommodate two pieces of the cod side by side. Sprinkle a third of the horseradish into the saucepan and top it with two of the cod fillets. Sprinkle the fillets with half of the remaining horseradish, then place the other two pieces of fish on top. Sprinkle with the last third of the horseradish.

Stir the vinegar into the fish stock and pour the mixture over the fish. Cover the pan and bring to a boil. Immediately lower the heat and simmer the fish for 10 minutes, until it is flaky but still moist. Be careful not to overcook.

While the fish is cooking, melt the remaining 2 tablespoons butter in a small saucepan and whisk in the rye flour. Cook for 1 minute over low heat, stirring constantly. Set aside.

When the fish is done, transfer it with a slotted spatula to a shallow serving bowl. Whisk the fish stock into the rye butter and cook over low heat for a few minutes, stirring constantly, until the sauce thickens slightly. Stir in the dill. Pour the sauce over the fish and serve immediately.

8
MEAT

Oven-Braised Veal Stew with Cherries

Телятина, тушёная с вишней

Russians are such cherry connoisseurs that they make a linguistic distinction between sweet cherries and sour ones, using two completely different nouns. Not surprisingly, it's the sour cherries that they really love—and whose imminent destruction in Chekhov's play *The Cherry Orchard* symbolizes the loss of an entire way of life.

This lovely stew is loosely based on a recipe from Elena Molokhovets's nineteenth-century cookbook, *A Gift to Young Housewives*. Hers is a veal loin roast braised with Madeira and cherry syrup, quite an elegant dish. Mine is more homely, though no less tempting. As with other stews, the flavor improves upon standing, so I usually make it early in the day to reheat for dinner. The veal goes nicely with parsley boiled potatoes or egg noodles.

Serves 4

2 pounds veal stew meat, cut into 1½-inch pieces

1 teaspoon salt

Freshly ground black pepper

1 tablespoon flour

4 tablespoons unsalted butter

4 cups pitted sour cherries

¼ cup water

2 tablespoons honey

1 cinnamon stick

1 whole green cardamom pod

1 bay leaf

1 tablespoon minced fresh parsley

Place the veal in a bowl and sprinkle it with the salt and pepper. Dust with the flour. Melt the butter in a 3-quart ovenproof casserole and brown the meat on all sides, in two batches. Set aside.

Preheat the oven to 350°F. Place the cherries in a medium saucepan and stir in the water, honey, cinnamon stick, cardamom, and bay leaf. Cover the pan and simmer for 10 minutes.

Pour the cherry mixture over the browned veal. Cover the casserole and bring to a boil over low heat on the stove, then transfer the casserole to the oven. Braise the veal for 1½ to 2 hours, until tender.

Transfer the stew to a serving dish and sprinkle with the parsley. Serve hot.

Braised Pork with Kvass and Honey

Свинина, тушёная в квасе с мёдом

This stew epitomizes the simple perfection of dishes cooked slowly in the Russian stove (see page 243). Stovetops weren't introduced into Russia until the eighteenth century, and even well into the twentieth century rural Russians continued to rely on a masonry stove for all of their cooking and baking. Meat, for those who could afford it, wasn't butchered into small cuts, and vegetables weren't sautéed as a requisite first step toward developing flavor, as the French do with *mirepoix* or the Italians do with *sofrito*. Instead, the raw ingredients were placed together in an earthenware or cast-iron pot and allowed to simmer for hours at gentle heat. For this recipe, a stainless-steel Dutch oven works fine, but if you use a heavy cast-iron or earthenware pot, the stew will develop an even richer flavor.

I like to braise the meat for a full four hours, until it is meltingly tender, and serve it with buckwheat and sour pickles on the side. If you want to serve the meat cold, as many Russians do, it's best to remove it from the oven sooner, for ease of slicing.

Serves 6

5 pounds boneless pork shoulder roast (pork butt), rolled and tied

Salt

Freshly ground black pepper

2 large onions, peeled and sliced

1 whole head of garlic

4½ cups Kvass (page 92)

¼ cup honey

1 teaspoon caraway seed

1 large bay leaf

Rub the pork liberally with salt and pepper and place it, fat-side up, in a 5-quart ovenproof casserole with lid. Strew the onions around the meat. Remove the papery outer skin from the garlic and cut about ½ inch off the top to reveal the cloves. Set the garlic head in the casserole, cut-side up. In a small saucepan, heat ¼ cup of the kvass with the honey, stirring until the honey dissolves. Pour this mixture over the meat, then add the remaining kvass, along with the caraway and bay leaf. Cover and allow the pork to marinate overnight in the refrigerator.

Take the pork out of the refrigerator about 2 hours before baking to bring it to room temperature. When ready to cook, preheat the oven to 325°F. Braise the pork, covered, for 3½ to 4 hours, until very tender.

Slice the pork and serve topped with the onions and pan juice.

Braised Duck with Turnips

Утка, тушёная с репой

The beauty of this dish lies in its minimalism, which highlights the full-bodied flavor of duck and turnips. The combination is so flavorful that it's hard to believe the recipe relies on only four main ingredients. I like to serve this braise with parsley boiled potatoes to make sure that none of the savory broth goes to waste.

Serves 2 to 3

One 4-pound duck, cut into six pieces

Salt

Freshly ground black pepper

2 medium onions, finely chopped

2 large turnips (1½ pounds), peeled and cut into ½-inch cubes

8 large garlic cloves

1 bay leaf

2 cups water

Prick the skin of the duck all over with a sharp knife and sprinkle the pieces with salt and pepper. Place them, skin-side down, in a 12-inch cast-iron skillet and cook over medium heat until browned, turning once, about 3 minutes on each side.

Remove the duck to a plate and pour off all but 2 tablespoons of the fat. Add the onions, turnips, and garlic to the skillet. Season with ½ teaspoon salt and ½ teaspoon pepper. Cook over medium-low heat until golden, stirring occasionally, 12 to 15 minutes.

Preheat the oven to 375°F. Nestle the duck pieces, skin-side up, among the vegetables in the skillet and tuck in the bay leaf. Pour in the water and bring the liquid to a boil over medium-high heat, then transfer the skillet to the preheated oven. Bake, uncovered, for 1 hour, until the vegetables are tender and the duck is nicely browned. Serve directly from the skillet.

THE RUSSIAN STOVE

There's a lot of talk these days about *hygge*, a Danish word that describes an ineffable feeling of comfort arising from warmth, nourishment, and companionship, especially when the weather is cold outside. For Russians, that feeling is epitomized not by a word but by an object: the traditional Russian masonry stove. So dear is the stove to Russians that in the past it was affectionately referred to as "our own mother"—not such a stretch when you think about it, since the stove gives birth to just about every traditional dish in the Russian culinary repertoire.

Russian folktales use the stove to evoke a character's laziness, though these simple folk usually end up reaping riches for their guilelessness and good nature. One beloved fool, Emelya, is so indolent that when he's ordered to appear before the tsar, he refuses to leave his perch atop the stove and commands it to carry him to the palace—which it does, knocking people down right and left as it zooms along. Another well-loved tale describes Ilya Muromets, a legendary hero from Russian epic poetry. Dreadfully ill as a child, Ilya lies on the stove, unable to walk, for thirty-three years. Then a miracle occurs. Not only can Ilya suddenly walk, he also gains superhero powers that enable him to kill the monster Nightingale the Robber, whose powerful song echoes throughout the forest, causing passersby to die.

But back to the stove. If you've never seen a traditional Russian stove, it may be hard to imagine lying on one, especially for thirty-three years. But at the rear of the stove, high above the floor, is a ledge built into the masonry that surrounds the oven. Because heat rises, this *lezhanka* (from the verb "to lie") was the warmest spot in the peasant cottage. The elderly and infirm slept there, and kids cuddled there with their grandparents to listen to fairy tales during the long winter nights. The stoves were built of bricks or stone rubble, then covered with a thick layer of clay and usually whitewashed. They provided storage areas for food, kitchen equipment, and wood, as well as niches for drying mittens and herbs—which meant they were massive enough to occupy a good quarter of the typical cottage's living space. Beyond the stove's practical uses, it played a highly symbolic role in Russian life, demarcating the traditional female and male spheres, with the cooking area to the left of the hearth and the icon-dominated "beautiful corner" to its right.

The design of the stove determined the very nature of Russian cuisine: many of Russia's most typical dishes result from the stove's ability to retain heat. Breads, pies, and even pancakes (Russia's famous *bliny*) were placed in the oven when the temperature was hot and embers still glowed at the back of the hearth. As the heat began to diminish, the oven welcomed other dishes: porridges that baked up crusty on top and creamy within, followed by soups, stews, and vegetables cooked slowly in earthenware or iron pots. For this low-and-slow method, known as *tomlenie*—a cross between braising and steaming—raw ingredients were layered in the pot with as little liquid as possible. The tightly covered pots kept both aromas and vitamins intact as the slow cooking imparted a deep, mellow flavor. In the last stage, when the oven was barely warm, it was just right for culturing dairy products and drying mushrooms and berries.

The stove was important in other ways, too. When planks were set up along the hot interior walls of the oven and water sprinkled on to create steam, the stove became a makeshift sauna. One at a time, cottagers crawled in. Some Russians took a "bread bath," believed to have healing powers, by using diluted kvass instead of water to create the steam. In some regions of Russia, women crawled into the huge cavity to give birth, because it was the most sterile place in the cottage. Not surprisingly, given its importance for sustenance, heat, and health, the stove gave rise to superstitions, and because fire represents life and strength, the stove was believed to hold magical powers, besides the alchemy of transforming dough into bread. Mothers would sometimes place sick infants on bread peels and ritually insert them three times into the oven in hopes of curing them. And beware disturbing the capricious house spirit, the *domovoi*, who resided beneath or behind the stove, lest misfortune befall. Even as the stove symbolized nurturance and life, the *domovoi* hinted at its potentially destructive powers. The chimney, which released smoke and ashes, was seen as a conduit between living and dead, so great care was taken to treat the stove with respect, for fear of tempting otherworldly spirits to enter the cottage and invade earthly life. Baba Yaga, the hideous witch of Russian folklore, is first encountered lolling on the stove, her nose grown all the way to the ceiling.

The Russian stove was, in its enormous way, quite efficient, providing all the heat, cooking all the food, helping to heal the sick, and contributing a source of beauty and pride, especially in more prosperous households where glazed tiles decorated the surface. And yet, in the wild post-Soviet years of the 1990s, hundreds of dacha owners demolished old stoves that had survived for centuries. Younger modern Russians wanted to make room for flat-screen TVs, not realizing that these new status symbols of village life would lose their novelty and fail to offer the comfort and warmth of the stoves they replaced. Now, thankfully, traditional Russian stoves are prized again. Skilled masons have rediscovered the art of constructing smokeless stoves and are installing them in country houses. Even more telling is the stoves' popularity in Russia's cities. Although an urban apartment couldn't begin to accommodate a massive Russian stove, the ovens have become centerpieces of several of Moscow's most fashionable restaurants whose food revolves around wood-fired cooking. Thanks to two of these restaurants, Severyane ("Northerners") and Uhvat ("Baking Peel"), the twenty-first-century Russian stove has even become a brand.

Beef Stew with Horseradish

Жаркое с хреном

Horseradish and mustard—what better ingredients to flavor a Russian-style stew? As in the recipe for Braised Cod with Horseradish (page 235), don't be alarmed at the large amount of horseradish called for here. The fiery root mellows as soon as it hits the hot stew, retaining its flavor but giving up its bite and allowing the underlying sweetness of the onions and carrots to come through. I like to serve this rustic dish with Potatoes and Mushrooms Baked in a Pot (page 196).

Serves 4

3 tablespoons
unsalted butter

2 large onions, chopped

3 carrots, peeled and
sliced into ½-inch rounds

2 pounds beef chuck, cut
into 1½-inch pieces

1¼ teaspoons salt

Freshly ground
black pepper

3 large garlic cloves,
minced

1 thick slice (3 ounces)
sourdough rye bread,
crust removed, finely
crumbled

3 cups water

1 bay leaf

6 juniper berries

1 cup freshly grated
horseradish (from a
peeled 4-ounce piece)

4 teaspoons Russian-Style
Mustard (facing page) or
other strong mustard

¼ cup minced
fresh parsley

¼ cup minced fresh dill

Melt the butter in a large stockpot. Add the onions and carrots and sauté over medium-low heat for 10 to 12 minutes, until softened. Stir in the meat and season well with the salt and pepper, then add the garlic and cook until the meat begins to brown, another 8 minutes or so. Stir in the bread crumbs, mixing well. Add the water, bay leaf, and juniper berries. Bring to a boil, then lower the heat and simmer, partially covered, until the meat is just tender, 1¼ hours.

Remove the lid from the pot and increase the heat to medium-low. Cook the stew uncovered for 15 minutes more, until the liquid has thickened slightly.

Stir in the horseradish along with the mustard, parsley, and dill. Turn off the heat and let the stew sit, covered, for 5 minutes. Taste for seasoning and serve hot.

RUSSIAN-STYLE MUSTARD

Горчица

Makes about ½ cup

⅔ cup brown mustard seeds

1 teaspoon salt

½ cup boiling water

2 tablespoons cider vinegar

2 tablespoons cold-pressed sunflower oil

We may think of English or French mustard as the gold (or yellow) standard, but Russia was once famous throughout Europe for its mustard seed grown in the village of Sarepta on the Volga River. Russian mustard is brown, made from the pungent seeds of *Brassica juncea*. Its name derives from the word *gorchit'*, which means "to taste bitter," although the innate bitterness of the seeds is tempered by allowing the prepared mustard to mellow for a few days before using, so plan accordingly.

Grind the mustard seeds to a fine powder in a coffee mill or mini food processor. Transfer the powder to a bowl, stir in the salt, then add the boiling water and mix well. Stir in the vinegar and oil. Cover the bowl and leave the mustard to sit for 3 days at room temperature for the flavors to meld. Store in the refrigerator for up to several months.

Roast Lamb with Kasha

Баранья нога, фаршированная кашей

Once you've tried roasting lamb with kasha, you may never turn to potatoes again. The lamb juices make the buckwheat soft and savory, its flavor beautifully complementing the tender meat. Russians usually stuff the groats into a breast of lamb, but that's a laborious process, and the breast doesn't yield much meat. So I've riffed on the classic recipe, using a small butterflied leg of lamb instead, just right for four people.

Serves 4

1 large onion, finely chopped

2 tablespoons unsalted butter

1 teaspoon salt

Freshly ground black pepper

1 cup water

½ cup coarse-cut buckwheat groats

¼ cup finely chopped fresh parsley

1 small butterflied leg of lamb (about 2 pounds)

Vegetable oil, for the pan

In a medium skillet, sauté the onion in the butter over low heat until golden, 8 to 10 minutes. Season it with ¼ teaspoon of the salt and pepper. Set aside.

Bring the water to a boil with ¼ teaspoon salt, then add the buckwheat. Simmer, covered, for 12 to 15 minutes, until the water has been absorbed. Stir in the sautéed onion and the parsley.

Preheat the oven to 400°F. Cut five 10-inch lengths of kitchen twine and set them aside. Open the lamb up to lie flat and pound it with a mallet to ½ inch thickness. Sprinkle the lamb with the remaining ½ teaspoon salt and pepper to taste. Spread about two-thirds of the buckwheat mixture over the meat, pressing down on it and leaving a 1-inch border. Bring the edges of the two long sides of the lamb up to meet in the center. Pinching the edges with the fingers of one hand, tie the meat with the twine in five places to enclose most of the filling. (It may help to have an extra set of hands here.) Don't worry if some spills out.

Lightly grease a small roasting pan and set the lamb in it. Spoon the remaining buckwheat around the meat. For rare lamb, roast for about 18 minutes per pound, until the meat registers 135°F on an instant-read thermometer. (If you want the meat to be medium-rare, roast for about 20 minutes per pound, until it reaches 140°F.)

Remove the meat from the oven and allow it to sit for 10 minutes before carving into ½-inch slices. Spoon the buckwheat onto a serving platter and top with the sliced lamb. Serve immediately.

Brine-Braised Giblets

Куриные желудки в рассоле

When I was little, whenever we had roast chicken, I begged for the *pupik*, which my grandmother said was the belly button. I never stopped to think whether chickens could actually have belly buttons—it was simply the part I loved most. Many years later, when I started studying Russian, I learned that the word for "belly button" is *pupok*! So there was the linguistic connection, even if the physiology remained suspect.

I wish we had a different word for "gizzards," which sounds as tough and gnarly as, well, a chicken's stomach, which is what they are. Both the Russian *pupok* and Yiddish *pupik* sound alliterative and playful, something you might want to eat even if you didn't know what it was. Please don't let the word "gizzards" deter you from making this recipe. When braised in a tart brine, gizzards are truly delectable! This is an easy dish to serve guests, as it can be made a day in advance and reheated. Cooked barley is a perfect side to soak up the rich sauce.

Serves 4

1 pound chicken gizzards

2 tablespoons unsalted butter

1 medium onion, finely chopped

2 cloves garlic, minced

¼ teaspoon salt

Freshly ground black pepper

1¼ cups pickle brine (from Half-Sour Dill Pickles [page 83], Alexandra's Sweet and Sour Cucumbers [page 57], or commercially fermented pickles such as Bubbies)

2 tablespoons sour cream

¼ cup finely chopped dill pickles, for garnish

2 tablespoons minced fresh dill, for garnish

2 tablespoons minced fresh chives, for garnish

Wash the gizzards well and remove any excess fat. Pat dry with paper towels.

Melt the butter in a medium saucepan. Add the onion and sauté over low heat until soft and golden but not brown, 5 to 7 minutes. Add the gizzards and garlic. Sprinkle with the salt and a few generous grinds of pepper. Cook over medium heat, stirring occasionally, until the gizzards are nicely browned and beginning to caramelize, about 10 minutes.

Pour in the pickle brine, cover the pan, and bring to a boil, then immediately lower the heat to simmer. Simmer gently for 45 minutes, until the gizzards are fork-tender.

With a slotted spoon, remove the gizzards from the broth and transfer them to a cutting board. Slice into ½-inch-thick pieces.

Stir the sour cream into the sauce, mixing well. Return the gizzards to the pan and stir to coat before transferring them to a serving dish. Garnish with the pickles and herbs.

Venison Meatballs with Roasted Celery Root and Mushrooms

Тефтели из оленины с запечённым корнем сельдерея и грибами

This meal is like a one-act play, with the elements of flavor, color, and texture magnificently concentrated on each plate. As with any performance, it takes careful timing to stage things right, but it's worth the effort. This dish is particularly welcome in the fall thanks to the warming, earthy celery root and mushrooms.

If you've never made venison meatballs before, you'll find them surprisingly light. The secret lies in handling the meat gently, so be sure to chill the bowl and blade of the food processor before using, and pulse the venison only briefly to grind. In a pinch, ground venison can be substituted for the shoulder steak (see Sources).

Makes about 30 meatballs, serves 6

Celery Root

1 celery root (about 1½ pounds), scrubbed

2 teaspoons vegetable oil

Meatballs

½ cup beef broth

½ cup grated fresh bread crumbs (see Notes)

1 pound venison (shoulder steak, trimmed of all silverskin), semi-frozen

¼ pound bacon, coarsely chopped (about 5 strips)

¼ teaspoon salt

Freshly ground black pepper

2 tablespoons minced fresh parsley

Fried Shallots

4 large shallots, peeled and very thinly sliced

¼ cup sunflower oil

Mushrooms

4 tablespoons unsalted butter

1 pound wild mushrooms or shiitakes, trimmed and sliced ½ inch thick

1 teaspoon salt

Freshly ground black pepper

¾ cup beef broth

¼ cup sour cream

2 tablespoons unsalted butter, cubed (optional)

3 tablespoons minced fresh parsley

A few hours before you're ready to make the meatballs, place the bowl and blade of a food processor in the refrigerator to chill. Reassemble the food processor just before you're ready to grind the meat.

To prepare the celery root, about 3 hours before serving, preheat the oven to 425°F. Slice about 1 inch off the top of the celery root and rub the root all over with the oil. Place it on a large square of aluminum foil, root-side down, and close the foil tightly. Roast until a knife slides easily through it, about 2½ hours.

Meanwhile, make the meatballs. In a shallow bowl, pour the broth over the bread crumbs and let sit for 5 minutes until the liquid has been absorbed.

Cut the semi-frozen meat into 1-inch cubes and immediately transfer the cubes to the bowl of the food processor. Pulse until

continued

the meat is coarsely ground, then add the chopped bacon and pulse the mixture until medium-fine. Be careful not to overprocess, or the meatballs will be tough.

Transfer the venison and bacon to a medium bowl and gently mix in the soaked bread crumbs, salt, pepper to taste, and parsley. Let the mixture sit in the refrigerator for at least 1 hour for the flavors to blend. Shape the meat mixture into 1½-inch meatballs, being careful not to compress them. (This step can be done well ahead of time. Just keep the meatballs chilled.)

To prepare the shallots, separate the shallot slices into rings. Heat the oil until very hot in a large nonstick pan. Drop in the shallots and cook over medium-high heat, stirring occasionally, until caramelized, about 6 minutes. Remove them from the pan with a slotted spoon and set aside, leaving the leftover oil in the pan.

Next, make the mushrooms. In a second large skillet, melt the butter. Add the mushrooms, season with the salt and pepper, and sauté over medium heat until the mushrooms acquire a sheen and are slightly browned, 8 to 10 minutes. (At this point, they can be set aside.) When ready to finish, whisk the broth and sour cream together in a small bowl. Heat the mushrooms gently and stir the sour cream mixture into the mushrooms. Simmer for a couple of minutes to blend the flavors.

Once the celery root is tender, cook the meatballs. Heat the nonstick pan over medium-high heat. When it is hot, add the meatballs and brown them over medium-low heat, turning with tongs to cook evenly on all sides. Be careful not to overcook—they will be done in just 6 minutes or so.

Place the celery root in the middle of a large platter. With a sturdy spoon, scoop around the edges of the cut top to loosen the roasted interior. If desired, drop in the butter cubes and stir to mix.

Arrange the mushrooms and their sauce around the celery root in six separate mounds. Fill the spaces between the mushrooms with the meatballs, five to a space. Spoon the fried shallots over the meatballs and sprinkle the 3 tablespoons parsley over everything to add color. Serve right away.

Notes

To make grated fresh bread crumbs, run a few slices of hardened bread against the large holes of a box grater. The result should be coarser than storebought crumbs and finer than hand-torn crumbs.

To substitute ground venison for the shoulder steak, simply grind the bacon to medium-fine in the food processor and mix it with the ground venison. Proceed as directed.

Beef in Aspic

Студень

Meat in aspic—whether beef, veal, pork, or chicken—stars on nearly every *zakuska* table, a shimmery prelude to the meal to come. It's also near mandatory for New Year's Eve. Just think of a richly flavored bone broth that's simmered for hours. Once it's been chilled and layered with meat (and sometimes hard-boiled eggs or carrots), the broth jells into sliceable portions.

Aspic goes by two names in Russian, *studen'* and *kholodets*, both words signaling that the dish has been chilled, though *studen'* most often refers to beef and *kholodets* to pork. Aspic is both resourceful—using collagen-rich parts that might otherwise go to waste—and extravagant in the amount of time needed to make it properly. Once prepared, it keeps for a long time. Hunters often carried some on their winter expeditions to energize themselves quickly with a protein-rich slice or be soothed by a warming broth after heating the aspic over a campfire.

Russians always serve *studen'* with a dollop of horseradish or a smear of hot mustard. I like to use beet horseradish for a spot of bright color.

Serves 12 to 16

2½ pounds calf's feet (2 feet), cleaned, split, and sawed into 1½-inch pieces by your butcher

8 cups cold water

1 pound boneless beef short ribs

1 medium onion, peeled but left whole

1 medium carrot, peeled

2½ teaspoons salt, plus more as needed

10 black peppercorns

5 allspice berries

2 large bay leaves

3 large cloves garlic, minced

½ teaspoon freshly ground black pepper

3 hard-boiled eggs, sliced

A few parsley leaves

Russian-Style Mustard (page 247), or horseradish, for serving

Place the calf's feet in a large stockpot with the water. Bring to a boil, skimming off any foam that rises to the surface. Simmer the feet, covered, for 1½ hours, then add the short ribs, onion, carrot, salt, peppercorns, allspice, and bay leaves and simmer for another 2½ hours, until the meat is tender.

Remove the pot from the heat and allow the broth to cool to room temperature. Refrigerate it for several hours or overnight, until a layer of fat has solidified on top. Scrape off and discard the fat, then return the pot to low heat and simmer, again skimming off any foam that rises to the surface. Strain the broth through a double layer of cheesecloth into a large heat-proof pitcher. You should have 2 quarts of liquid. Taste the broth and add more salt, if necessary. Stir the garlic into the warm broth.

Discard the onion, carrot, and calf's feet. Coarsely shred the short ribs, making sure to remove any fat, and set the meat aside. Pour half of the broth (4 cups) into a 9 by 13-inch glass baking dish and refrigerate until the broth has firmed up, about 1½ hours. Keep the remaining broth at room temperature. When

continued

Beef in Aspic, continued

the refrigerated broth has jelled, evenly distribute the shredded meat over it and season liberally with salt and the pepper. Pour the remaining broth over the meat. Arrange the hard-boiled eggs in a decorative pattern on top, nudging them slightly, if necessary, to submerge them in the broth. Tuck in the parsley leaves for color.

Refrigerate the dish for 1½ hours more, until the broth has fully set into aspic.

Serve the aspic well chilled, cut into squares. You can present it in the dish it was prepared in, but it looks more festive when the squares are arranged on a platter. (One stylish friend chills her aspic in shot glasses, which she passes with spoons at cocktail parties.) Be sure to offer Russian-Style Mustard or horseradish on the side.

PERFORMING
THE MEAL

It may come as a surprise that our typical American sequence of courses—
appetizer, soup or salad, entrée, and dessert—descends directly from the
medieval Russian style of table service. Although Peter the Great westernized
Russia, introducing foreign foods and compelling women to appear at the
table with men, one thing he didn't touch was the traditional Russian manner
of presenting a fancy meal. This practice contrasted greatly with the classical
French banquet, where French diners entered the room to find tables already
set with an artful array of dishes, many of them in fanciful trompe l'oeil. Each
course comprised dozens of dishes geometrically arranged on the table.
When one dish was removed, another immediately took its place so as not to
disturb the design. The table was dazzling, but eating the food may have been
less appealing. The display meant that hot foods were no longer hot, fats
were congealed, and the risk of food poisoning was real.

Russian service was the opposite. Diners were seated at tables devoid
of food. In medieval times, this meant that only salt and pepper cellars
and vinegar cruets appeared on the table. By the nineteenth century, such
sparseness had been replaced by lavish displays of flowers. The 1904 edition
of England's culinary bible, *Mrs Beeton's Book of Household Management*,
features a striking color lithograph of a table set à la russe, with flowers and
candelabra along its entire length. Dinner rolls couched in linen napkins are
the only visible food.

Once guests were seated, the performance began. Liveried waiters, often
one for each guest, paraded repeatedly into the room with platters held high,
displaying the food that would then be whisked off to the sideboard or kitchen
for individual plating. Chroniclers tell of a single huge sturgeon brought to
table by four dozen cooks struggling to hold the immense fish steady (a mature
beluga sturgeon can weigh up to 2,500 pounds). A pre-portioned individual
serving was then brought to each diner, a practice that entailed a huge number
of servants—something Russia was, until the liberation of the serfs in 1861,
never in short supply of.

Based on the journals of foreign visitors accustomed to the orderliness
and self-containment of a French-style meal, we can infer that Russian feasts
could be an ordeal. Diners found it confusing, and sometimes upsetting, not
to know how much food would appear at each meal. While the French style

made it easy to pace oneself, since all the food was laid out beforehand, the components of the Russian meal couldn't always be ascertained. But the Russian style of service delivered the food hot, since each dish was served at its peak of readiness.

This traditional feature of Russian dining survived Peter's reforms, though little could the tsar anticipate that within a hundred years, service à la russe would be introduced to Europe, and later America—a notable example of cross-fertilization in the other direction. Charles Dickens was one of the first to introduce the Russian manner of dining to English society, where it became all the rage. The Russian style met with real resistance only in France. Yet by the time of Escoffier at the end of the nineteenth century, the Russian style of service was fully entrenched throughout Europe, even in France. It's easy to understand why. Despite the bedazzlement of the classical French table, diners are ultimately better cared for with food that is hot and presented in sequence in individual portions, rather than having to reach for delicacies that have congealed in their sauces.

9

SWEETS

Sour Cream Honey Cake

Сметанник

Sour cream and honey, two of Russia's most iconic foods, are lusciously paired in this honey cake, with billows of sour cream complementing the cake's chewy texture. The recipe is courtesy of Svetlana Kozeiko, the brilliantly inventive chef of Tsarskaya Okhota (The Royal Hunt) in Murmansk. This cake is ideal for entertaining, since it has to be chilled before slicing. I usually make it the morning of a dinner party and refrigerate it all day. The longer you hold the cake, the softer it becomes, so leftovers make an indulgent breakfast. To whip the frosting into swirling clouds, you'll need to seek out high-fat sour cream.

Serves 8

4 tablespoons unsalted butter

3 tablespoons honey

1 teaspoon baking soda

1 egg

½ cup granulated sugar

1¾ cups flour

1½ cups (12 ounces) high-fat sour cream (see Sources)

⅔ cup confectioners' sugar

In a small saucepan, heat the butter and honey over low heat until the butter melts. Stir in the baking soda. The mixture will almost immediately bubble up, foam, and turn light in color. Remove the pan from the heat and leave the mixture to cool for about 15 minutes.

Meanwhile, crack the egg into a bowl and whisk it with the granulated sugar for a few minutes, until light. Stir in the cooled butter mixture, then sift the flour directly into the bowl, stirring to make a very soft dough. Cover the bowl with plastic wrap and leave to rest for 20 minutes. The dough will firm up and become nicely pliable.

While the dough is resting, beat the sour cream and confectioners' sugar in a stand mixer on high speed for 5 minutes, until stiff peaks form. Place in the refrigerator to chill for 1 hour.

When the dough has finished resting, preheat the oven to 350°F. Line a 12 by 17-inch baking pan with parchment paper. Divide the dough into four pieces (each will weigh just under 4 ounces). Rinse your hands quickly with cold water and pat each piece out on the parchment into 5 by 5-inch squares about ⅛ inch thick, 1 inch apart. Bake the squares for 8 to 10 minutes, until slightly puffed and golden. If the squares have spread slightly so that the edges are touching, use a sharp paring knife to separate them. Place the baking pan on a rack to cool. (If you don't plan to assemble the cake right away, store the cooled squares in an airtight container so they don't dry out.)

Place one cake square on a serving plate and spread it with one-quarter of the sour cream filling. Top with another cake square and continue to layer the cake and filling, ending with filling on top. Make decorative swirls with the filling but don't frost the sides of the cake.

Carefully transfer the cake to the refrigerator. Chill for at least 4 hours to firm up before slicing.

THE
SAMOVAR

When talking about Russian culture and cuisine with my students, I sometimes play a speed association game to break the ice. What, I ask, do you think of when I say "Russia"—besides Putin and oligarchs, that is? "Vodka!" "Caviar!" come the fast and furious answers. Then someone inevitably calls out "Samovar!" This response always pleases me, for if there's any quintessential symbol of Russian dining, it's this shiny brass urn for serving tea. Simultaneously a tangible object of beauty and a metaphor for well-being, the samovar, hissing with steam in its foot-and-a-half-high glory, stands ever ready to provide guests a restorative cup of hot tea, a symbol of Russian hospitality.

And yet, surprisingly enough, the samovar is a fairly modern vessel. Samovars became widespread only in the late nineteenth century, when the price of tea dropped and the beverage became affordable to the larger population. Before that, ever since being introduced from China in the early seventeenth century, tea had been exclusively enjoyed by the wealthy.

The word *samovar* in Russian means "self-boiler," which perfectly describes its purpose—to heat water for tea. The tea itself is brewed very strong in a small teapot that sits within a ring atop the urn. This ingenious method allows each person to make a cup of fresh tea precisely to her liking—strong, medium, or weak, depending on how much hot water she adds from the samovar's spigot.

The origins of the samovar's design are murky, and there's plenty of debate as to whether it arrived in Russia from East or West. Was the prototype the Mongolian hot pot or Dutch urns that had taps rather than spouts? Could the forerunners be Byzantine urns or European fountains for cooling wine? In any case, the Russians developed a useful object that became very much their own. The body of the urn contains a wide central tube that is filled with fuel—charcoal, pinecones, twigs, or hot coals plucked from the great masonry stove. Water, poured around the tube, heats up quickly, steaming and hissing, a sound that is joyous to Russian ears. If the samovar has a design defect, it's that the burning fuel produces smoke. Outdoors, that's no problem, making the samovar a highlight of dacha life in the summer, when it's used in the open air. For indoor use, though, well-to-do families had a metal pipe extension that fit onto the stove; it carried the smoke into the flue and out of the house. So-called "white cottages" with flues were a lot healthier than the sooty, fume-filled "black cottages" that the majority of poor peasants lived in. Even so, the samovar represented such an object of prestige that the smoke it produced was deemed worth it.

Grand houses in the past had a special table devoted to the samovar, where the vessel often stood on a matching brass tray to catch any drips from the spigot. Guests were offered an abundant spread resembling an English high tea. But equally for rich and for poor, the samovar signals comfort, and tea is now more often served with sweets: berry pies, crumbly cookies, the ethereal apple confection known as *pastila*, multilayered tortes spread with whipped cream or icing—or at the very least with syrupy preserves on the side, spooned onto tiny glass dishes. The preserves are enjoyed between sips of tea, although some drinkers stir them right into the cup.

These days, most people use electric samovars or simply put a kettle of water on to boil, though they always prepare strongly brewed tea beforehand and add water to taste. But no matter the vessel used, in true Russian style, tea should be served with each cup filled to the absolute brim, to ensure that one's life will be equally full.

Bird-Cherry Cake

Торт из черёмуховой муки

I couldn't resist including this recipe, even though bird-cherry flour is a challenge to find. This cake is spectacular, with an extraordinary texture and taste—a slight crunch and a flavor of almonds and cherries. Though it looks like every child's dream of a perfect birthday cake, it has a perfectly grown-up taste that hovers around bitter.

What, you may ask, is a bird cherry? It's a handsome tree, and sometimes a bush, known by its scientific name of *Prunus padus*. In Siberia, where it grows wild, the bird cherry is considered a harbinger of spring. Locals believe that when the tree blooms in May, its gorgeous white flowers presage another spell of cold weather before true spring arrives. The berries ripen in late summer, at which point they are dried and then ground into a dark mahogany–colored flour. The flour can be sieved multiple times to remove the last vestiges of the pips, but I like the less-processed flours that contribute an intriguing crunch.

Because bird-cherry flour is made from fruit, it is gluten-free. It is also caffeine-free, which is why it's sometimes used as a coffee substitute. To make a cake that will rise, you need to add some wheat flour—I use as little as possible to keep the cherry flavor front and center. The hot pink lingonberry cream is gorgeous against the chocolate-brown cake layers, but if you don't have lingonberries on hand or don't want to whip sour cream, you can simply spread regular whipped cream between the layers. Or try spreading on some cherry jam before layering with the whipped cream.

The cake should be chilled for several hours for ease of slicing. As it chills and the filling permeates the layers, it becomes even more moist. The sweet spot for me is six hours in the refrigerator. I've been known to eat leftovers of this cake very happily for breakfast and again for lunch.

Serves 10 to 12

1½ cups bird-cherry flour (see Sources)

1 cup whole milk

1½ cups all-purpose flour

1 teaspoon baking soda

1 cup sour cream

2 eggs

1½ cups granulated sugar

Unsalted butter, for the pans

Lingonberry Cream

1¾ cups frozen lingonberries, thawed, plus a few frozen lingonberries for garnish

2 teaspoons unflavored gelatin

3 tablespoons cold water

1½ cups (12 ounces) high-fat sour cream (see Sources)

1 cup confectioners' sugar

Place the bird-cherry flour in a bowl. In a small saucepan, heat the milk to just below boiling and pour it over the flour, stirring to mix well. You'll end up with a thick, aromatic paste. Let it sit for 1 hour.

In a small bowl, mix together the all-purpose flour and baking soda. Set aside.

Beat the sour cream into the bird-cherry flour paste just until incorporated. In a large bowl, beat the eggs with the granulated sugar until light. Add the bird-cherry batter and mix well. Gently stir in the all-purpose flour mixture.

Preheat the oven to 350°F. Butter two 9-inch cake pans and line the bottoms with parchment paper. Butter the parchment and the sides of the pans. Pour half the batter into each pan and smooth the tops. Bake for 30 minutes, until a cake tester comes out clean. Cool the layers in the pans for 10 minutes, then turn out onto racks to finish cooling.

While the cake layers are baking, prepare the lingonberry cream. Set aside ⅓ cup of the berries. Puree the remaining berries in a blender.

In a small saucepan, sprinkle the gelatin over the cold water. Let stand for 1 minute until it's absorbed, then heat gently until the gelatin dissolves, about 30 seconds. Cool slightly.

Beat the sour cream in a stand mixer on high speed, gradually adding the confectioners' sugar, for 3 minutes. Beat in the pureed lingonberries and the gelatin, adding the gelatin in a steady stream. Continue to beat the cream for 3 minutes more, until soft peaks form. Fold in the reserved whole lingonberries. Place the lingonberry cream in the refrigerator for 1 hour to firm up.

When ready to assemble the cake, cut each layer in half horizontally. Place the bottom layer on a serving plate, cut-side up, and spread with one-quarter of the lingonberry cream. Top with another cake round, cut-side up, and continue to layer the cake and lingonberry cream. Place the top layer cut-side down and spread it with the remaining cream. I like to let the cream drip decoratively down the sides of the cake.

Chill the cake in the refrigerator for at least 4 hours before serving. Decorate with frozen lingonberries or chocolate shavings, if desired.

Sasha's Grated Apple Cake

Пирог насыпной яблочный

My friend Sasha baked this cake in celebration of our visit to his tiny village south of Moscow. He calls it "dry" apple cake because it actually has no batter. The cake is super easy to make—just sprinkle the dry ingredients between layers of grated apples, which you don't even have to peel. The secret to its special texture is farina, which we know more commonly as Cream of Wheat. The apples bake down into a soft filling punctuated with chewy bits of dried apple and a slight graininess from the farina.

You can adjust the amount of sugar to your taste. For me, it depends on my mood—sometimes I like the cake tart, with some pucker; other times I prefer a sweeter cake. And although it's not à la russe, I can recommend serving this cake à la mode, with vanilla or caramel ice cream.

Serves 8

6 tablespoons unsalted butter, cut into tiny bits, plus more for the pan

¾ cup flour

½ cup fine farina or Cream of Wheat (not instant)

6 to 8 tablespoons sugar

1 teaspoon baking powder

½ teaspoon ground cardamom

Pinch of salt

1½ pounds (4 to 5) tart apples, such as Granny Smith, halved and cored (do not peel)

2 tablespoons freshly squeezed lemon juice

¾ cup finely chopped dried apples

Preheat the oven to 400°F. Lightly butter an 8-inch springform pan.

In a small bowl, mix together the flour, farina, sugar, baking powder, cardamom, and salt. Set aside.

Coarsely grate the apples. This is most easily done in a food processor with the grating attachment; you can also use the large holes on a box grater. Transfer the apples to a bowl. Stir in the lemon juice to mix well, then stir in the dried apples.

Evenly sprinkle one-third of the flour mixture over the bottom of the springform pan. Top with half of the apples, then cover with half of the remaining flour mixture. Spoon on the remaining apples and cover them with the last of the flour mixture.

Scatter the bits of butter evenly over the top, being careful to cover the entire surface so you don't end up with dry patches. Place the cake in the oven, then immediately lower the heat to 350°F and bake for 1 hour, until golden. Let cool slightly on a rack, then remove the outer ring of the pan. Serve slightly warm or at room temperature, cut into wedges.

Black Currant Cheesecake

Творожный пирог с чёрной смородиной

This deep-purple cake is my idea of heaven. The consistency is lighter than that of New York–style cheesecake, and the crust is tender and buttery. The cake tastes best at room temperature, so if you have any left over, remove it from the fridge about half an hour before serving.

Serves 8

½ cup (1 stick) unsalted butter, at room temperature, plus more for the pan

⅓ cup sugar

1 teaspoon vanilla extract

2 egg yolks

Pinch of salt

1 cup flour

Filling

¾ pound (packed 2 cups) farmer's cheese, homemade (page 79) or store-bought

½ cup plus 3 tablespoons sugar

1 egg, separated

1 teaspoon potato starch

2 cups fresh or frozen black currants

In a medium bowl, cream the butter. Beat in the sugar, vanilla, egg yolks, and salt. Stir in the flour, mixing only until the dough holds together.

Butter an 8-inch springform pan. Scrape the dough into the pan and, using well-floured hands, pat it evenly over the bottom of the pan and 1½ inches up the sides. Chill the dough in the pan for at least ½ hour while you make the filling, or up to overnight.

Preheat the oven to 375°F.

To make the filling, place the farmer's cheese and the ½ cup sugar in a large bowl and mix well. Stir in the egg yolk, then add the potato starch. Beat well with a wooden spoon.

Measure out ½ cup of the black currants, place them in a small bowl, and sprinkle with 1 tablespoon of the sugar. Set aside. Place the remaining berries in a blender along with the remaining 2 tablespoons sugar and puree.

Pour the puree into the farmer's cheese mixture and either blend well or, for a ribboned effect, stir the puree through the cheese with a spatula. Whip the egg white until soft peaks form, then fold it into the cheese mixture.

Gently scrape the mixture into the prepared crust, smoothing the top. Bake for 1 hour, until the filling is puffy. Cool the cake on a rack. When ready to serve, remove the sides of the springform and place the cake on a platter. Spoon the reserved black currants decoratively over the top.

Pear Charlotte

Шарлотка с грушами

The charlotte is an old-fashioned dessert that deserves resurrection. The earliest versions were a frugal French method for using up stale bread. A deep mold was lined with bread slices and filled with stewed apples before being baked into a hearty pudding. The Russian nobility eagerly adopted the original French recipe along with the French name. During the Soviet years, a quick charlotte became popular. It called for simply pouring a batter of eggs mixed with equal proportions of flour and sugar over chopped raw apples, then baking the mixture into an airy cake—comfort food. Here I create a hybrid of the two charlottes, combining the cooked fruit of the classical dessert with a quickly made batter. I use honey for the taste and pears because I love them, but it's fine to use apples instead. The resulting charlotte is surprisingly light, like a fruit-filled sponge cake.

Serves 8 to 10

3 pounds Bartlett pears (about 6), firm but not hard

4 tablespoons unsalted butter, plus more for the pan

¼ cup honey

3 eggs

1 egg yolk

2 tablespoons sugar

Pinch of salt

1 cup flour

Peel the pears and cut them into quarters. With a sharp knife, remove the cores, then cut each quarter crosswise into ¼-inch slices.

Melt the butter in a 13-inch skillet and stir in the honey. When the mixture begins to bubble, add the pears, turning them with a wooden spoon to coat on all sides. Cook over high heat, stirring occasionally, for 12 to 15 minutes, until the pears have softened and most of the liquid has evaporated. The pears should still retain their shape. Remove from the heat and allow to cool for 30 minutes.

Preheat the oven to 350°F. Place a round of parchment paper on the bottom of a 9-inch springform pan. Butter the parchment and the sides of the pan.

Using a stand mixer, beat the eggs, egg yolk, sugar, and salt on high speed until pale and fluffy. Remove the bowl from the mixer stand and fold in the flour.

Turn the batter into the prepared pan and spread it evenly with a spatula. Using a slotted spoon, distribute the pears over the batter. Bake for 1 hour and 15 minutes, until nicely browned on top. It's best enjoyed within a few hours of baking.

CHARLOTTE RUSSE

No discussion of charlottes would be complete without mentioning the charlotte russe, or Russian charlotte. The great French chef Marie-Antoine Carême claimed this cold dessert as his invention in 1815. For a classical cold charlotte russe, the mold is lined with ladyfingers and filled with a Bavarian cream. It's sumptuous, highly caloric, and sweet. In the early twentieth century, charlotte russe became famous in its American iteration, a layer of sponge cake topped with whipped cream and a maraschino cherry. Often raspberry jam was spread between the cake and the cream. This version was a seasonal treat especially popular among New York City's Jewish population. Part of its delight was the way it was presented, in frilled cardboard cups that could be pushed up from the bottom as the whipped cream was consumed.

Baked Apples with Caramel Sauce and Puffed Buckwheat

Печёное яблоко с карамелью

I was initially concerned when I saw the name for this dessert, called "Last Year's Apple," at Moscow's restaurant Björn, since I can be very literal-minded. But our server assured me that the name was just a playful reminder of the bad old Soviet days. The apple did arrive on the plate wrinkled and wizened, as though it really had been stored for a year, but oh, the flavor! My presentation's a bit more photogenic, especially if you char the apple with a butane torch just before serving. I love the interplay of textures in each bite—toothsome baked apple, silky caramel sauce, and crunchy puffed buckwheat.

Serves 4

4 Golden Delicious apples, with stems intact

1 quart kefir

1 cup vegetable oil

½ cup whole buckwheat groats

1 cup sugar

½ cup heavy cream, at room temperature

2 tablespoons unsalted butter, cubed

Seeds scraped from ½ vanilla bean

½ cup hot water

In a bowl just wide enough to hold the apples upright, soak them in the kefir for 4 hours. There should be enough liquid to cover all but the very tops, but if not, there's no need to weight them down.

Meanwhile, you have plenty of time to pop the buckwheat. Heat the oil in a heavy saucepan over medium-high heat until hot. Test by flicking a few drops of water into the pan; they should sizzle right away. Dump the buckwheat into the pot and deep-fry it for 2 minutes, until it puffs and expands. Be careful not to burn it, which can happen in a flash. With a slotted spoon, scoop the puffed buckwheat onto paper towels in a single layer.

About half an hour before you're ready to bake the apples, make a caramel sauce. In a medium saucepan, melt the sugar over medium-low heat, stirring constantly, until it turns dark amber in color, 8 to 10 minutes. Slowly pour in the cream, whisking constantly, then stir in the butter and vanilla seeds. Simmer for 1 minute. Remove the pan from the heat and leave the caramel to cool slightly.

Preheat the oven to 350°F. Remove the apples from the kefir and rinse them. Place them upside down on a cutting board and core them from below, carving an opening about 1½ inches in diameter and leaving about ½ inch of apple at the stem end. Fill the cavities of the apples with the caramel sauce. The amount you need will depend on the size of the apple, but each apple will generally accommodate about 4 heaping teaspoons.

Place the apples, cored-side up, in an 8-inch square baking dish. Pour the hot water around

continued

them and tent loosely with aluminum foil. Bake the apples for 45 minutes, until they're tender but still holding their shape. Remove the pan from the oven and let the apples rest for 5 minutes, just till they're cool enough to handle.

Place a handful of puffed buckwheat on each plate. Carefully pick up each apple and invert it onto the buckwheat, stem-side up. The caramel will spill out onto the buckwheat. For dramatic effect, use a butane torch to decoratively char the top of the apples. Serve warm.

Notes

Both the puffed buckwheat and the caramel sauce can be made well in advance. Store the cooled buckwheat in an airtight jar at room temperature. The caramel sauce will keep in the refrigerator for several weeks. Simply reheat it gently to a pourable consistency when you're ready to bake the apples. The kefir can be reused after the apples have soaked in it.

Buckwheat Honey Ice Cream

Мороженое с гречишным мёдом

I can't get enough of this ice cream—it's that divine. Sadly, my cravings can never be immediately assuaged, since the custard base must be prepared a day in advance in order to chill thoroughly. Don't be tempted to use mild floral honey here. It's the dark buckwheat honey that makes the flavor so thrilling.

Makes 1 pint

1½ cups heavy cream

1½ cups whole milk

2 tablespoons sugar

⅛ teaspoon salt

1 vanilla bean

4 egg yolks

⅓ cup buckwheat honey

Place the cream, milk, sugar, and salt in a medium saucepan. Slit the vanilla bean lengthwise and scrape the seeds out into the cream. Add the pod and heat the mixture over low heat.

While the cream mixture is heating, combine the egg yolks in a small bowl. When bubbles begin to appear at the edges of the cream mixture, whisk about ½ cup of it into the egg yolks to temper them, whisking constantly. Pour the egg yolk mixture into the pan and continue to cook over low heat until the custard thickens slightly, 3 to 4 minutes. (It should coat the back of a spoon.)

Pour the custard into a bowl through a fine-mesh sieve to remove any lumps that may have formed. Stir in the honey, incorporating it well. Leave the custard to cool to room temperature before placing it in the refrigerator to chill for at least 8 hours.

Pour the custard into an ice-cream maker and churn according to the manufacturer's instructions. The ice cream keeps for a couple of weeks in the freezer, though it will begin to develop ice crystals after a few days.

Black Currant Ice Cream

Мороженое из чёрной смородины

This deep-violet ice cream is beautiful to behold, and because it leans more toward the tart than the sweet, it's a refreshing palate-cleanser after a rich meal.

Makes 1 pint

12 ounces (3 cups) black currants, fresh or frozen

1½ cups heavy cream, plus 2 tablespoons

½ cup sugar

1½ cups whole milk

Pinch of salt

4 egg yolks

Thaw the currants, if frozen. Place them in a medium saucepan along with any juice from the thawing. Add the 2 tablespoons heavy cream and 2 tablespoons of the sugar. Simmer over low heat, covered, for 5 minutes. Put the currants through a food mill to make a puree. Set aside.

In a medium saucepan, heat the remaining 1½ cups heavy cream with the milk, the remaining 6 tablespoons sugar, and the salt. While the mixture is heating, combine the egg yolks in a small bowl. When bubbles begin to appear at the edges of the cream mixture, whisk about ½ cup of it into the egg yolks to temper them, whisking constantly. Pour the egg yolk mixture into the pan and continue to cook over low heat until the custard thickens slightly, 3 to 4 minutes. (It should coat the back of a spoon.)

Pour the custard into a bowl through a fine-mesh sieve to remove any lumps that may have formed. Leave the custard to cool to room temperature. Stir the black currant puree into the custard, incorporating it well. Place the custard in the refrigerator to chill for at least 8 hours.

Pour the custard into an ice-cream maker and churn according to the manufacturer's instructions. The ice cream keeps for a few days in the freezer.

Arkhangelsk Gingerbread Cookies

Архангельские козули

Of all Russian gingerbreads (see page 280), Arkhangelsk cookies, or *kozuli*, are the most fanciful. Traditionally molded or cut into animal shapes and prodigiously decorated with white-frosted squiggles that recall snow or the Dvina River's frothy whitecaps, they're a genuine form of folk art. This excellent recipe was a gift from Svetlana Kornitskaya, an Arkhangelsk native with a deep knowledge of the region. She cherishes the scrap of paper on which her grandmother wrote out the recipe before dying. I've adapted it only slightly, using part honey in place of all sugar, and adding a little cardamom. Don't be alarmed at the loose consistency of the dough when it's first mixed—it firms up after a few hours in the refrigerator. And if you're in no hurry to eat these tempting cookies (as I always am), you can let the dough rest for two or three days for the flavors to meld.

Kozuli are enjoyed for their artistry and their taste, but in the past they also had ritual uses. Their animal shapes spelled good fortune, especially during winter-solstice celebrations, when mummers dressed in animal costumes—shaggy furs to resemble bears, or frightening masks crafted of birch bark—received the cookies in return for singing carols that wished their neighbors well in the coming year. Each family made sure to keep some cookies for themselves, to ensure good fortune in their own household. They also made sure not to eat them up right away, lest good fortune disappear with the cookies.

Unlike older forms of gingerbread, Arkhangelsk *kozuli* are a relatively modern invention, relying as they do on sugar and baking soda. Their rich, deep color is achieved by caramelizing the sugar before mixing it into the dough, or by adding some strongly brewed tea.

Makes 36 cookies

½ cup sugar

½ cup water

1 cup honey

5 tablespoons unsalted butter, melted

3 cups flour

Pinch of salt

½ teaspoon baking soda

½ teaspoon ground cinnamon

½ teaspoon ground cardamom

¼ teaspoon ground cloves

1 egg, lightly beaten

Icing

6 tablespoons sugar

2 tablespoons water

1 tablespoon egg white

¼ teaspoon distilled white vinegar

Food colorings (optional)

Place the sugar and water in a medium heavy saucepan. Bring to a boil and simmer over medium-high heat until the syrup turns pale amber in color, about 10 minutes. Be careful not to let it burn.

While the syrup is simmering, heat the honey in another saucepan until hot, then stir it into the sugar syrup. Beat in the melted butter.

In a large bowl, whisk together the flour, salt, baking soda, and spices. Pour in the sugar mixture, stirring vigorously. Before it's entirely incorporated, beat in the egg, and continue to beat until a soft, sticky dough forms. Refrigerate the dough for at least 4 hours or overnight, until it is firm.

When you're ready to bake the cookies, preheat the oven to 350°F. Line two baking sheets with parchment paper.

Divide the dough in half and shape it into two disks. Roll out each disk ¼ inch thick on a well-floured surface. (Don't be tempted to roll it out thinly—these cookies aren't meant to be crisp.) Cut out shapes with cookie cutters (I like to make horses and bears) and place the cookies on the prepared baking sheets. Press any leftover scraps of dough together, roll out the dough, and continue to make cookies until the dough is used up.

Bake the cookies for 12 to 14 minutes, until puffy and golden. Cool on the baking sheets for 3 minutes, then transfer to racks to finish cooling.

To make the icing, bring the sugar and water to a boil in a small saucepan over high heat. Continue to boil until a syrup forms, about 3 minutes. In a bowl, beat the egg white until stiff but not dry, then slowly pour in the syrup, beating constantly. Add the vinegar and continue to beat for a few minutes more, until the mixture has cooled. If you want to create intricate designs, allow the icing to firm up slightly before using.

Divide the icing among several small bowls and add just a drop of the desired food colorings. Transfer the icing to a pastry tube fitted with the smallest round tip, or into a small squeeze bottle, and pipe decorative designs onto the cookies. Allow the icing to dry for several hours before storing the cookies in an airtight container. They keep for several weeks at room temperature.

Note

Although white icing is traditional, modern bakers frequently apply multiple shades. Just use a light hand when adding food coloring, to stay true to the muted northern palette. And if you don't have the patience to decorate, plain gingerbread still makes a delicious treat.

GINGERBREAD

Gingerbread, one of Russia's oldest sweets, originally contained only rye flour, honey, and tart berry juice. Known as honey bread, it baked up into cakes so hard and long lasting that they eventually had to be softened in water (or later, tea) to be enjoyed. Around the twelfth century, when spice caravans made their way into Russia from the East, the cakes came to be called *pryaniki*, or spice cakes, richly flavored as they were with coriander, cardamom, ginger, cloves, cinnamon, nutmeg, and black pepper. As spices became more affordable, Russian bakers turned gingerbread into an art form, devising dozens of different varieties. They were so famous that at America's first World's Fair in Philadelphia in 1876—which featured Alexander Graham Bell's telephone and Thomas Edison's automated telegraph system—the Russian section included an extensive exhibition of gingerbreads.

Russian gingerbread is made by three different techiques, the oldest of which is molding by hand (*lepnye pryaniki*). The dough is shaped by hand into small three-dimensional cakes whose forms often represent animals, a holdover from pagan times. In northern Russia, "sun deer"—reindeer with antlers resembling the sun's rays—are especially popular, as are seals, which are believed to ensure a good catch of fish. Historically, these figures were baked and exchanged at the winter solstice to bring good fortune in the year ahead.

Stamped (*pechatnye*) *pryaniki*, made by pressing dough onto carved wooden forms that emboss the cake, are nearly as old as molded gingerbread. Boards unearthed from the twelfth century feature geometric and organic forms, as well as crosses. The designs could be highly ornate, depicting not just simple figures but also narrative scenes; later boards often included verbal greetings or wishes. Some large boards were fashioned so that up to eighty individual squares could be broken off and sold in sections. This type of sectionable gingerbread was also used to signal the end of a feast: "farewell" cookies were broken off and distributed to guests to let them know it was time to leave. Gingerbread boards are not only a significant form of folk art, they also offer an iconography of history, from the two-headed Imperial eagle to the Soviet hammer and sickle.

Silhouette (*siluetnye*) *pryaniki* are a modern variety, first mentioned in print only in the mid-nineteenth century. These cookies are cut out or traced in elaborate shapes and profusely embellished with icing. Although fairly recent in origin, the cookies nevertheless generate magical thinking. In December they're hung like ornaments to guarantee coming good fortune.

Within these three gingerbread genres lie many variations: wheat flour instead of rye; yeast or baking soda to lighten the dough; and flavorings such as candied orange rind, fennel seed, or raisins. The dough itself can be quick, chilled, boiled, or fermented, and the classic sweetener of honey can be replaced by sugar, either in granulated or syrup form. Most striking, though, is the degree to which all the different types of gingerbread remain local. My hosts in the tiny village of Kimzha marveled that the "black cake" they had only recently discovered—even though it had been made in the neighboring town of Mezen for more than a hundred years—called for sour cream, an addition they'd never considered.

The Kargopol region is famous for another local variation called *tetyory*—ropes of rye dough elaborately coiled into the shape of the sun or other symbolic forms. Unlike Arkhangelsk *kozuli*, these coiled cookies were usually made at the spring equinox, to summon the sun. The city of Tula, near Tolstoy's estate, lays claim to the most famous regional gingerbread, one so widespread that it's sold online and in Russian groceries in the United States. Tula gingerbread is a dense rectangular loaf sandwiched with thick jam, usually cherry or plum, and glazed with sugar over its surface design.

The Volga River town of Gorodets was once known not just for its large population of Old Believers (members of the Russian Orthodox Church who practice old forms of the liturgy) but also for the smell of honey that wafted from the large number of gingerbread factories there: until the end of the nineteenth century the town produced close to thirty different kinds of *pryaniki*, from bite-size to giant. The first Volga guidebook, published in 1838, noted that the fifty gingerbread manufactories once housed in Gorodets had diminished to nine. And yet, if the authors are to be believed, these nine factories produced an astonishing 360,000 pounds of gingerbread each year. The authors go on to describe individual gingerbreads weighing up to 36 pounds apiece that were sold at one of the wintertime fairs, when booths offering *pryaniki* were built right on the frozen river.

The residents of Rostov, on the Golden Ring north of Moscow, celebrated prenuptial activities with enormous gingerbread cakes that the groom presented to his bride. Up to three feet by three feet—their size depending on the groom's wealth—they were topped with molded gingerbread figures decorated with shimmering foil. A small mirror was placed in the center of the cake, which the bride kept as a talisman for a long and love-filled life.

Gingerbread pervaded many aspects of Russian life. A crowd-pleaser at harvest fairs was a game simply called "Gingerbread," whose goal was to see who could throw a cookie the farthest without breaking when it hit the ground. The prize? The *pryanik*, of course.

Gooseberry Mousse

Мусс из крыжовника и манки

This ethereal pudding will surprise and delight your guests. Surprise them because the secret ingredient is Cream of Wheat and delight them because it's absolutely delicious—an airy dessert with a subtle fruit flavor. It's healthy besides. For an especially pretty mousse, use pink gooseberries.

Serves 8

¾ pound fresh or frozen gooseberries (see Sources), preferably pink

1 cup water

⅓ cup sugar

6 tablespoons fine farina or Cream of Wheat (not instant)

¼ teaspoon finely grated lemon zest

If you're using frozen gooseberries, thaw them at room temperature.

In a medium saucepan, bring the gooseberries (including any juice from the thawing) and water to a boil. Lower the heat and simmer, covered, until soft, about 5 minutes. Transfer the mixture to a blender or the bowl of a food processor and puree. Strain the puree through a fine-mesh sieve into a 2-cup measuring cup. You should have about 2 cups; if you have less, add a little water to reach that amount.

Pour the strained puree into a clean saucepan and stir in the sugar. Bring to a boil and add the farina in a slow stream, whisking constantly so that it doesn't clump. Turn the heat to medium-low and cook, stirring, until the mixture thickens, 3 to 5 minutes. Remove the pan from the heat and transfer the mixture to the bowl of a stand mixer. Leave to cool for 15 minutes.

Beat the mixture on high speed until it doubles in volume and turns pale pink, about 10 minutes. Stir in the lemon zest and spoon the mousse into a bowl. Chill for at least 2 hours before serving.

Note
It's important to use finely ground farina so that the pudding remains light. If you can only find a coarser grind, just give it a whir in the food processor before using.

Rhubarb Pudding

Кисель из ревеня

Some years ago, New York City's Mount Sinai Hospital saw their immigrant patients, many of them Russians, failing to thrive due to the bland standardized diets they'd been prescribed by well-meaning nutritionists. I was asked to identify foods that might encourage the Russian population to eat. My immediate response was a quick fix: substitute *kisel'* for rubbery Jell-O and they'll eat it right up! This fruit pudding is rich with vitamins and very easy to digest. Most important of all, it's a taste of home—comfort food, plain and simple. And it tastes really good.

Kisel' is one of Russia's most ancient dishes. Originally made from oats or split peas, the pudding eventually came to be made with fruit. But it's not a sugary dessert. The name comes from the Russian word *kislyi*, or "sour," and a proper *kisel'* has a sparkling tartness. I like it best when barely thickened and soupy, but it's easy to increase the starch for a sturdier pudding.

Although just about any fruit can be turned into *kisel'*, I typically use rhubarb for its tang and also because it has a long history in Russia. A medicinal variety was prized for its dried roots—Catherine the Great's physicians are said to have given her a rhubarb cure after she fell ill from eating too many oysters. When the European market began clamoring for this miraculous plant, Russia became the middleman between the major supplier, China, and the West. Rhubarb was a lucrative commodity until the nineteenth century. At the height of the craze, in the mid-seventeenth century, it sold for three times the price of opium.

Serves 4

1 pound rhubarb, cut into 1-inch pieces (about 4 cups)

2½ cups plus 2 tablespoons cold water

5 tablespoons granulated sugar

1 vanilla bean (optional)

2 tablespoons potato starch or cornstarch (or more, for a thicker pudding)

Place the rhubarb in a medium saucepan along with the 2½ cups water, the sugar, and the vanilla bean (if using). Bring the mixture to a boil and simmer, uncovered, for 5 minutes. Remove the pan from the heat and allow the rhubarb to cool for 10 minutes.

Remove the vanilla bean, then pass the rhubarb through a food mill. Transfer the puree to a clean saucepan. (If you want the *kisel'* to be very clear, first pass the rhubarb puree through a fine-mesh strainer.)

Dissolve the potato starch in the remaining 2 tablespoons water. Bring the puree to a boil and stir in the starch mixture. Turn the heat to low and simmer for 3 minutes, stirring occasionally, until the rhubarb turns slightly thick and shiny. Transfer the pudding to a 1-quart serving bowl or, for a more elegant presentation, use four individual bowls. Cover with plastic wrap so a skin doesn't form, and chill in the refrigerator for a couple of hours before serving.

Black Bread Pudding with Apples

Пудинг из чёрного хлеба с яблоками

Leo Tolstoy's wife, Sofia, was a saint as well as a martyr. Besides caring for thirteen children, each day she turned her husband's messy scrawl into clean copy. In fact, she copied out *War and Peace* a full seven times. Sofia also took an interest in the kitchen, as we discover from the family cookbook she compiled with her brother Stepan. One recipe, for black bread pudding, is an elegant version of a frugal apple charlotte that makes use of stale bread crumbs. Sofia chops her apples finely, but I prefer to slice them to create a bit more texture in the filling. Although ice cream isn't traditional with this dessert, it's awfully good, especially when the ice cream is made with buckwheat honey (see page 276).

Serves 6 to 8

8 ounces stale black bread, preferably Borodinsky rye (see Sources)

1¼ pounds Granny Smith apples (about 5)

1 teaspoon unsalted butter

Fine dry bread crumbs, for the pan

¼ cup sugar

¼ to ½ teaspoon ground cinnamon

½ cup (1 stick) melted unsalted butter

Preheat the oven to 350°F. Remove the bread crusts and cut the bread into 1-inch chunks. Transfer to the bowl of a food processor and grind into coarse crumbs. You should have about 2 cups.

Peel and halve the apples. Remove the cores and cut the apples horizontally into ¼-inch slices.

Generously grease a 1½-quart charlotte mold with the 1 teaspoon butter and dust it with the fine bread crumbs. Place one-quarter of the apples in the mold and sprinkle with 1 tablespoon of the sugar and a little cinnamon. Top with ½ cup of the black bread crumbs and pour 2 tablespoons of the melted butter over them. Repeat with the remaining apples, sugar, cinnamon, black bread crumbs, and butter, making four layers in all. Bake, covered, for 1 hour and 30 minutes, until the apples are soft and the pudding holds its shape. Let cool for 30 minutes, then place a decorative plate over the top of the mold and invert the pudding onto it. Serve warm.

Apple Pastila

Яблочная пастила

Winter is the season that defines Russia for most of us. We remember Napoleon's retreat from Moscow or, more fondly, Doctor Zhivago and Lara in the frozen cottage. But Russians themselves celebrate early autumn, which is apple time and the "old wives' summer" of golden, sun-filled days. The apple confection known as *pastila* captures the essence of the Russian fall, and it's become something of an obsession for me. Classic *pastila* is an intensification of apples, with the pulp cooked down to a puree, then mixed with a little sugar and a bit of whipped egg white. When freshly made, *pastila* is ethereal, like a fragile honeycomb, with a deep, slightly tart flavor. For years I've tried to place it within the hierarchy of meringues that range from soft to crisp but have ultimately decided it deserves its own special standing.

Pastila isn't especially tricky to make—you just have to attend to its baking. That process usually takes six hours, although if the apples are particularly juicy, the *pastila* may take a little longer to firm up. In any case, convection heat is necessary to dry the apple puree sufficiently.

Makes about 36

1 pound Granny Smith apples (see Note)

6 tablespoons mild raw honey

1 egg white

Preheat the oven to 400°F. Line a baking sheet with parchment paper. Cut the apples in half and set them cut-side down on the prepared baking sheet. Bake for 18 to 20 minutes, until the apple halves are soft and begin to collapse.

Place a food mill over the bowl of a stand mixer and puree the apples. Discard the solids. Stir the honey into the puree and mix well. Chill the puree in the refrigerator for at least 1 hour and up to several days.

When you are ready to bake, set the bowl on the mixer stand and beat the puree on high speed until the mixture is airy and pale in color, about 8 minutes.

In a small bowl, whip the egg white until foamy, then add it to the puree. Beat on high speed until very light and fluffy and doubled in volume, another 8 minutes.

While the mixture is beating, preheat a convection oven to 200°F. Line a 10 by 15-inch jellyroll pan or rimmed baking sheet with parchment paper. Use a spatula to spread the mixture about 1 inch thick over the parchment paper, gently smoothing the top to distribute the mass evenly.

Place the pan in the convection oven and bake for 3 hours. Take the pan out of the oven and carefully lift the parchment holding the pastila from the pan. Place the parchment directly on the oven rack and continue to bake the pastila for 3 hours more.

Remove the pastila from the oven and invert it onto a large wooden cutting board or rimless baking sheet. Carefully peel off the parchment—it should come off easily. (If it sticks, return the pastila to the oven and bake for 30 minutes more.) Once you have peeled off the parchment, place the parchment on the kitchen counter and carefully invert the pastila onto it so that the crust side is up.

Cut the pastila into squares. It can be eaten right away or kept for several weeks at room temperature when stored airtight between layers of waxed paper. If it begins to hydrate and become a little sticky, use a knife dipped in cold water to cut it.

Note

The number of apples you need will vary, depending on their size. What's important is the weight of the apples in proportion to the honey and egg white, so aim for exactly 1 pound.

Variation

To make a pastila Napoleon, cut the pastila into 2-inch squares and sandwich the cut sides together with raspberry jam.

PASTILA

Pastila is one of Russia's oldest and most wondrous sweets, capturing the essence of autumn in a confection that balances sweet and tart, delighting the tongue without ever becoming cloying. In its original form, the confection was no more than fruit leather, a means of preserving the harvest by cooking tart, pectin-rich apples until soft, then sieving them into a puree that was smoothed into sheets and slowly air-dried. Over the centuries, *pastila* evolved into the ethereal confection it is today, lightened with beaten egg whites.

Pastila offers a wonderful example of culinary innovation. The earliest version—thin, rolled sheets of dried puree—easily kept for a year, till the next harvest. At some point, probably in the fourteenth century, cooks began to whip air into the puree by beating it before drying, a method credited to the medieval town of Kolomna to Moscow's southeast, which was renowned for its apple orchards. Honey was added to balance the apples' acidity. When, in the late eighteenth century, sugar became more widely available through the English maritime trade in Arkhangelsk, it began to replace honey as a sweetener. The next stage in *pastila*'s evolution occurred in the nineteenth century, when Amvrosy Prokhorov, a merchant from the town of Belyov, incorporated beaten egg whites into the puree to make the mixture even lighter. *Belyovskaya pastila*, with its melt-in-the mouth properties, soon became the gold standard.

At Kolomna's charming Museum of Pastila, you can see old-fashioned implements for making the confection—a mechanical contraption for peeling and coring, hair sieves, wooden frames for bedding the puree. Nothing went to waste in production. The apple peels and cores were saved to make vinegar, and any residual juice from straining the puree was mixed with sugar to boil down into hard candies. The process demanded both labor and skill. The puree had to be beaten until a stiff mound of foam stayed on the hand without dripping off. Artisans listened closely to the pureed mass as they beat it: if the foam wasn't firm enough, it seemed to squeak. Only when it was silent did they know it was ready.

Even more laborious and expensive was the delicate *muftovaya pastila*, named after the downy muffs aristocratic women used to keep their hands warm, and said to be Dostoevsky's favorite. To make this type of *pastila*, egg whites were added not to a chilled puree but to the baked apple puree while it was still hot. The mass was then beaten by hand for ten hours or more. Some sources claim that the lightest *pastila* was achieved only after forty-eight hours of beating. It's hard to imagine the number of serfs, working in shifts, required for such a protracted process.

No wonder that the traditional art of making *pastila* was lost during the industrialized Soviet era. Only in the past decade has *pastila* seen a revival, as old recipes are rediscovered and new ones are invented. I've traveled all over Russia in pursuit of the finest *pastila*. And I'm still searching for a nineteenth-century variety made with hops, touted as a hangover remedy.

Although it is tempting to connect the word *pastila* with the Latin root that gave rise to *pasta* and *paste*, a Slavonic etymology is much more likely—and much more evocative—deriving as it does from the word *postel'*, which means "bed"—a place where sheets have been smoothed out. *Pastila* is fruit puree that has been smoothed into sheets, into a bed of sorts, light enough to please a real princess.

My recipe draws on *pastila*'s evolution even as I depart from it. I tested this recipe many times, trying different apples, ingredients, and cooking methods, until hitting upon this version, a contemporary spin that hearkens back to honey instead of sugar and yet is as light as the "muffs" I tasted in Russia. Best of all, you don't have to whip the puree for forty-eight hours to attain a bed of clouds.

Easter Cheesecake

Пасха

The luscious cheesecake known as *paskha*, made from ingredients forbidden during the long six weeks of Lent, is a highlight of the Russian Easter table. In the pre-refrigeration past, *paskha* was most often boiled so that it would stay fresh throughout Easter week. I prefer uncooked *paskha* for its lighter texture. Many cooks add diced candied fruits, raisins, toasted almonds, or citrus zest—all luxury ingredients to honor the miracle of Easter—but I'm a purist at heart and like my *paskha* plain, in all its creamy glory.

Paskha is traditionally shaped into a pyramid meant to recall Golgotha, the site of the Crucifixion. Master woodworkers displayed their talent in crafting *paskha* molds with intricate designs. These molds were almost always inscribed with the Cyrillic letters *XB*, which stand for "Christ is risen," but the molds could also sport tendrils, flowers, and other decorative elements, all carved in mirror image to appear correctly on the finished loaf of sweet cheese. Lacking one of these wooden molds, you can use a clean clay flowerpot.

The secret to a successful *paskha* is to begin with firm *tvorog*, or farmer's cheese. If you're using a commercial brand, it may not need to be drained beforehand, but whether homemade or store-bought, the cheese should be pressed through a sieve to ensure that it's lump-free. Firm *paskha* slices easily. It is classically spread on *kulich*, a towering golden loaf of enriched bread, though I like to serve it on the side. If your *paskha* happens to turn out too soft to slice, simply scoop it into a bowl. It will still be scrumptious.

Serves 8 to 10

4 cups (2 pounds) tvorog or farmer's cheese, homemade (page 79) or store-bought

½ cup (1 stick) unsalted butter, softened

1 cup sugar

5 egg yolks

1 vanilla bean

1 cup heavy cream

Dried currants for decoration

Softened raisins, toasted almonds, diced glacéed fruit to taste (optional)

Drain the tvorog for several hours in a cheesecloth-lined sieve set over a bowl to make sure that it's firm and dry.

When you're ready to make the paskha, cream the butter with the sugar in a stand mixer. Beat in the egg yolks until the mixture is light.

Press the drained cheese through a fine-mesh sieve into a bowl. Turn the cheese out into the butter mixture and beat until completely smooth. Slit the vanilla bean lengthwise and scrape the seeds into the mixture.

continued

In a bowl, whip the heavy cream to soft peaks, and fold it into the cheese mixture.

Cut a piece of double-thickness cheesecloth large enough to line a 2-quart paskha mold or a 6-inch unglazed terra-cotta flowerpot with several inches overhanging the top. Moisten the cheesecloth with water, then wring it dry and carefully line the mold. Pour in the cheese mixture, folding the extra cheesecloth over the top to cover the cheese completely. Set the mold securely in a bowl and place a small saucer on top of the enclosed cheese. Place a heavy can or other weight on the saucer to help force out excess liquid. Let the paskha sit in the refrigerator overnight. Check it after several hours and discard any liquid that has accumulated in the bowl.

Unmold the paskha by placing a serving plate on top of the mold and inverting it. The paskha should slide right out. Remove the cheesecloth. Let the paskha stand for 30 minutes at room temperature before serving.

If the mold you use isn't carved, use dried currants to decorate the sides of the finished paskha with the letters XB. Covered with plastic wrap, it keeps well in the refrigerator for several days.

Easter Bread

Кулич

The tall domed loaf known as *kulich* is always paired with the pyramidal Easter cheesecake called *paskha*. And like *paskha*, *kulich* is baked but once a year. Superstition holds that the success of this sweet bread is mood dependent, so don't try making it if you're feeling impatient or testy. The reason isn't merely superstition: *Kulich* needs to be treated gently when it's removed from the oven. Old-fashioned cooks actually turn the loaf out onto a down pillow and carefully roll it from side to side until it's completely cool so that the loaf doesn't lose its shape. Once cool, the loaf can be placed upright without worry. *Kulich* is always decorated in celebration of the holiday, glazed with white icing and topped with dragées or flowers.

Pious Russians bring their *kulichi* to church to be blessed at the Easter Eve service. Only then is the loaf placed on the Easter table.

Makes 1 large loaf

1 package active dry yeast (2¼ teaspoons)

¼ cup lukewarm water

½ cup lukewarm whole milk

¾ cup granulated sugar

5¾ cups flour

12 tablespoons melted unsalted butter, cooled to lukewarm, plus more for greasing

4 whole eggs, at room temperature

4 egg yolks, at room temperature

¾ teaspoon ground cardamom

¾ teaspoon salt

1 vanilla bean

⅓ cup currants

¼ cup candied orange peel

¼ cup blanched sliced almonds

Icing

1½ cups confectioners' sugar

¼ teaspoon almond extract

2 to 3 tablespoons hot water

In the bowl of a stand mixer, dissolve the yeast in the warm water. Stir in the milk, ¼ cup of the granulated sugar, and 1 cup of the flour. Cover and let the sponge rise in a warm place for 1 hour, until puffy. Transfer the bowl to the mixer stand.

Using the dough hook on the lowest speed, mix in the butter, the remaining ½ cup granulated sugar, the whole eggs and egg yolks, the cardamom, and the salt. Slit the vanilla bean and scrape the seeds into the batter. Add the remaining 4¾ cups flour to make a soft, rather sticky dough.

Knead with the dough hook on low speed for 10 minutes, until the dough is very smooth and pliant. Remove the bowl from the mixer and with a wooden spoon gently stir in the currants, candied orange peel, and almonds until evenly distributed. Place the dough in a greased bowl, cover, and let rise until doubled in bulk, 1½ hours.

continued

Butter a tall 2½-quart pudding mold. Line the bottom and sides with parchment paper, turning the edges of the paper out over the top of the mold and crimping them to make sure the paper stays in place. Butter the paper.

Preheat the oven to 375°F. Flour your hands well, then punch down the dough and knead it lightly a few times. Drop it into the prepared mold. The dough should come no farther than two-thirds of the way up the sides of the mold. Let the dough rise until it comes just to the top of the mold, no more, about 15 minutes.

Bake for 10 minutes, then turn the heat to 350°F and continue baking for 35 to 40 minutes, until nicely browned on top and a cake tester comes out dry.

When the kulich is done, set it on a rack to cool in the mold for 10 minutes. Carefully turn it out onto a wooden board, on its side, parchment paper removed, to cool completely.

While the kulich is cooling, prepare the icing. Sift the confectioners' sugar to remove any lumps, then stir in the almond extract and enough of the hot water to make a pourable icing that isn't too thin.

Once the kulich has cooled, turn it upright and glaze with the icing, letting the icing drip down the sides. Decorate the iced kulich with flowers or sprinkles. To serve, cut off the top—the mushroom crown—and set it aside. Then slice the loaf horizontally, replacing the crown to keep the bread moist and its symmetry intact.

Notes

If you can't find a tall 2½-quart mold, you can bake the kulich in one or two smaller molds. Just be sure not to fill any mold more than two-thirds full, because the crown really mushrooms. Alternatively, you can shape any remaining dough into a round and bake it as you would a loaf of bread. Depending on the size of the pans you use, smaller loaves may not take as long to bake, so check them periodically.

It may be blasphemous, but I like to serve kulich as a dramatic sweet bread for breakfast or brunch. Instead of icing it, I simply glaze the unbaked loaf with 1 egg yolk stirred with ½ teaspoon water to give the top a lovely sheen.

Variation

For saffron-flavored kulich, dissolve ½ teaspoon crumbled saffron threads in 1 tablespoon warm whole milk and leave to infuse for 10 minutes, then add to the dough in place of the cardamom.

SOURCES

Most major cities have markets that specialize in Russian products, including the NetCost chain, which has a number of stores in New York, New Jersey, and Philadelphia. You can also buy a wide assortment of Russian foods online from sites such as Russian Food USA (russianfoodusa.com) and Russian Table.com (russiantable.com).

Below are additional online sources for specialty products.

Beet juice: I like the Biotta brand of lacto-fermented beet juice available from amazon.com.

Berries (black and red currants, gooseberries, lingonberries, sea buckthorn, and more): Northwest Wild Foods at nwwildfoods.com

Bird-cherry flour: Biokarma brand from biokarma.eu

Borodinsky rye: I like the Latvian AmberRye brand from russianfoodusa.com.

Brown mustard seed: Amazon.com

Buckwheat flour: Ground whole-grain flour is available from Anson Mills (ansonmills.com), Pereg Gourmet (pereg-gourmet.com), and Bob's Red Mill (bobsredmill.com).

Caviar: American Caviar Company sells a variety of sustainable American roes at americancaviarco.com. Imported caviar is sold by many companies, including Browne Trading Company at brownetrading.com.

Halibut cheeks: Northwest Wild Foods at nwwildfoods.com

High-fat sour cream: I like the Amish Style All Natural brand with 39 percent fat sold by russianfoodusa.com.

Malted barley and rye: Muntons Maris Otter Malt and Briess Caramel Rye Malt are available from Rebel Brewer (rebelbrewer.com) and Great Fermentations (greatfermentations.com).

Morello cherries in syrup: Trader Joe's Dark Morello Cherries in Light Syrup are available at Trader Joe's or at amazon.com

Sea buckthorn juice: Amazon.com

Venison: If you don't know a friendly hunter, you can purchase high-quality venison from D'Artagnan (dartagnan.com). Substitute chops for the shoulder steak or buy the venison preground.

Whitefish roe: Browne Trading Company at brownetrading.com

This book came to be thanks to Jenny Wapner, my visionary editor at Ten Speed Press, to whom I owe so very much. I'm also enormously grateful to Stefan Wettainen, who took the gorgeous photographs for the book (as he did for *Fire + Ice*). I can't imagine a more fun, or more intrepid, creative partner. The studio shots came alive thanks to the brilliant styling of Anastasia Lundqvist and Niklas Hansen in Stockholm. I'm thrilled that Betsy Stromberg, who designed *Fire + Ice*, turned her attention to Russia with equal verve. And I'm grateful to the others at Ten Speed who made this book happen: Emma Rudolph, for so adeptly shepherding the book to completion, and publicist David Hawk, for his infectious enthusiasm; Windy Dorresteyn, for her excellent marketing; and production manager Jane Chinn, for her expert eye. Without the wonderful creativity of Olga Katsnelson and Hannah Davitian at Postcard PR, the book's reach wouldn't be nearly so broad. Heartfelt thanks go to my fabulous agent, Angela Miller, not just for her professional skills but also for our friendship.

I couldn't have dug so deeply into Russian culture without the help of many extraordinary people, friends and new acquaintances alike. Luba Kuzovnikova of the art collective Pikene på Broen in Kirkenes, Norway, started the ball rolling by introducing me to Oksana Arzhanova, who immediately took me under her wing, introducing me in turn to the Murmansk restaurateurs Svetlana Kozeiko of Tsarskaya Okhota and Sergei Balakshin of Restaurant Tundra, as well as to her husband, Maxim, and friend Katya Bruyaka, a master of ferments and preserves. Luba of the art collective also connected me with Svetlana Mashkova, the owner of Kayut-Kompaniya Café on Solovki Island, and with her parents, Alexandra and Yuri Kuzovnikov, who shared their dacha life with my husband and me for a day of cooking and bathhouse construction.

Nowhere was excitement for this book more palpable than in Arkhangelsk, where Svetlana Kornitskaya and her team at the Tourist Information Centre set up a dream itinerary. I never would have met such remarkable people or seen so many fascinating places without her help and imagination. These people include Natalia Kuzmina of Kiar-Dom in Arkhangelsk; Yevdokia Mushukova, Elena Mitkina, and Natalia Kruptsova in Kimzha; Nadezhda Ulanova at Forest Hotel Golubino; Zhanna Dement'eva and Arina Nazarova in Velsk; Maria Egorova, Ekaterina Osina, and Marusya Klocheva in Kargopol; Natalia Tsokorova in Ustiany; and Yevgeny Tenetov at Arkhangelsk's Maritime Museum. Further south, Natalia Kochnyova generously opened her home to us, as did Sasha Kremnyov, to whom I was introduced by one of my oldest and dearest Russian friends, Nadia Shokhen. In Moscow, I had lively conversations about food history with Olga and Pavel Syutkin.

Whenever possible, I bookended my trips to Russia with visits to Helsinki, where I came to rely on the exceptional warmth and hospitality of my devoted friends Maria and Micke Planting, who always provided the necessary R & R in addition to being lots of fun. I recorded my travel notes in *Le livre à venir*—

ACKNOWLEDGMENTS

"The Book to Come"—a very thoughtful retirement present from Karen Olson. And speaking of thoughtful presents, when John McMath of Wild Winds Farm heard I was writing a Russian cookbook, he sent me a case of his New York State buckwheat.

Treasured friends who helped with this book include Elena Siyanko for her brainstorming, Olga Shevchenko for her astute readings, and Julie Cassiday, Leyla Rouhi, Leslie Morgenthal, Deborah Rothschild, Ilona Bell, Eva Grudin, and Lauren Gotlieb for their enthusiasm—and for taking so many leftovers off my hands. My sister, Ardath Weaver, tirelessly posted to the Facebook page she created and was always there to share helpful ideas. I also want to thank Cortney Burns and Jim Poris for their tasting notes (and Jim for his heroic delivery of calf's feet for the *studen'*), and Jim Dodge for his long-distance baking advice for the pear charlotte.

My most profound thanks go to my husband, Dean Crawford, with whom I've shared Russian adventures for nearly forty years now, from a squalid dorm room at Moscow State University to luxurious digs at the Metropol Hotel. Not only is Dean my favorite traveling companion, in-house editor, and taste tester, but he also makes the most perfect blini. I dedicate this book to him with love.

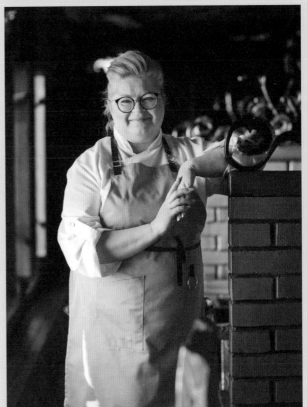

Published in the United States by Ten Speed Press, an imprint of Random House,
a division of Penguin Random House LLC, New York.
www.tenspeed.com

Ten Speed Press and the Ten Speed Press colophon are registered trademarks of
Penguin Random House LLC.

Library of Congress Cataloging-in-Publication Data is on file with the publisher.

Hardcover ISBN: 978-0-399-58039-0
eBook ISBN: 978-0-399-58040-6

Printed in China

Design by Betsy Stromberg
Food and prop styling by Niklas Hansen
Food styling by Anastasia Lundqvist

10 9 8 7 6 5 4 3 2 1

First Edition